Light of Awakening

Prophecies and Teachings of Saint Germain
and the Ascended Masters

GOLDEN CITY SERIES
BOOK TWO

Received and written by

LORI ADAILE TOYE

Host and questions by
Lenard Toye

Foreword by
Penny Greenwell

Praise and Glory to the Seven Rays of Light and Sound

"To understand a law in action is a holy thing, indeed. To understand this law within you is Divine."
~ Saint Germain

THANKS FROM THE AUTHOR AND PUBLISHER:

I would like to thank the Master Teachers Saint Germain, El Morya, and Kuthumi for their continuous guidance and support while receiving, writing, and producing this book. Of course the channeled works in this second volume of the Golden Cities Series are their invaluable teachings; and, the seminal stages of outlining the topics and terms, the months of research, and the final edits of *Light of Awakening* were overshadowed by their steady presence. This helped with a number of important questions and suggestions. They chose many of the subjects presented in the appendices, and this priceless direction literally shapes the pages of this book. I send a heavenly nod of thanks to Carol, who transcribed the lessons on the Rays; and I express deep gratitude to my friend Mary, whose support and advice at critical junctures was invaluable. The appendices of *Light of Awakening* are edited by Felicia Megdal, whose talent once again proves immeasurable. I express deep appreciation to Penny Greenwell, my friend and co-worker with the Masters who wrote the foreword. I credit my daughter Bryn for her contribution with the cover design and Pat Thompson for her professional polish on the jacket copy. Last, but far from least, I recognize the contribution of my husband and spiritual partner Len, who is a continuous power-house of the Yellow and Blue Rays. I thank him for his years of precious love, service, and devotion to the work and message of I AM America. OM SHANTI.

© (Copyright) 2011 by Lori Adaile Toye. All rights reserved. ISBN: 978-1-880050-08-8. All rights exclusively reserved, including under the Berne Convention and the Universal Copyright Convention. No part of this book may be reproduced or translated in any language or utilized in any form or by any means, electronic or mechanical, including photocopying, recording, or by any information storage and retrieval system, without written permission from the publisher. Published in 2011 by I AM America Seventh Ray Publishing International, P.O. Box 2511, Payson, Arizona, 85547, United States of America.

The author and publisher have made every effort to secure proper copyright information. In the event of inadvertent error, the publisher will be happy to correct it in subsequent printings. I AM America Seventh Ray Publishing recognizes the previous works of Lori Toye and derivative components that may be contained in this book by permission: I AM America Map, © Lori Toye, 1989; New World Atlas Series, © Lori Toye 1991-97; Freedom Star Map, © Lori Toye 1994; I AM America Golden Cities Map, © Lori Toye, 1998. Cover: *The Milky Way Galaxy*, by NASA and ESA. Cited works appear in footnotes at the end of each appendix and in a detailed bibliography published in the back of this book.

I AM America Maps and Books have been marketed since 1989 by I AM America Seventh Ray Publishing and Distributing, through workshops, conferences, and numerous bookstores in the United States and internationally. If you are interested in obtaining information on available releases please write or call: I AM America, P.O. Box 2511, Payson, Arizona, 85547, USA. (480) 744-6188, or visit:
www.iamamerica.com

Graphic Design and Typography by Lori Toye
Host and Questions by Lenard Toye
Editing by Felicia Megdal

Love, in service, breathes the breath for all!

I AM
AMERICA

Print On Demand Version

10 9 8 7 6 5 4 3 2 1

Contents

LIST OF ILLUSTRATIONS	v
FOREWORD *by Penny Greenwell*	ix
PREFACE	xiii
CHAPTERS:	
1. *Light a Candle*	17
2. *Emanation*	21
3. *Behind the Interplay*	35
4. *A New Day*	41
5. *A Quickening*	53
6. *Golden City Rays*	63
7. *Blue Illumination*	73
8. *The Light of a Thousand Suns*	79
SPIRITUAL LINEAGE OF THE VIOLET FLAME	87
GLOSSARY	89
APPENDICES	105
BIBLIOGRAPHY	241
DISCOGRAPHY	245
INDEX	247
ABOUT LORI TOYE	261
ABOUT I AM AMERICA	262

Appendices

Appendix A
    TOPICS AND TERMS FOR LIGHT A CANDLE   105

Appendix B
    TOPICS AND TERMS FOR EMANATION   127

Appendix C
    TOPICS AND TERMS FOR BEHIND THE INTERPLAY   165

Appendix D
    TOPICS AND TERMS FOR A NEW DAY   171

Appendix E
    TOPICS AND TERMS FOR A QUICKENING   179

Appendix F
    TOPICS AND TERMS FOR GOLDEN CITY RAYS   191

Appendix G
    TOPICS AND TERMS FOR BLUE ILLUMINATION   211

Appendix H
    TOPICS AND TERMS FOR THE LIGHT OF A THOUSAND SUNS   233

List of Illustrations

FIGURE 1-A

    Rays Blue through White   108

FIGURE 2-A

    Rays Green through Aquamarine-Gold   109

FIGURE 3-A

    Mithra and King Atiochus   119

FIGURE 4-A

    Taq-e Boston: Investiture of Sassanid Emperor of Shapur II   119

FIGURE 5-A

    Mithra, the Sun God   119

FIGURE 6-A

    The Deities of the Rays, Blue through White   122

FIGURE 7-A

    The Deities of the Rays, Green through Aquamarine-Gold   123

FIGURE 1-B

    Eight-Sided Cell of Perfection Location and Movement of the Rays   129

FIGURE 2-B

    Directional Movement of Energy through the Eight Palaces of the Eight-Sided Cell of Perfection   130

FIGURE 3-B

    Eight-Sided Cell of Perfection Overlaid the Human Body   131

FIGURE 4-B

    Fifth Dimension: Golden City Vortex   135

FIGURE 5-B

    Fourth Dimesnion: Golden City Vortex   135

FIGURE 6-B
- *Third Dimension: Golden City Vortex* — 135

FIGURE 7-B
- *Vitruvian Man* — 136

FIGURE 8-B
- *Vesica Piscis* — 137

FIGURE 9-B
- *Flower of Life* — 137

FIGURE 10-B
- *Rod of Power* — 141

FIGURE 11-B
- *Caduceus* — 142

FIGURE 12-B
- *Mithra as Boundless Time* — 142

FIGURE 13-B
- *Kundalini System and the Golden Thread Axis* — 142

FIGURE 14-B
- *The Dharmic Bull of Truth* — 143

FIGURE 15-B
- *Layers of the Human Aura* — 146

FIGURE 16-B
- *The Auric Blueprint* — 147

FIGURE 17-B
- *Golden Thread Axis* — 148

FIGURE 18-B
- *Kundalini System* — 157

FIGURE 19-B
- *The Will Chakras* — 158

FIGURE 20-B
- *Flow of the Rays through the Human Hands* — 160

FIGURE 21-B
- *Movement of the Rays through the Human Feet* — 162

FIGURE 1-E
- *The Co-creative Thought Process* — 181

FIGURE 2-E
- *Thoughts and Time Compaction* — 182

FIGURE 3-E
- *Native American Butterfly Symbol* — 183

FIGURE 4-E
- *The Dagaz Symbol* — 183

FIGURE 1-G
- *Golden City of Gobi* — 214

FIGURE 2-G
- *Lineage of Shamballa to the Golden Cities* — 215

FIGURE 3-G
- *The Four Kumaras* — 222

FIGURE 4-G
- *The Ancient of Days* — 223

FIGURE 5-G
- *Kartikkeya* — 224

FIGURE 6-G
- *Ahura Mazda Investiture* — 224

FIGURE 7-G
- *Akhenaten and Family* — 228

FIGURE 8-G
- *Akhenaten and the Blue Crown* — 228

FIGURE 9-G
- *The Golden City of Gobean Lineage of Gurus* — 229

FIGURE 1-H
- *Golden City of Denasha* — 239

Cover Note:
  NASA, and ESA. "Plik:The Milky Way Galaxy Center (composite Image).jpg – Wikipedia, Wolna Encyklopedia." Wikimedia Foundation - Secure Portal. 12 Mar. 2010. Web. 29 Oct. 2011. <https://secure.wikimedia.org/wikipedia/pl/wiki/Plik:The_Milky_Way_galaxy_center_(composite_image).jpg>.

The NASA/ESA Hubble Space Telescope, the Spitzer Space Telescope and the Chandra X-ray Observatory have collaborated to produce an unprecedented image of the central region of our Milky Way galaxy. In this image, observations using infrared light and X-ray light see through the obscuring dust and reveal the intense activity near the galactic core. Note that the centre of the galaxy is located within the bright white region to the right of and just below the middle of the image. The entire image width covers about one-half a degree, about the same angular width as the full moon. Each telescope's contribution is presented in a different colour: Yellow represents the near-infrared observations of Hubble. They outline the energetic regions where stars are being born as well as reveal hundreds of thousands of stars. Red represents the infrared observations of Spitzer. The radiation and winds from stars create glowing dust clouds that exhibit complex structures from compact, spherical globules to long, stringy filaments. Blue and violet represent the X-ray observations of Chandra. X-rays are emitted by gas heated to millions of degrees by stellar explosions and by outflows from the supermassive black hole in the galaxy's centre. The bright blue blob on the left side is emission from a double star system containing either a neutron star or a black hole. When these views are brought together, this composite image provides one of the most detailed views ever of our galaxy's mysterious core.

Foreword

You are about to enter a new dimension that will bring you closer to yourself, your loved ones and the earth and her inhabitants – seen and unseen. Whether you are an experienced Ascended Master student, a chela or just discovering these teachings, *Light of Awakening* surely will bring insights, confirmations, and assistance.

I first found *I AM America*—Lori and Len Toye in 1991 as I was recovering from a life-changing fall off a cliff (the path literally went out from under my feet). In one short evening of basking in the radiance of the loving etheric presence of the Masters, Len spun the golden thread of the teachings through, in, and around all the truths I had discovered in libraries, books, museums and life. Here was a tale that ran through centuries and disciplines, ancient civilizations and modern physics, from the beginning of time to the space between the molecules. And all of these greats, these pillars of hope for me in a bleak world, not only knew each other but there was a plan. A Divine Plan that held coherence to weave Pythagoras, Margaret Mead, Gene Rodenberry, Maria Montessori, Sacred Geometry, Sufi, Lao Tzu, Bach, Einstein, Akhenaten, Walt Disney, symbols, Angels, DeVinci, the colors, Blake, crystals and gems, Beethoven and Abraham Lincoln not to mention Buddha and Jesus together—all working on the same team. And the columns of Light from my dreams as a child had names and identities. For me it was the welcome home to my real family. Not the birth family who I love dearly and who constantly prompted a quizzical look and "why are (we) doing this this way?" from me as a child. These sorts of questions weren't appreciated or really understood in my neighborhood. I had a well-established sense of what I wasn't and didn't aspire to in those days. Here were teachings from all parts of time, circling the globe that were loving and logical. These teachers I could use as models, this was a way of being I could aspire to.

In 1988 as a teaching assistant at Vermont Studio School, a student introduced me to the esoteric study and implications of Astrology. In Art Schools we had studied the great masters and discussed how we aspired to Mastery in our own disciplines, with a modern twist of course. Concurrently this strange image of a trifold flame burst from my own hands in clay. It became a maquette for a forty-eight inch bronze flame-like figure. I also began the carving of a hooded form from pink Laurentian marble. The impetus to complete these images was something I had never before experienced. Upon meeting Lori four years later, the meanings of these images became apparent. As Lori moved through the room gesturing and teaching or demonstrating hands-on techniques, tiny Violet

FOREWORD

Flames burst from her fingertips. The shrouded ones—robed figures of white, pink, green, gold, and blue encircled the room. I was discovering the power of words, images, and intention. I began the study of my deep truth, purpose in being and the Truth of the Ancients.

Lori and Len have become great friends as the touchstone of reality; our reality as we all negotiate the often wobbly, challenging 'times of the transition.' And together we have learned how to hold the focus for a gentle transition and to be the change we dare to dream.

I was blessed with the opportunity to assist and participate in the creation of the *Freedom Star Map* and the visions of the culmination of a new world emerging from the process of Earth Changes. I remember the moment the responsibility hit me of sculpting the new forms the earth could take, the diminished continents and the new lands. The visions of prophecy staggered me, literally, and I slid to the floor. Lori held my hand (yea, the tiny violet flames erupted) and Len my feet. Violet Flame decrees and the loving eminence of Kuan Yin poured through me; soon we were laughing and giggling about the joint memory of the moment when we raised our hands to volunteer to come to earth for these times. The seriousness of dedication and responsibility can only be lightened by the memory and opening of the heart through friendship and true communion. In a sense this is what we find in the literature of the Truth, in the meeting of like (same) minds. The path of the prophet is narrow and treacherous and like Cassandra rarely heeded.

Many of the Masters' suggestions in *Light of Awakening* were included in the teachings of the *School of the Four Pillars* the energy work and Ascension school I AM America had in Pennsylvania. It is my prayer that this volume will serve as the first text in the resurrected school. The resonance and positive experience gleaned from these instructions reshaped my life and I consider responsible for my complete healing of the injuries from my fall. Not to mention the love and radiance I was enveloped within. I have diligently followed these indispensable teachings through the roller coaster of life for the past nineteen years. I can attest to their value, the shifts and blessings they initiate. The path has been long and varied, incorporating new friends and an expanded, deepening of purpose. The Violet Flame and meditation are the oars that steady my boat on my personnel River of Life and consciousness; sometimes stowed in the eddies and portages, clung to and repeated firmly in 'white water'.

The material new to me is welcomed at this time of heightened energetic and proving to be invaluable in the constant juggling act of rebalancing through the ensuing wide swings of humanity's emotions. The Bija-seed mantras and tones are welcome additions to my toolbox, bringing renewed clarity and enthusiasm to my work in service to the Masters and the Divine Plan.

FOREWORD

Lori's brilliance and deep understandings garnered through extensive research, study and experience, enrich the discourses—transmissions—with appendices, which provide historical relevance, integration and clarification of the metaphorical orations. It is a joy to have a contemporary transmission and expansion of these ancient teachings. As in any extensive study, it is important to strive for the primary resources. My inside joke is that is what these teachings really do. Take you to the *Source*. They draw the dots and point the way; your own practice, surrender and personal engagement will lead you to the unique expression of the love you are and your service.

There are many paths and avenues that incorporate similar and divergent material. Lori's personal experience, dedication and perspective as a Jyotish practitioner enrich and integrate often confusing poetic passages and references bringing new relationships and meanings to light. The layers and subtly within the Master's words bring depth and delight when reread, incorporated through direct experience and the rhythm of repetition.

I have been witness to many moments when the spark is lit through the re-introduction and re-membering of the Masters and their light while conveying their words or radiance through my hands. What a joy to see the seed in the heart burst into flame and radiate throughout all those glorious charkas and Vortices. The human body is an amazing temple for an awakened soul. Through tears or laughter there is a sudden realization of coming home to a family and being enfolded in truth as deep as we can perceive. It is an ecstatic experience of being present to a miracle. I am so honored to be part of this reunion. These moments lead me to a moment of humility and gratitude for all the beings of the Brotherhoods and Sisterhoods of Light and for Lori and Len and their continued focus and distribution of the Truth of the Ancients. Their tutelage and friendship helped me to reignite the flame and allow me to hear the still small voice(s) that now is my ever-present, constant guide.

Light of Awakening is a validation of all of our individual and collective incarnations and our unique and interdependent individuations of Love, Wisdom, and Power. May you enjoy your journey into the Light of I AM.

Penelope Greenwell

Penelope teaches and serves the planet and individuals interested in evolution and Ascension. She is a practitioner of Craniosacral Therapy and energy work specializing in children, their teacher, parents, and grandparents. She has formulated e-lyte products, high frequency infused creams and balms to assist the body in integrating the new vibratory frequencies. She is author of "Birthing the Babes of the Light." Her websites are Bluesphereoftruth.com and Violetbabes.com.

Preface

The steady radiance of Love, Wisdom, and Power that twinkles, glows, flames, and blazes throughout Ascended Master Teaching is known as the classic Seven Rays of Light and Sound; however, for simplicity, I refer to this esoteric light as the *Rays*. The teachings in this book begin with the metaphoric flicker of the light of a single candle, and end in the brilliant luminosity of a thousand suns.

Light of Awakening purposely contains a wealth of information on the Rays, both historical and contemporary. The Appendices contain vital correlations between the ancient myths and the ageless wisdom to the conventions and beliefs held by many of the great esoteric teachers of the Ascended Master Tradition. Wherever possible, illustrations segue abstract thoughts and clarify critical ideas. A picture is worth a thousand words.

Years ago, my personal introduction to the vital energy of the Rays was almost obscured by its own cryptic, yet incandescent language. A Ray of Light was once described as a tube, with focal points and sparks, which reflected attributes of the supreme Godhead. As I continued my education into the sacred light, I was encouraged to call upon its radiance, and somehow this would develop my aura's ability to broadcast the Rays—a divine emanation from the Great Central Sun. This technique carried the implicit caveat that there were indeed good Rays and bad Rays. Kind of like *film noir*, this suggests that in the shadows of the Rays lurks disease, enmity, maybe death.

My graduation to the concept of Ray Charts added even further confusion. I carefully memorized the qualities of each of the Seven Rays, one through seven, only to learn that one had to develop the Christ Consciousness to diffuse their ethereal color. This, of course, was territory where only Cosmic Beings, Elohim, Ascended Masters, and Archangels could tread.

So I made a sharp turn to Theosophy to learn that in this philosophy the word *Ray* was paradoxically interchanged with *logos*, whose meaning is linked with the creative word of God and the English etymology for *logic*. However, in Theosophical terms the seven procreative Rays are also known as the *seven builders*.

PREFACE

In 1996, during a family vacation, I stepped into a bookstore. I immediately walked towards the metaphysical section where I noticed the title, "Ancient Hindu Astrology for the Modern Western Astrologer," by James Braha. The book magnetized into my hands. For weeks, I poured over its pages that fully explained the vast underbelly and intricate systems of the wisdom of the Rays as *Jyotish*, which in Sanskrit means *Science of Light*. Here, at last, was the practical knowledge I sought that described and interpreted the Rays as both a tangible and an accessible power.

Jyotish (pronounced Joe-teesh) is the ancient astrology of India, and likely originates from a time of greater light on earth—the epoch of *Dvapara-Yuga* over six-thousand years ago. Legend states that the wise Rishi Teachers of India knew our earth would soon enter a time of psychic corruption and darkness, the time we are now experiencing: *Kali-Yuga*. Jyotish, the personal exacting science of the Rays, was humanely bestowed so one could ably contact and achieve *moksha*—the natural and innate ability to liberate our human consciousness (aka the Ascension Process) in this prophesied time of spiritual shadows.

The foundation of Jyotish is based on the traditional Hindu Vedas—ancient spiritual scriptures—as one of the six disciplines (*Vedanga*) necessary to understand the Vedas. An experienced *Jyotishi* (astrologer) can accurately interpret the language of the stars and affirm with stunning accuracy personal predictions or forecast worldwide events; yet, most importantly, the practice of Jyotish opens subtle doors beyond this world and reveals the creation beyond our earthly awareness, or better yet, the *creation behind this creation*. My Jyotish counselor explained how Jyotish ideally opens our instinctive psychic abilities, while simultaneously grounding each vision in its spiritual law that was observed thousands of years ago.

I took a full year's sabbatical from my work at I AM America to study Jyotish and discovered the complex and compelling parallels to the Seven Rays and Ascended Master Teaching. During this period my dreamtime became unusually vivid. I found myself entering celestial classrooms where many of the intricate topics of Jyotish were addressed. Often I would wake in the morning with a particular assignment from the heavenly instructor, such as: "Today, you will study *Shad-Bala*." Or, "Re-read and memorize the properties of the *grahas* (planets)." This process of conscious and dream-state education continued for approximately one year, and for months afterwards I still had numerous questions. Many of these inquiries were telepathically relayed to the Master Teachers and addressed in our channeled sessions. Several of these lessons are contained in *Light of Awakening*.

As my education progressed I experienced the spiritual passage of *Re-membering*. This involves retrieving deep-seeded past-life memories. Its processes use mind, thought, and perception to recalibrate memory into conscious activity. To me, many of the familiar Sanskrit terms which accurately portray the dance of the Seven Rays throughout human

PREFACE

experience are inherently visceral, like the beating of my heart. Later, I would learn that the education of a Master Jyotishi requires three lifetimes.

Light of Awakening includes teachings and prophecies from the Master Teachers Saint Germain, El Morya, and Kuthumi on the Seven Rays and their significance in today's world events. This light, as stated in the beginning of this preface is indeed metaphoric, and employed through the development of our spiritual consciousness. And this profound light is experienced through touch, sound, taste, scent, and sight. Its prophetic appearance is designed to align, integrate, and awaken the innate memory of our true self: the HU-man.

This sensory journey travels onward and inward, morphed into the visions and dreams of a New World traversed with the spiritual migration of Golden Cities and their wondrous *Adjutant Points*; the phenomenon of *Time Compaction* alongside the healing consciousness of *Unana* (Unity Consciousness); and graced with the ever-present flowing light of the Rays that re-awakens our Co-creative ability and the boundless perfection which lies beyond human fear and limiting beliefs.

Perhaps this is the light that signifies the end of darkness, a brief reprieve from the restraints of *Kali the Destroyer*, and empowers the leaderless resistance of Occupy Wall Street, and galvanizes the voice of scientific reason over the politically-driven science of Global Warming and Climate Change, while envisioning a sustainable earth with clean air and water for our children and their children. An internet journalist recently coined this insightful phrase regarding our current times, "This is the *beginning of the beginning.*"

So, don't ever underestimate the light of one small candle! Buddha said, "Thousands of candles can be lit from a single candle and the life of the candle will not be shortened." The Master Teachers reiterate, "The Time is Now!"

In the Light of a Thousand Suns, I AM,

Lori Toye

Light a Candle
Saint Germain

GREETINGS, BELOVED, IN THAT MIGHTY VIOLET LIGHT, I AM SAINT GERMAIN.

I stream forth on that Violet Ray of Mercy, Transmutation, and Forgiveness. Dear hearts, at this time I ask permission to come forward.

"Dear one, you have permission, please come forward."

Greetings and salutations! I AM most happy to be able to come forward this day. It has been some time since we have had such technical discourse, but, it was the feeling of the hierarchy that this (discourse) would be imperative; for there is, you see, an opportunity for great war upon your planet. We had hoped, through this discourse, that we could ready those who claim to be, or state and say they are, light-workers. Come forward and bring the balance of light for the earth and her planetary evolutions!

At this time there is great dissension that is brewing among your world political leaders, and this is of great distress and disturbance for this hierarchy and its purpose and intention. For, you see, our work is for those among humanity who are willing to bring a greater harmony, a greater understanding of LIGHT. This LIGHT, of course, is the illumination of the mind, but is also the opening of the heart. So, one may understand that it is indeed the equilibrium, or balance of peace that all are seeking, and so as we see through the choices that humanity makes, a time could come for imbalance, resulting in great war upon your planet. It is important, shall we say (for light-workers), to tip the balance of that scale. And those who are willing to go into the silence of the Great Silence; willing to tap into the universal consciousness, can bring forward a Time of Peace and imbue the planet, humanity and the planetary Rays with the qualification of greater harmony and greater unity—peace.

May our minds and hearts not divert to the lower energies of competition, greed, avarice and fear. May these energies be transmuted into the greater energies of light and peace, and be directed toward our political leaders. May both sides of any conflict be given support at the higher level, and never treated with dissension or disrespect. Instead, in the most silent ways, may these greater energies imbue all who may partake of them (and our world leaders) at an unconscious level.

For more information and study topics on *Light a Candle*, see Appendix A, page 105.

LIGHT A CANDLE

While certain leaders may not be aware of these Ray Forces and subtle energies working upon them, you know, Dear chelas, that they are powerful indeed. For, at one time in your past, were not you, too, led to the path of light through the same subtle force!

May Divine Grace empower the little wills of man!

We see this brewing—this time which was also a Prophecy. We ask for those who are willing to serve through the greater cause Divine to meet in unison of mind and heart. Begin first in daily meditation and prayer for planetary peace for the earth and harmony among its peoples. Even as this disturbance is the choice of those who would do so, it is our hope that a greater union and peace should prevail, and this serves the greater cause—Divine.

It is all a choice, as you, Dear hearts, would understand this most astutely. It is indeed a choice, if we should have wars and famine, or peace and prosperity on this planet. These are the choices that humanity must make!

But students who understand the Greater Laws Divine, know that it is also a consciousness, or an energy—a qualification of the Ray Forces, that imbues the planet for good or bad. Undesired energies can be diverted, shall we say, "Glanced into a greater harmony," that may prevail upon the earth.

There are those who are the doubting Thomases, who feel that prayer does not indeed affect things. Instead, it is the Will of man and the Will of the forces of nature that are causing such at this time. But indeed, it is, shall we say, the higher "Point of Perception," as we have taught in earlier discourses, that can change the course of events.

Again, this is based upon that subtle premise, "Is the glass half full or is the glass half empty?" It is the Point of Perception—the way in which things are seen.

From there, it is the way in which things are qualified or acted upon. Through this premise, one may begin to understand a greater working in the unison of Greater Mind.

Dear hearts, it is our request that this be posted among your students, among the chelas, among those who are interested to help the greater cause of the Great White Brotherhoods and Sisterhoods of Light. May meditation and prayer be part of the vigil at this time. We ask that all light a white candle for planetary peace. May this candle symbolize the ONE light that all share.

[Editor's Note: It was also taught in this discourse that the lighting and burning of white candles in certain geophysical locations would enhance the energies for world peace. While it is our opinion that the entire earth is sacred, these areas earmarked by Saint Germain are: The apexes (also known as the Stars) of all Golden Cities. These areas are approximately forty

Light of Awakening

LIGHT A CANDLE

miles in total diameter. Here are some apexes that we have identified: GOBEAN: Baldy Peak, Arizona. MALTON: Mattoon, Illinois. WAHANEE: Augusta, Georgia. SHALAHAH: Lolo Pass, Montana. KLEHMA: Cope, Colorado. (Again, please remember that the area extends in a 40-mile circle around these center points.) Another area in the United States that the Masters say is extremely important in affecting World Peace, because of its connection to the planetary grid, is Kansas City, Missouri. This is often referred to as the Heart of the Dove.]

Emanation
Saint Germain on Ray Forces

GREETINGS, BELOVED IN THAT MIGHTY CHRIST, I AM SAINT GERMAIN, AND I STREAM FORTH ON THAT VIOLET RAY OF MERCY AND FORGIVENESS. AS USUAL, DEAR HEARTS, I REQUEST PERMISSION TO COME FORTH.

"Please, Saint Germain, come forward."

Dear ones, it is most important that you observe the energies that are moving now upon the Earth Plane and Planet. For, remember, we told you there would come a time when those with the eyes to see and the ears to hear would place their hands into action. You see, beloveds, it is very important we continue our work upon the Earth Plane to increase light upon the planet. The increased value of this light is that the Earth Changes, or, cataclysmic geological changes are held back, and those who have the eyes to see and the ears to hear have the opportunity to assimilate the higher energies at this time. These higher energies are coming forward through the Golden City Vortices and also through those areas that are known as the ancient Vortices. There are also many Portals of Entry, so to speak, as we have taught before in other discourses. All of these are sensitive points upon the Earth Planet, beloved Mother Babajeran, and indeed are taking in light forces at this time. Many among humanity absorb these light forces. This great cosmic force, as it works upon the planet as a great wave in the same way that the ocean tidal system exists upon your planet, has the ability, to speed up consciousness into a greater evolution, into a greater consortium of the ONE. It is important for you to understand that it is this Unity Consciousness that we are speaking of, and it is important, as the light energies increase upon the planet that you understand its ability to affect all humanity— to affect all in a much better way. For you see, Dear ones, there are those who live with great fear, those who live with the fear of impending doom, those who would live, shall we say, seeking only protection and safety from fear which resides within themselves. Now, this fear has occurred for many generations and lifetime after lifetime, and, you see, it can adhere to the genetic structure and is passed on from one family to the next and to the next. When an opportunity like this occurs, this allows one to transmute, even genetically, lifetime after lifetime of genetic-held fear—Cellular Fear. The light that emanates from the Great Central Sun is the light that shall free you all. It is the *Light of Awakening*. When we gave you instruction of the Cellular Awakening, this is, too, what we were referring to, and the increase of light is available for all to partake of. There are many opportunities that will come to accelerate this light process upon the earth. It is indeed an acceleration of the light

---

For more information and study topics on *Emanation*, see Appendix B, page 127.

EMANATION

process, an acceleration of love, and an acceleration of Unity Consciousness. This is the only solution that can stop cataclysmic change and heal all as ONE.

Prophecy, as you know Dear beloveds, has been brought forward, to expedite this process, to bring forward the unconscious fear within yourself. Facing fears enables purification and redemption; then one is able to face the future with hope and love and a willingness to create for the good of all. Indeed when all are in this Consciousness of Light then—truly then, and I say this from a firmness of knowledge—all benefit; all are then received as ONE. So you see, during this process you spin off the past; spin off the Karma of many lifetimes of fear, of war, of poverty, deceptions, betrayals, and the little hurts that occur to one. Now we see the results of past Dharma and your purpose is connected to letting go of fear, letting go of the little wants, letting go of the little trappings that can keep you trapped within the world of your perception.

We have discussed perception many times. But perception, Dear hearts, Dear chelas, is indeed a pivotal point when one has the choice to how they shall see something; the choice of how it will be contained within their being, and how it will create in their worldly experience. This Time of Acceleration, of Cellular Acceleration and of genetic acceleration is a Time of Light and Bliss. This is the time in which the purpose of the Mighty I AM is revealed to all. This purpose is revealed at an individual level and then released as to the many. So you see, beloveds, it is important to firmly hold this vision of light for all upon the earth, to not see that it should go to just a select few, but light is to go to all. For all will gain through this experience and through this acceleration. The upliftment of the earth is of the utmost importance and this upliftment is through the medium of consciousness. Also, the medium of conscience and many choose their greater purpose, and a greater way that will serve all. For you see, beloveds, the future is always in your hands. It is held in the power of your choice.

Let me get to the work at hand. I have come forward to give further instruction upon Ray Forces, as this has been the topic of many conversations between the two of you, and also conversations between many of the chelas who request information on Ray Forces and how Ray Forces color light, and sound vibration which activates one toward greater harmony, greater understanding of unity and a greater understanding of the current time, the Cellular Awakening. There are indeed seven Ray Forces that work in the HU-man, the man who is to be God, the man who is to be realized through self-understanding. As I have taught before, the Rays are indeed anchored within the heart, and emanate through various Kundalini points along the spine with various meridians and points upon the body. The Ray Forces arc out of the bottom of the feet as well as through the hands. Also Ray Forces arc through various chakras situated along the spinal cord. Ray Forces carry the encoding. They carry the information of who and what you are as substance. They carry the past. They carry the present, and they carry the future. The Rays come under the direction of the Great Central Sun. This is a force emanating throughout your universe and acting like a collective consciousness to unite one purpose to the next, one Karma to the next, one Dharma to the next. Do you understand?

Light of Awakening

EMANATION

Answer: "Yes."

Unity brings all together into a greater harmony. One would think at times that they are being punished for an experience they may experience, but indeed this is not so. There is harmony in all things. You must seek to see it. And when one understands the Ray Forces, they understand that the grand conduction of energy is only working through Law, and the Law is based upon the first Jurisdiction, Harmony. So you see, Harmony pervades all activities upon the Earth Plane and Planet as it comes under the conduction of the Great Central Sun. Many of the Ray Forces that emanate from the Great Central Sun arc off of other planetary forces as they travel toward the earth. Known as astrology, this science has been studied for many ages and is indeed true. It is the subtle science of the Astral Body, the first Body of Light that can be viewed by a HU-man, a God-realized man. This is the emanation, or the light-field force. This magnetic and electromagnetic force-field is indeed the emanation of the energies of the Rays in their commingling of experience. And this experience is indeed broad. It may vary, shall we say, from one Ray to the next in a current lifetime, but, you see, in as much as one event is committed, as you have learned in the Point of Perception, indeed it becomes a point of departure for another event, and so on, and so on, and so on. That one event is never dissolved—it is continuous. It is always an *experience*. So, all history, as you would perceive, is indeed always accessible. There is truly no past, there is truly no future. There is only the Ever-present Now. So that you may understand...this—as your brain, as your intellect, is a binary system—one that relates more to duality—and I will explain it first from a more dual perspective. First, there is the perception that time exists as wasting away into nothingness. Yet, there is the present when time is *potential*, shall we say, much like a spore or an egg that has the ability to expand and grow into the future. Now do you understand this?

Answer: "Yes."

I will proceed so that you may gain even a broader understanding of Ray Forces and how they work. You know the Seven Ray Forces, as they exist, identify and relate to a color. Each color is a particular harmonic for the Earth Field and Planetary Field of Experience. Each harmonic creates through various experiences for the individual. For instance, one who is imbued with the Green Ray is more apt to have more experiences with one's own physical body in relationship to disease or disorders that exist within the physical body. The Green Ray, then, naturally brings one to seek his own healing. So, through the experience of one's own healing, one comes forward to help many others on the path of healing. The experience of the Green Ray may be one that is not totally understood within the context of one lifetime. But often there have been many lifetimes in which one has suffered or one has had diseases that appeared to be incurable. So in a predominance of the Green Ray Force will provoke one to seek greater Harmony. The harmonies will first come through aligning the light-bodies, and that alignment sometimes comes through artistic and musical expression, but is primarily used as a force-field to bring healing to others, and to ease suffering and develop compassion. This is just one explanation of a Ray Force. My intention is to not go into great detail of descriptions of Ray Forces, for these are contained in many other materials, and also can be found in many Ascended Master teachings. Most of them are quite accurate. For those

EMANATION

who are requesting greater accuracies on these, I will be willing to concord and provide such information. But for now, I would like to stay with the work at hand so that you may understand how Ray Forces work together. There is always a Chohan (Lord) of a Ray. This is a Master Teacher of that particular Ray Force. This Master Teacher is responsible for the way in which the energies of a Ray Force from the Great Central Sun is utilized upon the Earth Plane and Planet. Now, you understand in the science of Astrology that there are planets that arc certain energies, and the force of this particular Chohan resides as a consciousness between that planet and the earth. For instance, the Chohan of the Green Ray resides as an energy force, a force of consciousness that is timeless and perpetually immortal between Mercury and the earth. The energy exists simultaneously not only as a light force and a sound force that is recognizable to one upon the Earth Plane and Planet, but as a Ray Force that is a resonance, a harmonic, so to speak. Those of science often identify this as a laser Ray or as a life force that can be sensed, measured by an existing scientific principle—but a Ray Force does not work in a direct current. Indeed, it emanates like a coal in a fire. It emanates a certain warmth that later ignites the fire, and so a Ray Force is as an emanation, an emanation a quality, and it brings this quality to the painting of the greater picture. Do you understand?

Answer: "Yes."

This emanation is an important factor in understanding Ray Forces and how they work together. For instance, take your hands and rub them together. As you rub them together, do you not feel a heat?

Answer: "Of course."

The heat is indeed the emanation of friction. This is how a Ray Force indeed works. It emanates, radiating and generating a greater and greater energy as it travels throughout space or time. And so, as one begins to recognize the workings, the qualities of a Ray Force through lifetime after lifetime, it begins to emanate a greater and greater surgence throughout the being. We have explained before that once the emanation exists, and if you were to measure this along a mathematical line once it is functioning above fifteen percent within the HU-man being, it may then be qualified. Again, an emanation may be qualified in several ways, for good or for bad, as the Earth Plane is dual. Things are hot; things are cold. Things are up; things are down. Again, Dear hearts, beloveds, it is *perception* as to how the emanation is realized and understood. This emanation, travels forward from lifetime to lifetime, and is qualified in this same manner. As it is qualified by the grand conductor and it is of course given as a free gift to the HU-man. For the HU-man, indeed, has the choice of how to utilize this energy for *experience*. For instance, referring back to the Green Ray, one may use the Green Ray for greater harmony to bring forth a great compassion and understanding of scientific knowledge, which frees another from suffering—this creates compassion in the world. But if there is not complete understanding of the emanation, the Ray Force is expressed as *dual*. You may meet one whose life is emanating, the lower qualities of a Ray, choosing only to produce or manifest the energies in this dualistic quality. When this occurs, the invidivual

---

Light of Awakening

EMANATION

becomes overly analytical and scientific, and relies more upon the *processes* of the Ray, and not upon the *results* of the Ray. Have you not seen this many times?

Answer: "Very true."

So one has a choice concerning how to utilize a Ray Force as it arcs from the Great Central Sun and gives each of you the life of Co-creation. The HU-man develops this faculty of choice. Within choice lies the ability to make the earth a heavenly paradise or filled with the torments of hell. The darkness that has covered the earth oddly, is but a choice—a choice of the qualification and utilization of emanation. When one speaks of the Ages of Darkness that have covered the earth, do you now understand with greater wisdom and knowledge how the darkness *had* to exist in order so one could begin to understand and experience how Ray Forces are qualified and used for greater and further evolution?

Answer: "I see what you're saying."

It is not a matter of judging a time and saying that it must not exist, or it is of a darker or of lesser quality. It fully serves the function of reason. It fully serves the function of choice. Choice is indeed the wholistic pivotal process of how the Rays work, and how the Rays send their emanation.

Now, let us talk about the interplay of the Rays. Again, I have mentioned there are Seven Ray Forces that are utilized for the education of the soul and the enfoldment of the incarnation. These Seven Ray Forces, as I have stated before, enter into the Eight-Sided Cell of Perfection. The Eight-Sided Cell of Perfection is activated upon the first breath upon the birth of the child. That is why many upon the Earth Plane and Planet record a specific time of birth, but it is not so much the birth process itself, but the intake of the first breath. This breath activates the Eight-Sided Cell of Perfection, the Kundalini along the spine, and all of the Chakra Systems. You know that a chakra spins in a clockwise or counter clockwise position. The spinning utilizes the Ray Forces. This spinning can indeed tell you how the emanation of the Ray Force is conducting its Karma or Dharma within that particular individual system. So, when you see, for instance, a chakra spinning in a counter clockwise motion, producing, a cloudy Green Ray color, like a muddy green, you know the individual is still learning through the lower energies of the Green Ray and yet to qualify into the higher energies. This emanation sets up many experiences through the light and energies of the aura.

Now, you begin to see that the Human Aura is an interplay of the many Ray Forces as they interact along the Golden Thread Axis and emanate through the Chakra System. When you encounter a life force, at times you may meet one from whom your destinies are very different, from whom your experiences are very different, from whom your beliefs are very different. Upon meeting and greeting one another, you feel a sense of repulsion toward one another. Now, you have experienced this, and many others have experienced this. It is not a matter of judgment, of good or evil, it is a matter of understanding emanation. It is a matter of

EMANATION

understanding the science, the Astral Body. This science of the Astral Body may be utilized in many forms. As one, we begin to understand the greater harmony and the greater working of mind, soul, and body. Now, this Astral Body that you carry with you at all times, your first light force, so to speak, the first interplay of all Rays coming together, also to some extent controls the field of experiences that you may have. For you see, Dear ones, as you carry this light field and force with you, it carries, shall we say, the programming of the Ray Forces so that throughout your day it can control the types of experiences you will have, the type of people you will meet, the types of interactions that you will have. Too, it sets up a force-field for your co-creative abilities. At night, when you sleep, there is a type of detachment from the physical body, and the greater light force is then freed up and allowed to explore the worlds that exist beyond that of only physical understanding. Many of you have had these dreams. Sometimes the dream experiences end up actually bringing forth a creation in your world. That is because the imprinting of that was already contained through the Ray Forces. Now do you understand?

Answer: "Yes."

This is very important to understand the emanation of Ray Force and how it works for creation, how it works to bring all forward in a greater harmony. And now I will open the floor for your questions. [The Master momentarily leaves the teaching, and then returns.]

Greetings, Dear ones. Now I shall continue on this discourse of emanation. Did you feel the disconnection of our energies?

Answer: "No, not really."

What you felt was the continuing emanation. Now, for instance, when a Master Teacher enters a room, before that Master Teacher enters into the room do you not first feel the emanation?

Answer: "I hear your sound, I smell a fragrance and I see your light."

That is indeed an emanation, and when a Master Teacher leaves the room there is still a heat. There is still a fragrance. There is still a sound and a vibration within the room. This, too, is emanation. As you can see, emanation, much as the coal has been lighted to fuel the fire, is an energy that builds. That is why, whenever we come in to bring discourse, we build an energy. We build an emanation. This is very important so that people understand that the Ray Forces of the subtle astral bodies are built lifetime after lifetime after lifetime. There may be one life force that comes forward into a very strong incarnation. the strengths of those Ray Forces within that individual have been built lifetime after lifetime after lifetime. One is not born with a strong Ray Force without, of course, putting the work forward, without having effort.

Light of Awakening

EMANATION

So, you see, all comes together in a perfect harmony. This harmony, of course, is the result of actions that you have taken and choices you have made in previous incarnations. So, you see how important the ever-present now is, for this, too, will create your future, create the lifetimes that you will have in the future, create the experiences, the types of friends, and so on and so on. And so, Dear hearts, as you can see, emanation is indeed an important understanding when you begin to understand the work of Ray Forces and their conductivity within the human body.

Now, Dear ones, when you understand how a Ray Force is gathered, in this case an individual lifetime after lifetime, when we begin to understand the Golden City Vortices and that each of them is part of an individual Ray Force, now you can understand that they, as new planetary Vortices, are building energies, their emanations starting, of course, and building and building and building. And so in the beginning to birth of a new Vortex, it may be difficult at first to feel the energies of a Golden City, to feel the emanation of that Ray Force. However, over time the emanation builds. And in the same way that a Ray Force emanates throughout the Astral Body of an individual, that Ray Force in the beginning may only be functioning, maybe at a low rate of five percent, seven percent, 10 percent, but then as this grows, shall we say, in its force-field, the Ray Force is then able to start giving its subtle indications. Remember, as I have taught, indeed this is a dual system, and so very often in the beginning of development of Golden Cities the more lower energies of that Ray Force will then exist. For instance, in the Golden City of Gobean, where you are dealing with transformation, harmony, all indications of the higher use of the Blue Ray, you may get shortsightedness; you may get coldness; you may get disharmony. You see, it is a matter of qualification of taking the energy forces as they exist and using them at the higher level. This requires an understanding of perception, an understanding of your choice as we have always taught. Is the glass half-full? Is the glass half-empty? Again it is a matter of your perception of how do you utilize a Ray Force. This is known as qualification. These two principles, emanation, qualification, need to be understood so that the chela, the student of these teachings, may move forward in understanding how to utilize the energy of Ray Forces within their own being.

I should like to discuss the idea of conductivity. In the same way that we have described the pyramidal structures of the Golden Cities and outlined its circular motion, shown you the apex of a Vortex, the doorways of a Golden City, and the parameters in miles and kilometers, we must also explore this within the human body. You are all well aware of the idea of pressure points and meridians within the body. Many of you are also exposed to the idea of Kundalini currents of this force moving within the spinal system, activating the Chakra System. Conductivity relies upon geometrical structures, each geometrical structure peculiar to each planetary system. The conductivity is carried out, of course, through this sacred geometry. Remember, Dear hearts, when we brought forth the teachings of sacred geometry so that you would understand its language, its purpose, and its intent? In the human body, most of the movement of conductivity occurs upon a circular motion. Sometimes this is also seen as a wave. This is why the Kundalini current is sometimes known as the snake energy, as it mirrors the movement of a snake in the sand, but this is ideally a circular motion. That is why, throughout your life, you may have periods of time when you feel that two ends of a circle now meet. However, you also feel, through the series of experiences, that you have

EMANATION

had a higher perception, a higher knowledge, in the closure of understanding a completed lesson. This spiral of energy is indeed circular when viewed from certain perspectives, but this is also how the Ray Forces work in their conductivity in your present field of experience. Within the Golden Cities, this sacred geometry, or shape, is based on a triangular system. As you were taught in previous discourse, triangular forces duplicate energies—duplicate them again and again—whereas, circular forces expand energies. The Golden City Vortices have been placed upon the planet to duplicate the Ray Forces, the Ray Forces of the higher emanation, qualification of understanding of their teachings. So, do you see, Dear ones, this harmony working together, the expansion of the HU-man, the God-man, the triangular forces duplicating the higher end of these energies so that they may be given to many others upon the Earth Plane and Planet at this time, and to move humanity into a greater evolution and understanding of its manifested destiny? Now I shall open the floor for questions.

Question: "Can Ray Forces be enhanced?"

Ray Forces are enhanced through your understanding. When one begins to understand the force-field of the Ray Force itself, the existence of the Ray, the intention of the Ray, its higher and lower usage, indeed it is enhanced perceptibly by the individual, the HU-man. Then it is utilized in its greater understanding, in its greater workings for choice, and for the greater capacity for love, compassion, service and charity. Many of these higher forces are understood in the Twelve Jurisdictions, but then one is moved to utilize, to make the choices, with these Ray Forces for greater understanding. Enhancement may occur in many ways. Of course, the one method that we recommend for enhancement is meditation upon the Ray Force itself to gain an understanding of that Ray Force in your life. To simply meditate upon the Green Ray and its existence in your life will, of course, bring the Green Ray to a greater force-field within your experience. But it is better to bring it to the element of mind and to choice, consciousness, and conscience so it can be utilized at its greater understanding. It is recommended that you meditate upon the greater use of this force-field as a Ray, as an emanation within your life, in this individual's lifetime, to bring forth the desired result. Meditation, when used along this line and with this complete understanding, can be very beneficial to the chela. Forces indeed exist within the Mineral Kingdom, these coming from beloved Babajeran, herself. Ray Forces can be increased through certain Golden Cities. These Golden Cities have been brought forth to help and assist those who would like to take a particular focus with a Ray Force or a Ray energy. The crystalline forces also contain many different emanations of the Seven Ray Forces, and it is best for the chela to choose one that they feel drawn to and that they feel magnetized toward. For, you see, Dear ones, it is always *choice*. So, Dear hearts, yes indeed, Ray Forces can be significantly strengthened throughout the body, throughout the mind, throughout the soul.

But perhaps the strongest of these, in terms of forces, is through the use of vibrational sound. Now you have known that when the Vibration of OM is given that it snaps the Kundalini, or, shall we say, that Golden Thread Axis, into complete alignment with the

EMANATION

sun and with the earth, and then there is indeed a sense of grounding, a sense of purpose, an expansion of the solar forces within the Astral Body. I have given you many decrees that vibrate to the Violet Flame. "Violet Flame, I AM, Come Forth. Violet Flame, I AM." You see, the Violet Flame forces help to aid one in overcoming especially trying circumstances. The Violet Flame is an emanation of the higher use of your Karma. It allows the trying circumstances, suffering, tears, problems and anxieties that surround the release of Karma of the misuse, or the lower emanation of a Ray Force. It drives the energies of that Ray Force up into its higher use, so that one is then freed, liberated, so to speak, from the lower understandings, from the lower emanations, of a planetary force. So, Dear hearts, it is entirely and absolutely recommended that the use of the Violet Flame is always of the utmost importance in strengthening any condition that may seem trying. It is sound vibration that comes forth within the Chakra System. It is sound vibration that comes forth within the consciousness. It is sound vibration that allows the conscience to have the clarity to choose the right way at the right time. That is why I have repeatedly recommended the Violet Flame to my students and my chelas, as this is the clearest, the quickest path to liberation and to understanding the Ray Force of emanation, and to allowing a greater field of experience. Indeed, it does expand your astral field, your field of experience, the force-field that you have come to live through and to experience through.

Questions?

Question: "Since the Ray Forces come together to make the Astral Body, or the Astrological Body, and that is the conductive control for the experiences or the life that a person leads, what attracts to them, what repels from them. If there are certain Rays that are functioning at smaller percentages than others, is the Violet Flame the best usage for, I would say, the neutralization of any of the afflictions of the Rays of Light?"

The Violet Flame has been brought forth to free, or liberate one so that they may understand the higher use of energies. When one has achieved a certain understanding of liberation through the use of the Violet Flame being used, of course, as sound vibration, then one may begin to explore the use of other vibratory forces through the use of sound to actually enhance or increase the force-field in another direction. But until that moment has happened, it is, of course, always best to free the individual first. It is through freedom that one is allowed to expand, until one is able to see that they can see it from a whole other viewpoint. This is the freeing of perception. And it is, of course, recommended that all sounds be used to bring healing forth for the individual, but the Violet Flame, as you can see, is, of course, the one that is used, shall we say, at the first levels so that consciousness is freed and ready to explore other harmonies that exist within them.

Question: "So what you're saying is that the Violet Flame is, of itself, also a transmutating Ray and that is the first focus?"

EMANATION

It is Alchemical, as well, as it fuses in an interplay of the Rays, allowing each of the Ray Forces, for instance, a Yellow Ray, a Pink Ray, a Blue Ray, to come together in greater harmony. These forces, at times, are not in harmony at will within the individual, for that individual had chosen to allow the Ray Forces to war against one another, to be in disharmony with one another. It is the Violet Flame, indeed, that allows the Ray Forces to work together. Have you ever seen a team that seems to have all the strengths and all the qualities to achieve its goals, but yet the individuals within that team war among themselves and are not able to cooperate to achieve one thing?

Answer: "Yes, I have."

This is the same metaphor for understanding the Ray Forces within the Astral Body. One may have a great quality and another great quality, but they are not able to bring them together, to make them work together. The use of the Violet Flame brings, through sound vibrating, a lessening of the Karma and a lessening of the disharmony; and it brings together a fusion of cooperation between the Ray Forces, that one may now work together. If you would begin to view the Seven Rays as a *team force* that is working for you, through your choices and through your consciousness within your Astral Body, then you begin to understand how the Violet Flame, and use of this mighty Violet Ray, will bring you to a greater freedom for you to achieve your goals.

Question: "Can you give us a decree, specifically, to harmonize the Rays?"

> Violet Flame, come forth in harmony of the Seven Rays. Transmute the cause and effect and all records that have been genetically inscribed within me, genetically used by me. And now, Violet Flame, blaze forth in greater harmony to the Divine Plan and the Divine Will.

It is as simple as that: decreeing this unto yourself as a prayer. Let the Violet Flame be poetry to your soul. Let the Violet Flame come forward to bring greater harmony between you and the Seven Rays, so that each of the Ray Forces becomes a team player within you.

> Mighty Violet Flame, come forth in the Light of God that never, never, never fails. Mighty Violet Flame, come forth and heal all that ails me. Mighty Violet Flame, come forth and bring cooperation in, through and around me. I seal this forth in the name of the Divine Plan and Divine Will. Mighty I AM!

So, you see, Dear hearts, decree this unto yourself and it is so. It is the affirmation of your divinity. It is the affirmation of your Co-creatorship. Yet, this prepares you for a greater conductivity of the emanation and the qualification of the Ray Forces within you. As the Great Central Sun is the grand conductor of these Rays, do you see how you now become as a conductor of the Ray Forces?

EMANATION

Answer: "By pronouncing the decree, yes, we actually enhance the conductivity, and you harmonize that conductivity."

This is the idea of liberation and freedom so that one is then led to become as ONE with the forces of the universe. This leads one naturally to the Consciousness of Unity in Unana. This is the principle that we apply. This is the principle that we utilize.

Question: "Truly, this is most enlightening. To consider that for all the embodiments and all the eons, we can, at this moment, transmute much of that. How often would you suggest that this decree be done and at what time of day?"

It is, of course, based upon each individual need. It is best, of course, that the individual prescribe this for himself, for only he would know the discomfort he is feeling. Only he would know the harmony that he is seeking. It is best for an individual to choose this for himself. Perhaps for one individual to use the Violet Flame once a day is all that is required. And yet, for another, whose discomfort and suffering is so great, perhaps he should use the Violet Flame a thousand times a day. Of course, this depends upon the person and his choices. But you see, Dear heart, when one begins to vibrate totally to this concept of the Violet Flame, to this concept of liberation and freedom, to this concept of greater unity within the self, one may speak this as a mantra and say it all day, throughout his being. It is not spoken, of course, through that spoken word but emanated through actions, emanated through choices, emanated through interactions with others. They carry this like a force-field, as part of their Astral Body, incorporated within their being. They carry it forward each day. This is just as sacred as sitting in front of your temple and shouting these decrees for all to hear. You see, Dear ones, it is possible to carry the mighty Violet Flame in, through and around your being all the time.

Question: "And how does one achieve this?"

Through focus and through the focus of one's intention through imbuing these qualities within oneself and bringing them forth into actions and choices. Do you see, Dear one, how the emanation is built? Like the coal, fueling the fire, the Violet Flame is present and builds a greater and a greater energy. This is the concept again of emanation.

Question: "Through this focus, what is it that you would suggest or direct anyone to visualize or out-picture or focus upon?"

It is individual choice, but if I were to recommend a program, perhaps it would be to say the Violet Flame seven times seven, forty-nine times. This would assure that a momentum would be gained for each of the Ray Forces within the being. Again, this is only a recommendation, and this is only brought forth in reference to your question so that you may begin to understand. The Violet Flame is then used forty-nine times per day, and from there the individual notices a lessening of the burdens within his life. Then perhaps

EMANATION

he would like to bring forth an element of the Violet Flame, actually an act of forgiveness, an act of mercy, an act of compassion as an intention of the demonstration of the Violet Flame. We know that intention and demonstration carry this forth into the physical world, and there we have an expansion, of the emanation of the Violet Flame. Do you understand?

Answer: "Yes, it is a step-by-step process."

It is a step-by-step process. There is no formula or exact way for this to work. It is about the chela's union and harmony with the Seven Forces, the Seven Rays. It is the chela's choice, and this choice is revealed through action.

Question: "I understand. The number seven, or the Rays of Light and Sound, are really as far as our consciousness can perceive, aren't they?"

Let us start one step at a time, and as our consciousness emanates and grows into that Mighty Flame, that Mighty Light of God that never, never fails, then one is ready to be introduced to greater light, to greater understanding and to greater endurance in the Unity of Consciousness.

Question: "So, in the use of the Violet Flame, when you asked us to decree for peace, we could ask for the harmonization of the Rays of all governments, all businesses, all global consciousness, could we not?"

This is the ideal use of the Violet Flame: what moves beyond selfish motive and into a motive that serves the greater good. As I stated before, when suffering is lessened for your neighbor, indeed is not the suffering lessened for you?

Answer: "True, that is truly compassion. So this would probably be the most useful pivotal point for all types of healing. Yes, your personal challenges, but for the Earth Changes themselves."

Of course, beloved, this is the intention of the Violet Flame, to free and liberate one from fear, to free and liberate one from all that would inhibit the greater union with that Mighty Light of God. So, Dear heart, as we seek completion of this lesson, if there are no more questions I shall take my leave.

Answer: "No, I have no further questions, but, as usual, much more work to do."

> In that Mighty Light of God that never fails, I AM the Ember of the Violet Flame burning through all desire, burning now to seek the ONE service, the mighty union of all. So be it. Hitaka.

EMANATION

Answer: "So be it, and thank you."

Unless you have further questions, I shall take my leave from your realm and will be glad to return with further Prophecies of Peace. Hitaka!

3

Behind the Interplay
Saint Germain Gives Further Instruction on Ray Forces and Sound

GREETINGS, BELOVEDS, IN THAT MIGHTY VIOLET FLAME I AM SAINT GERMAIN, AND I REQUEST PERMISSION TO COME FORWARD.

"Please, Saint Germain, come forward."

Dear ones, at this time I would like to speak to you about service. Service comes forward to release you from your own Karmic burden, your own Karmic debts. However, Dear ones, service, as you well know, is an expression of the intention of your own soul. And that intention is sometimes clouded with the ego, other yearnings and other desires. You have known at times those who have come forward offering to help you, yet they have come forward wanting only something of their own desire, and expressing their own desire. Service in its purest form is without desire. It gives only for the want of giving. Service lifts your Karmic debt. It can release your bondage to the wheel of life. It is another opportunity for you to free yourself, to be spiritually liberated. Service is another way that your life is lifted into spiritual light. Service allows one to see things from a more detached perspective, so that you may qualify the Rays of Light within your (astrological) chart to a higher understanding, to a higher learning, so that you may free the Rays of Light functioning within your aura to a higher qualification. Service also is again very much like the coal in the fire; it brings a greater emanation, and builds energy. But it is always intention that will determine how and when the emanation shall occur. So, it is important to scrutinize your intention. It is important for you to understand the motive behind all that you do and the reason for so doing. For service, you see, can create Karma within itself. That from which you set out to free yourself can indeed turn around and create more. You see, Dear ones, the chelas upon the path, when they offer themselves to be of service, may indeed encumber themselves even more Karma in their own web of ego demand. It is important to understand desire, the working of desire, and where desires may lead you. Clarify your intention in all offers of service; also clarify your intent before offering yourself of service. Do you have questions?

Answer: "Not at this time."

For more information and study topics on *Behind the Interplay*, see Appendix C, page 165.

BEHIND THE INTERPLAY

Light continues to flow within the Human Aura; light flows at its highest intention to fulfill the demands of the cosmos, the Great Central Sun. The light emanates from the planetary life forces, and you see, Dear ones, planets also are life forces. Life streams through a planet in the same way life streams through your body. We have explained this before in the teachings of Beloved Babajeran, but this teaching is congruent within this planetary system, such as Mars, Venus, Jupiter and Saturn, and so on and on. Even your moon contains a life force unto itself. Although it may seem to be a more collective life force, or a collective being. But, in the same way you contain many harmonizing systems—a circulatory system, a respiratory system, and an immune system within your body, the planets work similarly. They contain systems that must come together and harmonize for them to properly arc energies to planet earth.

Planet earth at this time, Beloved Babajeran, is the ONE schoolhouse where HU-mans are learning. This learning is a very important process. It requires many lifetimes and allows the soul, the HU-man soul, to evolve through the course of experience. Experience is the only teacher from which one develops the idea of one's will, choice, and conscience. So, Dear hearts, it is indeed many lifetimes that you spend here on planet earth learning and growing through the many experiences contained within these lifetimes. The planets, the greater servants, and Beloved Babajeran, a greater servant unto herself, offer themselves to be of service to you during this your evolution. They offer themselves, arcing light and sound to you, and bring forward throughout your own Astral Body a multitude of experiences that create an evolutionary and experiential understanding. It is the apex of each experience that leads you to greater understanding, greater force, and a greater will for you to choose. Choosing seems to be the vehicle for the HU-man to begin to distinguish one experience from another.

When one begins to understand the Ray Forces and how they work and orchestrate the many experiences throughout one's body, one begins to understand how to differentiate the various experiences. It is the Ray Forces that give us the multitude of experiences throughout the solar system. And on planet earth a variety of experiences are afforded through the Ray Forces. As the Ray Forces arc themselves from the Great Central Sun to the planets who are indeed of service to this force greater than themselves, they, in turn, arc the energy to Beloved Babajeran. It is here that the energies are picked up through the Astral Body, and human experience unfolds. History is created, and the whole drama, the whole play is then set forward for learning to gain ever important experience. Beloved Sananda has said in past discourse, "What is the difference between you and me?" What the difference is indeed, Dear ones, but *experience*. And it is the Rays, through the interplay of the harmonies of the spheres, that light and sound blend and create your all-expanded awareness.

Intention exists behind the interplay of the Rays. This intention is orchestrated, not only through your will and through your choices, but also by your Karma and your past; Karma is one action for another, and seeks the balance within and the balance without. Many upon the Earth Plane and Planet define Karma to be a punishment, the meter of judgment. But it is not, Dear one, for judgment and punishment exist only within yourself and the way in which you view circumstance, through your beliefs and your choices; and the way in which you

Light of Awakening

BEHIND THE INTERPLAY

deal with any given situation, or the actions in those situations, and how you create balance. The Higher Self is ever-present through each incarnation, and ever-present through all experiences, is there as the guiding angel, the guiding force, to see that balance is kept and restored within all situations. This allows for a greater harmony in the interplay of the Rays and for the interplay of sound within the astral field. You see, Dear ones, it is almost as if the Astral Body is a grand book to be read, a grand book with an ever-changing plot, an ever-changing beginning, and an ever-changing end. It is this book that you must learn to read and begin to write for yourself, page by page, your own script, your own part, to achieve Mastership of the Ray Forces and the forces of sound.

It is important that you begin to understand each Ray Force is also complemented by a great sound. Many cultures have brought forward the various sounds that they resonate to in terms of light. I have given to you the "HU" sound. The "HU" sound vibrates to the Mighty Violet Flame of Mercy and Forgiveness. When I give you the "HU" sound to use as a vibration, or to use as a mantra, it is used to bring a completeness to all that you do. All is held within that vibration of finer tuning, with respect to forgiveness, mercy, and Divine Intervention. The Vibration of "HU" is used so that you may be brought into a greater understanding, into a greater Oneship with all things. It is the "HU" vibration that vibrates to the higher levels of the Violet Flame. The Violet Flame is birthed out of the Blue Flame, the Blue Flame of Will and Conscience, the Blue Flame of Choice, that Blue Flame of Direction and Directive Power. But it is indeed the Violet Flame, when it is blended with the Pink Flame of Love, that Divine Compassion becomes a higher qualification of this force. And it is the "HU" vibration that you shall use alongside it to intensify its work.

For instance, when you practice a Violet Flame decree: *"Mighty Violet Flame blaze in, through and around all my past Karma. Mighty Violet Flame blaze in, through, and around all of my present choices. Mighty Violet Flame blaze in, through and around me, raising me into the glory and the life of the Ascension."* Then repeat, "HU, HU, HU" three times three. This commands the Law of the Trinity and seals the energy. The sealing is very much like a seal that exists upon a chakra. Those who have developed their Auric Vision can see, when they work on an energy field or when they view their own energy field, a seal exists at the end of every chakra or center where light is taken in and released. This seal is of vast importance, for sealing the Chakra System enveloping the Human Aura seals the intention of a new creation. This allows the intention to carry through from the point of creation, the choice and the conscious will of the Co-creator. So, you see, sound acts as a complement to light and sound, and light, like best friends, create harmony similar to the Seven Rays and their work in the interplay of light. Sound comes seals and delivers the essence of the *lighted command.* Sound sets the intention, allows, and creates its manifestation or action. Do you understand?

Answer: "Yes, I do."

Dear one, do you have questions?

Answer: "Not at this time."

BEHIND THE INTERPLAY

So, sound within itself is of major importance to bring forward each command to a higher level, a higher understanding, and to allow it to bring forward its actions from your Divine Source.

Let us continue. Of course, each of the colors of light has its own sound vibration. It is best, though, that each chela find the sound vibration himself. It is best that each chela begin to meditate upon each of the Ray Forces, and through meditation a sound will be revealed. Why is this so? Each chela is individualized through his differing experiences, through the many choices they have made throughout their travels upon the Earth Plane and Planet. Sound within itself is a harmonizing effect, and seeks its own level. There are certain sounds that can be given to you, and they carry a very high frequency. But if the chela is not prepared or ready to absorb that certain sound energy, it will not, and cannot, bring the Rays into their consummate interplay. So, it is more important for the chela to find the sound vibration that will meet the interplay of his or her own Rays.

The process for this is quite easy. Within meditation, you will begin to hear a sound vibration. Soon, you will identify this sound starting with a consonant. It will contain a vowel sound. Very often these sound vibrations end with the "M" or the "ING" sound—this creates, of course, the vibration within the human to activate the Kundalini. This is of vast importance to understand that each find one's own sound vibration to the Ray Force that one is integrating within one's system.

It is also of vast importance to continue to use the Violet Flame, for the Violet Flame will lift the chela to a higher realm, and a higher understanding. Within the time of meditation, there will also be occurrences of hearing mathematical harmonies associated with each sound vibration. Sometimes these sound vibrations are rythmatic, tapping out within the mind their own repeated rhythm. This is an important note for the chela, for these mathematical harmonies work to bring a correction or a harmonization effect for the Ray Forces. I will not give you a set formula on how to activate sound and light to work together as ONE. It is more important that each chela, through the medium of his or her own experience, find this path. As I have stated before, Dear ones, it is most important to know thyself, and this becomes your grand experience, as your time in meditation and the interplay of the Rays become your *own* laboratory. Through your own practice, you will experience the force of God working within you, and this indeed will give you a new experience, a new evolution, and a greater understanding. Above all, Dear hearts, meditate with a clear intention, with a clear understanding of your own service to that Mighty Light of God that never fails. Do you have questions?

Answer: "Not at this time."

BEHIND THE INTERPLAY

So, Dear hearts, I shall take my leave from you, for this is the discourse of the day, and I shall return at a later time to bring forward more information.

Response: "Thank you very much."

4

A New Day
Saint Germain and El Morya Present Prophecies and Teachings on Beliefs

GREETINGS, BELOVEDS, IN THAT MIGHTY CHRIST, I AM SAINT GERMAIN, AND I STREAM FORTH ON THAT MIGHTY VIOLET RAY OF MERCY AND FORGIVENESS.

As usual, Dear ones, I ask permission to come forward.

"Dear one, come forth."

Beloveds, the work at hand is indeed important, for I have explained before in previous discourses that the information that is soon to be received is, shall we say, of a finer quality and lies beyond the tip of the iceberg. As I have explained before, the prophetic material, the I AM America Maps, the Freedom Star Map, were all given like an appetizer to a main course. For now, the information must be given to prepare humanity for a greater evolution, and for a greater understanding of their Divine Destiny. For you see, Dear ones, the work that is now in front of the Spiritual Hierarchy is that of raising the vibration through the spiritual evolution of humanity. Those who have the eyes to see, the ears to hear and the hands to do, will now come forward in this New Time, this Golden Age that is indeed the important part of this Prophecy.

For you see, Dear ones, it has long been determined that humanity shall raise its vibration to a greater understanding, and to a greater knowledge of their internal light. This has long been known as the Ascension. There have been those who have raised their vibration, understanding, and consciousness, and who now reside in New Dimensions, in a new understanding of breath, light, sound, thought, feeling and action. So, Dear hearts, in this New Time it is important that you understand so that you may prepare yourself for the great opportunity that now awaits. This great opportunity is one that many have prayed for, sought after, lusted after and now thirst for, for many embodiments, and they now wait for this most especial time. This is a time when mankind will be adjusted in many ways. Frequencies will change, not only in the electromagnetic field, which is the Human Aura, but there will be an understanding, a telepathic Oneness, a union between all of humanity. We have explained this before as Unana. You know this now as Unity Consciousness. Prior to any significant change, there must be changes that happen inside. Today, we see dissent among humanity— Brother against Brother, Sister against Sister, strife among families, but this is just a greater prepara-

---

For more information and study topics on *A New Day*, see Appendix D, page 171.

A NEW DAY

tion for the understanding of Unity Consciousness. The old ideas, the old beliefs, must first be shattered. Beloved Sananda has said in previous discourses that in order for new wine to be poured, a new wine skin must be structured. This, too, is the process of Ascension. It is indeed structuring a new wine skin, a new belief, a new concept.

The first of these beliefs is, as I have said before, "Down with death; conscious immortality arise." You see, Dear hearts, beloveds, your consciousness is indeed immortal, your thoughts stream forth lifetime through lifetime, ready for you to access at any moment so that you may understand in full knowledge and in full light all circumstances in front of you. The idea of a Shroud of Darkness over your consciousness is one you have instilled through your present beliefs. The information may not be carried from lifetime to lifetime. But you see, Dear one, this an old belief, and in order to maintain and understand the New Consciousness, one must access information from lifetime to lifetime so that the proper choices are made. When one begins to understand that they are consciously immortal, that there is a part of them that never dies, but only the physical body, this prepares the new wine skin. When thoughts are continuously upon immortality, feelings and actions will soon follow. These feelings and actions create a new body, a body that is not only linked consciously from one to the next in Unana, in Unity Consciousness, but is also linked as ONE to Beloved Babajeran, to the Mother Earth. For you see the dramas, the tears, the fears in each lifetime with its own desires, wants and trappings, along with its Karma, and with its Dharma has been played out on Mother Earth. Mother Earth has served in essence as a witness, as a witness to all the events that you have staged in your journey here upon schoolroom Earth, learning, loving, and living. She, too, comes forward to bring assistance as the grand teacher that she truly is. This assistance helps you to unify from within and create unity within all experiences. This unification of self is extremely important, for unification of self brings forth the birth of conscience, and it is only when Unity Consciousness is united with conscience, or your chosen course of direction, then and only then may Ascension and the work as a Co-creator come forward in its greatness and in its fullness. So, it is true that at this time the Beloved Babajeran has offered herself to be of assistance.

We have explained certain geophysical locations upon the Earth Plane and Planet. These are known as the Golden City Vortices. We have explained these quite thoroughly in other discourses, but we hope through this material to explain exactly and directly their purpose, their manifestation, and the role they will play in the times to come. Each Vortex is an energy source upon Beloved Babajeran—one that has been manifested directly by her to bring forth a cosmic lesson and, therefore, a cosmic unity within each individual. You realize now that, as a small child when you touched a hot stove, the result was your burned finger. This is the idea of cause and effect. Within a Golden City Vortex, one begins to understand cause and effect in its most simple manner. Today, with Time Compaction, the speeding up of events and the society that mankind has chosen to live through, and the constant and the steady hammering of this illusion, one is unable to recognize cause and effect. This has caused deterioration within humanity, an inability to recognize the truth that lies within, the truth of their Divine Destiny, and their own immortality. Consciousness and conscience work together as ONE and create a unity to body, mind and soul. So, when one is in a Golden City Vortex, because of the arrangements of energies through the assistance of the Beloved

Light of Awakening

A NEW DAY

Cosmic Beings—the Elohim of this earth and Mother Babajeran—these teachings are quickly understood. The individual enters into a New Consciousness through body, mind, and soul, an acceleration that not only brings a telepathic response through Unana but also an immortality of such, an understanding that all is connected as ONE. All life is for life, and death is indeed the ultimate illusion. This begins with the removal of fear held at a cellular level—fear that you have held from embodiment through embodiment, lifetime after lifetime. This fear that has kept you trapped within the shell of the physical body. It is a time to release this fear, primarily the fear of physical death. As I have said before in previous work, as the thought continues, the feelings and actions model themselves in the same way a potter's wheel forms clay. The hands of God are indeed your hands upon this piece of clay, and it is through your choice and your will that you begin anew. It is your choice if you begin anew.

Perhaps this shall be the first place we will begin. We will begin with this discourse, "Beginning Anew," "Starting Anew," "A New Day."

I would like to introduce the one who shall start this discourse on "A New Day." He is Beloved Brother El Morya. (Saint Germain steps back and Beloved El Morya comes forth.)

El Morya: "Greetings, chelas. I ask permission to come forward."

Answer: "Please come forward, El Morya."

Beginning anew is an important concept for those who wish to have a new mind. A new mind begins within the intention. This intention is extremely important. It comes within the depth of the soul. This intention determines the outcome—the outcome of all events, and all of the actions that the chela has come to experience. Many upon the Earth Plane and Planet lay down their best plans. They play them out, and then in anguish and sorrow wonder why such plans did not unfold as they had wished and hoped. The reason is quite simple, for not once did they consider their intention, and intention must be closely aligned to Will. To begin anew, one must identify and understand one's own Will—the Will that runs through him—then you begin to understand the Will that encompasses all choice, the flora of choice that has allowed your creation. Choice is the backbone of any person upon this planet. Therefore, choice very often can be seen in the Human Aura. It can be seen as a Vertical Power Current that runs along the spine, and attaches itself to the Mother Earth, and the lines to Father Sun. We have encountered those throughout life who we may judge and say, "He has no backbone." "She has no will." They are those whose will is indeed broken, whose idea of their own choice is no longer theirs, who give their will over to collective illusion, collective thoughts, collective feelings. Their actions mirror only those of the collective mind, caught up in fads, in whimsies and in what only others tell them to do. When one makes the choice to begin anew, he makes the choice within himself through an internal process. It is sparked within himself. It is not sparked from any outer influence, but comes through an inner influence, and this grows in its strength and in its current. This you have seen many times upon the Earth Plane and Planet as electricity crackling down as lightning. This is indeed the entity, Beloved Mother Babajeran making Her choice, aligning Her will to the Divine.

A NEW DAY

In the beginning, to begin anew, one may not particularly choose to align to the Divine Will. In the beginning, one may choose to align to his own wishes, to his own Heart's Desire. This is perfectly normal, and is a developmental stage. But, as you well know, the result of all action is but education, and soon the chela becomes quite educated and begins to understand a greater working, pulse and magnetic pull. One begins to understand that beginning anew is not a selfish action, but their intention becomes aligned to conscience. And there is the true birth of Divine Will, where one begins to understand the purpose, the direction, and the flow and that all must contain within it the Divine Plan as a plan Co-created among all God forces. Unity Consciousness does not see one God force as greater than another. It sees all God force *equal to*. This allows for a greater understanding of cooperation and of harmony. The concept of "equal to" is again a step in beginning anew. In beginning anew, one prepares the body, the mind and, inevitably, the consciousness to start fresh. Have you ever heard of a fresh start, a day in which all things seem changed, a day when you can breathe a sigh of relief and begin anew?

This is the same consciousness that must be utilized to gain your Ascension. You must discard and throw away the old beliefs, old choices, old collective illusions that will not serve your movement into the ONE. What is holding you back? What are the things that are holding you back? Ultimately, when you examine each and every one of these, you will find it is fear of death, conclusion, fear of ending, fear of decay and destruction. When one releases such fears, one becomes ready to begin anew. Throw them away. Make the choice from within. Find you own backbone. This is your Will. It is your Divine Gift, given to you so you may become a true *Divine Inheritor*. Contemplate and meditate upon this concept. Now, I shall turn the podium back to Beloved Saint Germain; of course, if there are no questions.

Question: "Intention, as you have brought forward, both of you, intention, as you have shared before, determines the outcome. In observing humanity, the fear that drives them forward to want Ascension is truly the fear of death, the fear of aging, the fear of decay. This I have observed in everyone, including myself. However, the great desire to be of service to the upliftment of humanity, the great desire to see humanity come to its Divine Plan, its true design, its entering into the ONE, many times overpowers any of those, oh, doubts. So, if there were a one, two, three process to be described by you for those who will hear this tape and who will read this as a transcribed book, I would assume from your discourse that the first is to determine your intention. Why would you want Ascension? Why would you want immortality thought of as consciousness? Why? And so I ask you, give us the reason Why for this."

The greater union that exists beyond the HU-man is a Body of Light that no longer requires physical incarnation. The drudgery then is released of the physical plane, but it is no longer perceived as drudgery, instead it is embraced as *life for life*. As I have said before, "Live life for life." When one begins to understand the greater plan Divine, they see the interconnection between all circumstances, and between all situations. This is Unana. As a simple program, what would I prescribe? Of all things, Beloved Saint Germain, my Brother in Service to Light and Sound, would call upon that Mighty Violet Ray. Of course, what is contained

Light of Awakening

A NEW DAY

within the Violet Ray but that Ray of Truth, the Blue Ray that understands the alignment of the Will. When I speak about intention and the alignment of the Will, it is important that one spend time alone, that one spend time in simplicity to allow the unessential to drop away. How long would I prescribe? As long as it takes—as long as it takes—Dear one, to spend your time in solace and reflection. Spend your time in meditation upon the ONE. What is the ONE intention that you hold? What is the ONE will that you are of? What is the ONE choice that is of most importance to you? If this takes but one day, then so be it. If it takes ten years, so be it. Many say *time is of the essence*, but, in this one particular instance, I would say *time must be cast aside*. It is more important that you understand and totally embody *experience*, for there is the ONE unity that exists within you. And it is the connection of you to the All. Of all things that must be understood, first is that the hypnotic illusion living upon the earth in the temporary encasement of the physical body perceives a separation that exists between that one individual life and the many other individual lives that exist upon the earth at any given time. To understand a grander plan, to understand the connection between all, one must integrate from inside and feel a unity within. Do you understand?

Answer: "So, what you're saying is that your appearance to us as Mahatma El Morya is only for our understanding. The Brotherhood and Sisterhood of Light and Sound are ONE."

This is so, Dear ones. We take on form at Will, so that we are able to convey particular and certain focused ideas, focused thoughts, focused vibrations for the work at hand. In this case, it is a preparation of consciousness so that humanity may begin the greater and grander change.

As a second reflection upon your question, I would propose to use that Mighty Violet Ray of mercy and compassion and forgiveness. Of course, this is blended with the Pink Ray of Love. When one develops this greater connection, this greater understanding, transmutation is the end result. If you would like more instruction upon this Violet Ray, Beloved Saint Germain will speak.

Response: "Yes, but I have one other question."

Proceed.

Question: "Since all transmutation starts with intention and the redefining of the Alignment of Will, it would seem that your individual existence has now been collectively stuck together so that it is not one will, but it is a unified will. For an individual, such as myself, choosing to join you, you have given reflection and the Violet Flame as the first two steps. The question that I ask is, once we have fulfilled all these desires that we have, all these little magnetic attachments to incarnations repeatedly, and it seems like the same things, new day, I think that humanity gets to the place where it becomes pointless. So, the only thing that is left is the inevitable, and that is to align one's own choices, will and intention to the unified choice for the movement of humanity and the uplifting of consciousness."

A NEW DAY

But the illusion of your thinking is the same things, new day. A New Day does not come forward with the same things. It is the altering of the thoughts. It is the altering of the feelings and the actions that creates a New Day. A New Day comes forward when one has simply stated the intention of one's purpose. It is that simple. It takes a time of release, releasing that which no longer serves the Greater Will Divine. How does one apply such a concept to release that which no longer serves that Greater Plan Divine? You must evaluate your own life and see what is within your life that no longer serves your greater plan. Have the courage to create a greater plan for your life. Have the courage to write it down. Have the courage to meditate upon it. Have the courage to live it, feel it, act it out. Then you will understand what is that that is serving you. What is serving the Greater Plan Divine of your life? Do you understand?

Answer: "Yes, you have answered my question sufficiently."

And now I shall turn this over to Beloved Saint Germain.

Response: "Thank you."

El Morya: At this moment, I would like to take a brief break.

Response: "As you so choose."

Saint Germain: In that the Mighty Violet Flame, I come forward. Again, I must ask permission to continue this discourse.

Response: "Please come forward. You are most welcome."

As Beloved Brother El Morya has stated, to use the releasing of old energy patterns, old thoughts of disease, old thoughts of decay, all thoughts of death, which can bring forward a greater understanding and a greater unity of the soul, how is this achieved? Of course, in the beginning it is difficult. You have been hypnotized, you see, through collective illusion. Each day in your world when you read a new book, talk to a new person, turn on your television, read a newspaper, what are you participating in? A collective hypnotic illusion of what others think the world must be, reflecting it back to you. You take that unto yourself, digest it as food, assimilate it within your being, and then your cells reflect that thought through feeling and action. How does one begin to embrace the New Day? How does one begin to embrace a new body, a New Consciousness? One must begin through the gift that was given eons ago through the Lords of Venus, and that is the use of the Violet Flame. As I have said repeatedly, it is only through the use of the Violet Flame that one can begin to release, to let go of, these past patterns that no longer serve, and no longer allow a New Day to emerge. When you become discouraged, when you wonder, will this ever end? That is the time, in that most perfect instant, to call forth the Violet Flame.

A NEW DAY

Violet Flame, I AM. God, I AM, Violet Flame. Come forward in this instant manifesting perfection in, through and around me. Violet Flame, I AM. God, I AM Perfection, Violet Flame.

And you see, Dear ones, in that instant the Violet Flame has provided the gift, that one Divine Intervention, in the same way that lightning cracks on Beloved Babajeran. In that instant, the Violet Flame cracks within you, aligning your will, releasing all thoughts, feelings and actions that no longer serve you. When you begin to ponder upon the past through worry and guilt, what is it that you are really engaging in? Fear. The fear of lack or a perceived lack of perfection. These are the things that must be addressed in order for the New Day to come forward in your hearts and in your mind. These are, indeed, the most important key elements. The use of the Violet Flame, may it ever be within you, within your hearts and shared with all of humanity, for the Violet Flame is indeed Divine Intervention— Divine Intervention structured to lift you out of suffering, limitation, death, destruction, and into the New Day.

Violet Flame, I AM. God, I AM, Violet Flame.

Before I proceed with more instruction, are there questions?

Answer: "Yes."

Proceed.

Question: "If we go back to intention, we address that many people, to this day, probably do the Violet Flame, and yet their bodies become old, they decay, they die. And they are still caught in the illusion as we are here in those of us who choose to help you. If the intention were to redirect for personal freedom, to redirect to be ONE with you, to be ONE in the Great Divine Plan, and the Violet Flame were applied to that intention, would that be a much more expedient transmutation?"

This is quite perceptive, for indeed, the Violet Flame may be applied with a specific idea in mind, a specific focus in mind. If one is practicing Brother El Morya's technique of simplicity and feels that his life is still cluttered, use of the Violet Flame to gain simplicity will only enhance and unencumber the consciousness, the thoughts, to allow the New Day to come forward. To allow a New Day to come forward will allow a new week to come forward. A new week becomes a new month. A month becomes a year. And before long what is it that has been created? But an age, a New Age, a Golden Age, and an age that is quite different from the time humanity is now experiencing. But we must start with our little steps. We must start with the necessary education that is needed now to begin. Questions?

Question: "Yes. As the intention, we will take me, as an average person, and we will say, "It is now my intention to become ONE with the Great Divine Plan." And I will sit and decree

A NEW DAY

upon that intention. Instead of focusing on the imbalances that I perceive, is it now more expedient to focus upon the unity of the Great Divine Plan?"

It is expedient to focus upon that which you wish to Co-create, and focus through the use of the Violet Flame on all that would hinder you, or keep you from the fulfillment of that singular intention or focus to be released in a form of transmutation to the Violet Flame of transformation, mercy, compassion, forgiveness. You see, Dear one, until one has truly forgiven oneself, it is almost impossible to move forward into the New Day. This may be compartmentalized into a series of exercises that the chela may then practice. For instance, say that they have decided to embark upon Brother El Morya's lesson of simplicity to find a New Day, but they are still hampered by feelings of guilt concerning an event that happened, perhaps, five years prior. Call upon that Mighty Violet Flame. Transmute the cause, effect, the record and memory of that event, and then one is able to move forward without a harness around one's neck holding him back. When we are held back in this way it is not so much a sin against humanity, but a great sin against the self. It is the little sins of the self that keep us trapped in the ideas of death, delay, destruction and catastrophe. To set yourself free—to truly set yourself free—will require perseverance. But it will only require perseverance in one application, and that is the plea to the Violet Flame for Divine Intervention to allow its Ray of Light to come forward into your life. Do you understand?

Answer: "Yes, I understand that it transmutes."

Questions?

Response: "But I still haven't figured out, even for myself, what the specific intention would be to move myself forward, which now requires immense meditation."

Know thyself, Dear chelas of my heart. Know thyself, and there shall be the first component of your freedom. To create your New Day, you must indeed know thyself.

Answer: "So, truly that is the format that everyone must follow, and I assume it is the one that you, too, followed to reach the place where you are now."

It is true, Dear one, that it was only through Grace and Divine Intervention that I was allowed this experience to be truth for myself. Now, I would like to proceed with further instruction.

A NEW DAY

It is through the consciousness of Unana that humanity can and will move forward. First, this will be achieved through understanding the need for change. When one accepts that things must change, they can accept that the change must happen first within them, and that the change must reflect to the outer, to their family, loved ones, partner, those with whom they may work, their neighbor and onward into their community. These changes are absolutely necessary in order for the New Day to come forward. From there, the change may reflect to a collective level, and then the change becomes collective reality. Do we need Earth Changes in order to create such changes within ourselves? In some respects, some would say it is necessary, for others will not change unless an outer influence is forced upon them. But is this truly the type of change that is needed? As you can see, Dear ones, Dear hearts, Dear chelas, it is the inner change that truly brings about the constructive change. It is the inner change that brings about the New Day, hence the New Age and the New Time. So, how shall this be achieved? The Greater Plan Divine working with all of us is designed first toward forgiveness—forgiveness of all past mistakes, injustices, understandings where one feels inequities, hurts and harms. These must first be released and dropped from a person's life so that he can move forward in the light of a New Day. When the Ray of Light is so firmly planted within one's heart, one begins to reflect upon the alignment of his will to a Divine Purpose. Beloved Babajeran has offered herself at this time to be of service to humanity, to allow an acceleration of understanding, an acceleration into the realms of light, an acceleration into the New Times.

The five areas known as the Golden City Vortices shall indeed be put forward as locations upon the earth, specifically now, within the United States, so that people may travel to them. Feel these energies at an experiential level, and, when within them, occurrences will take place through collective thought form. Do you understand?

Answer: "Yes, so it is your recommendation that people move to the Golden City Vortex centers and have an intention for moving there."

Such movement will allow a movement within themselves. If you feel you cannot release injustice, a sense of inequity within your life, it is suggested that you take a trip to assimilate the Vortex of Wahanee. There, the energies of the Violet Flame, if they cannot be felt, will be absorbed. As I have said before, to drink the water, breathe the air, raise vegetables and to ingest them in an area such as this will increase the Vibration of that single focus within yourself. You see, Dear hearts, Beloved El Morya has put forward to bring forward the ONE, to bring forward truth, harmony and inevitably cooperation; and to bring forward feelings of peace within oneself. One would then travel to the Vortex of Gobean, for that will instill and insight this action within the chela who is seeking to understand, who is seeking to gain a knowledge of Unana. You see, Dear hearts, this is the Greater Plan Divine. Questions?

Question: "Similarly, for each of the Ray qualities that are represented and brought to life in the Golden Cities, if that truly is the intention for the person to experience and to transmute, and in some instances just to absorb, then at the very least, a trip to these areas and at the very most, a new residence?"

A NEW DAY

Whatever one would choose. When one feels he has assimilated these energies, he may move on, move back to where he lived prior, or move on to another Vortex. You see, Dear ones, these energies have been presented so that one may gain a greater understanding of the ONE—a greater union with Mother Earth, a greater union within the Self and his own God, I AM; a greater union with the Hierarchy. It is this union that is sought, a union of body, mind and soul, so that the New Day may begin. One may not perceive a New Day until one has released the past, which holds him from the future. One may not live in the present until the past is no longer in front of him, tripping him up much as a block that one might stumble over. To live fluidly in the now is to release all that has kept you from your Ever-present now, from your ever-present Oneship. These are the teachings that we will elaborate on, each of the Golden Cities, so that chelas and students will understand what they are present for at this time and the great gift they can bring in a grander service.

You see, Dear ones, the Prophecies were given to tantalize those to see the need for change, and now we must move within the greater context of that teaching. It is change that must be made inside. There will be those who will not need to travel to a Golden City to take in the energies. It may not be necessary, but they are brought at this time to bring a greater acceleration: a greater acceleration vibrationally, electro magnetically; an acceleration of thoughts; an acceleration of feeling. In fact, there will even be an acceleration of the concept of time when one is within a Golden City. That is why the physical body requires less sleep when one first enters a Golden City. These are all concepts that we hold to lay down one by one in the next few weeks and months, as we spend our time releasing this information for humanity.

Now, I would like to lay down a template for the way in which we shall work together. As you well know, Dear chelas, I, along with those who work with me, prefer to build an energy. In building energy around a project, it allows a greater harmony and a greater clarity to be brought forward in the works. This we taught with the I AM America Map. Do you remember when we instructed you to place your left hand over your heart, your right hand to project it outward and to bring that visualization into its fullness? We were building an energy, and we shall do the same within that context in releasing the teachings of Gobean. It would be best if we selected a time each day to meet, one in which we can comfortably provide the information and not interfere with your day, yet dispense the information so that it may help all of humanity.

Question: "What was the time that you used previously?"

Early morning hours are always best for the collective consciousness. However, if this is impossible, we can work with other times. However, it is our suggestion that we work at 6 a.m. each morning.

Response: "We will do that, then."

A NEW DAY

We will instruct on the days we will come forward. We will take frequent breaks. This will allow rest and relaxation, but a more important aspect for the assimilation of the information, so that it may be organized and then utilized.

Now, some visualizations. Bring out the template of the Gobean Vortex, and each day I ask you in your meditation and your visualizations to perform the same technique of the left hand over the heart and projecting the energies out of the right hand toward the Gobean Vortex. Is this understood?

Answer: "Yes."

Then proceed every day until completion of these teachings. Master El Morya will serve as the Master Teacher instructor. I shall serve as Master of Ceremony and will provide an interface. Do you understand?

Answer: "Yes."

Are there any questions, Dear heart?

Answer: "Not about the process and the project."

Then, let us proceed in Grace and Divine Intervention. Let us proceed in the light of a New Day and the hope of a New Age. OM Manaya Pitaya Hitaka. So be it, Beloveds.

Response: "So be it. Hitaka."

5

A Quickening
Saint Germain and El Morya Offer Prophecies and Teachings on the Golden Cities

Greetings, Beloved, in that Mighty Violet Ray. I AM Saint Germain, and I request permission to come forward. .

"Please, dear Master, come forward."

In that Mighty Violet Ray that streams forth from the Logos, that streams forth from the heart of Helios and Vesta, I come on that wave, a wave such as time. Upon the Earth Plane and Planet, this time period known as Time Compaction is, indeed, a time when you may ponder and question, "Can I take much more of this?" You see, Dear ones, this time that you are now living is a Time of Opportunity, a time where action upon action is a time where you may now transmute those many fears, longings and desires that you have held through each lifetime. It is only through the use of the Violet Ray that one may move forward in the desire of their choice. You see, Dear ones, this time that has been brought forward, a time that is indeed for the evolution for all of humanity; a time when Unana will reign supreme upon the Earth Plane and Planet. Unity of Consciousness will come forward to bring forward that Law of the Best and the Highest Good. But, Dear ones, Time Compaction, itself, must be understood so that you will understand the use of the Violet Ray so you may move forward. You see, Dear ones, as we have discussed in "The Point of Perception" it is thought, feeling and action that Co-creates this reality in which you are living. But it is also your choice, Dear ones, and choice upon choice, desire upon desire. This is indeed a Time of Endings, a time when we enter into the fires of purification. What is this fire of purification? But only Time Compaction. It is as if one event is compressing upon another, tightly compacted, neatly one up against the other. And you feel as though you are stressed and harried. But, Dear ones, let me assure you that this is indeed also a time that has been given so that you will understand your own actions, your own thoughts, and will hone that faculty of choice. You see, Dear ones, to move into the Point of Perception, to understand your role as true Co-creator of your reality, you must understand your choice, the importance and the value of such. Time Compaction has been given as a great gift for you to instantly understand your thoughts, your feelings and your actions. It is as an Instant-Thought-Manifestation.

Now, let me diagram:

For more information and study topics on *A Quickening*, see Appendix E, page 179.

A QUICKENING

(He is giving a Vortex structure, almost a swirling one. They are beside one another. The two larger funnels are meeting one another.)

You see, Dear ones, in Co-creation where one meets another, one idea that is, there is almost a collison course. And the two shall become as ONE.

From these two meeting one another, he is drawing the third, which comes from the bottom and the top and creates a circle around it. You see from this diagram that thoughts, when they seem to collide upon one another, compact upon one another, create a more whole thought, a newer thought. It is sometimes perceived that there are disharmonious thoughts that do not work together, but this is entirely untrue. What happens, indeed, is that some of the thoughts may not be acted upon, but they do, indeed, work together as ONE. All things work together as ONE, and in Time Compaction, one action upon the next, also comes together as ONE. You see, Dear ones, this is the beginning of the understanding of Unity Consciousness that all things will work together as ONE, as ONE unit, as ONE being of light.

In the New Dimension that you will be living in, the New Times that you are being brought to understand, Unity of Consciousness is the most important thing to grasp and understand. There are those who say, "Well, if I do not agree with this one, then I shall go my separate way." This is true in most instances that you do go your separate way, but the thoughts, the feelings and the actions that you perceived as a disharmony still created. All thoughts create. All actions create. And feeling is the beautiful tie that binds and can lift a thought into harmony. We have viewed this before as a Point of Perception, but the emotion is the most valuable key. We have discussed this before in prior discourses, known as the E-motion. The E-motion sometimes is known as sound. It is this sound vibration that harmonizes all things to come forward into this greater unity, this greater cause of action.

Then you collect yourself with another group who decide that their thoughts, their feelings and their actions are in harmony. And they say let us unite in our minds, our hearts and our hopes, our desires and our wishes. And yet nothing comes forward. Why is that so? The collective action was charged with disharmony. It became the impetus and the force, you see. Impetus and force enable an action and then another action to exist. This presence of this charge is most important in all things. The charge that you have created and the disharmonious situation are just as important as the creation of harmony. Also, this thrust of your character into your creation is most important. This again is the E-motion. It is for you, Dear chelas of my heart, to decide what charge you shall put forward. Shall it be one of joy, one of enthusiasm, one of complete and total ecstasy, thrilled beyond? It is yours to choose. Within this time, Beloved Mother Babajaren, along with help from your beloved Brothers and Sisters, are here to assist during Time Compaction so that you may understand why it is that so much is currently thrust upon you all at once.

We're preparing for a New Time, and as Beloved El Morya has said, "This New Day begins one step at a time." Before the New Day can start, we must close down the old one. Now we must leave behind all that is ready to be closed and turn the page. In turning the

A QUICKENING

page, one must understands how harmonious situations and disharmonious situations are created. How may one choose to create more harmony within one's life? How may one choose to walk away from disharmony? Now the charge, itself, that you may feel in a disharmonious situation that you do wish to walk away from? Of course, I would say, "Blaze it in that Mighty Flame of the Violet Flame. God I AM, Violet Flame." Using this Violet Flame on a daily basis, and I mean a daily usage, will indeed help and assist through this purification. But it is also very important, Dear ones, that you understand the choices that you continue to make while in the *charge of disharmony*. Take time away in meditation. Take time away to calm yourself, your mind and your thoughts; to quell your E-motion. Resting this E-motion is of vast import, to understand that it is the charge, like the trigger of the small pistol that leads one into yet another event and another.

This Wheel of Karma, as I have now explained to you, is engendered in your choices. Dear ones, Dear hearts, begin to understand this. Seek the solace of the soul, and there you will begin to find the true Fire of Freedom. Find this first in all things, and then you can return to a creation in its wholeness and fullness. Understand the times that you are living in. See it as an opportunity that has been given for you, and you can then move on in grace and in harmony.

Now, Dear ones, I shall open the floor for a brief set of questions.

Question: "Time Compaction has long been a question that most people have asked me. It has always been my opinion that the planet and the solar system were changing their position relative to the galaxy, and in the movement of that change, Time Compaction was one of the results. As this Time Compaction progresses, the electromagnetic charges, as we call them, that have been built up over the eons in the earth's atmosphere and in the atmosphere of the individual must go through a transmuting process, more so than ever, because of the new dynamics of electromagnetics and levels of consciousness that completely affect the planet at all layers and realms. Is this why you have stressed the Violet Flame so much?"

The Violet Flame can set you free from any trying circumstance, from any sense of dissension, from all disharmonies within the soul. It can also begin to foster the growth of peace and stillness. It is the sun and moon that create the pull of life upon the earth, and it is through the collective thoughts, feelings, actions and desires of humanity that any sense of gravitation exists upon the earth. There would be those of science who would argue with this concept, but it is this force, this total force of your thoughts holding together the collective reality of the earth. As I have said in many past discourses, the earth is a vast schoolroom where many can be taught, if they choose to learn. Through this gravitational pull, we are pulled in essence to understand ourselves. Know thyself, Dear ones, and the truth within shall set you free. During this period of Time Compaction, the choices, thoughts and desires of many other lifetimes are opened. Prior to this lifetime, an Akashic Record exists of your prior embodiments and is comprised of your many thoughts, feelings, desires, and actions. Now, the Karmas you wish to experience are poured into your life, for you to qualify into action, and

A QUICKENING

will again create harmony or disharmony. Do you see, Dear one, that it is a simple choice? If you choose to live with harmony or with disharmony, the gifts that have been given to you are the work of the Violet Flame. To call upon It, to live It and to breathe It. The Violet Flame is that Divine Intervention that can lift you from the most trying of circumstance, that can lift you from all suffering. It is brought as a Law of Mercy and Compassion and given to you so that you may find within yourself whom you truly are. Dear Divine ones, it is the work of the Violet Flame that will set you free, not only in mind, not only in feeling, but from the path that you feel encumbers you; from all transgressions that you perceive, from all guilt that you perceive. In the time to come, it is hoped that through the use of the Violet Flame the earth shall be lifted into that shiny Star of Freedom. And from that point a New Age will dawn, humanity will experience a New Time. Do you see the hope and wonder that awaits? It is indeed this simple.

Call upon the Vibration of "HU." Call upon the help of those who are here now to give you assistance.

Mighty Violet Flame, come forth through I AM That I AM. Mighty Violet Flame, from the Grace of the Divine Heart, I AM. Violet Flame, come forth. Blaze in, through and around all that keeps me from my Divine Path. Violet Flame, I AM. God, I AM. So be it.

When you command such a force into the action, it affects all around it.

Now, let us return to the drawing table. When we have looked at each of two thoughts as if they were colliding upon one another, they still create. They create a force. The Violet Flame affects the ONE. It acts as a point of harmony and unity, the birth of peace. Do you see now, as I describe these waves...it starts from the center in the same way that a pebble, when it is dropped into the center of a small puddle of water, sends its rippling effect to the outer edges? In the same way, the Violet Flame works in your creation and works within you. When you call upon the Violet Flame, it works from that perfect cell, the Eight-Sided Cell of Perfection within the heart of the Unfed Flame. There were times upon the Earth Plane and Planet when humanity used the Violet Flame so regularly that the plume grew among the masses, and the skies actually took on a Violet hue throughout the day, and the sun and the moon cast a Violet hue upon the earth. It was carried electromagnetically in the aura as light, and as sound. So you see, Dear ones, to call upon it collectively only increases this force. But why is it that we now live in a different time? It is this simple. It is forgetting. It is this forgetfulness through eon upon eon of fear, rejection, dejection and giving to *that* creation more power than the power of harmony or the power of joy. It is most simple to understand in this context, but it is the application of this use, of this Mighty Law in action that shall set you free. Questions?

Light of Awakening

A QUICKENING

Question: "Beloved Saint Germain, is there any additional information that you would like to share with us at this time?"

There is indeed much more information that I shall impart this day, but I wanted to open this discourse with the use of the Violet Flame, its application so that it could be understood in its fullness. To understand a law in action is a holy thing indeed. To understand this law within you is Divine.

Now I shall proceed.

Beloveds, the work in the Golden Cities is of great import. As you know before, we have identified many different areas of these Golden Cities so that you could understand them energetically, so that you could understand their purpose. The Golden Cities are interacting with Beloved Babajaren and the Ascended Masters, this Hierarchy of Service, at this time, to bring forth a stillness, a peace, a harmony, an understanding of the ONE in this Time of Tribulation upon the Earth Plane and Planet.

We've explained many facets about these cities so that you may understand how they interact with you. But it has been pointed out most succinctly through Beloved El Morya that the Stars themselves coalesce. It is the most direct force of the energy Rays, and it is in the Stars that we would like to give discourse so that you may begin to understand how they can be used to bring forth qualities within your life.

Now, I would like to bring forward Beloved El Morya. (El Morya steps forward.)

Greetings, chelas. I request permission to come forward.

Response: "Please come forward. Please come forward."

Dear ones, we have spoken upon a New Day. Now we must proceed, for there is more than a New Day. There is a New Time. To understand a New Time, you must change the way you perceive. To change the way you perceive, you must understand. To understand, you must begin with choice. You have had many choices of which way to go, to turn left or to turn right, to move forward or to move backward. Now, it is important that you review such choices and say, "Has this helped me?" "Am I now in a position in which I feel content?" Or "Am I just stagnating in the mire of my thoughts?" That I cannot tell you, Dear ones, but you must decide within yourself whether you are content—whether you feel peace, or do you only perceive contentment out of the fear of moving forward.

The Star of Gobean is now activated. This has been placed in Divine Order to bring a magnetic effect for the New Time. Have you not noticed that now many are being drawn and pulled, and are moving and gravitating toward the Star. This is because of the radiation that is within it. It is not a radiation that exists within the earth itself, even though Beloved Babajaren

A QUICKENING

is offering herself to be of service. It is an energy that we are building. It is a template of perfect thought, perfect feeling and perfect action. It is a template, or a network, of understanding so that you may model this in your own lives and use it to move forward into these New Times.

There are Strategic Points that exist geophysically. You see, Dear ones, there must be physical demonstration of this New Time. Physical demonstration of the energy is built for those who have the eyes to see and the ears to hear. We have laid this template down so that a New Time may be birthed—a New Time that is now much needed upon your Earth Plane and Planet.

Engendered within this template is a transformative harmony. You have noted that when you live in disharmony in such a Vortex city, that it is almost impossible to move forward without the use of the Violet Flame. But it is that Blue Ray of Will, that Blue Ray of Choice that fills the mighty Vortex of Gobean. It is there where chelas may learn through this energy, learn about the manifestation of their choices, and transform through working in groups with the principle of harmony. It is through this Star of Knowledge, and understanding that we ask you to move forward to utilize these energies for yourself, for the work that you are bringing forward. They are present for you to understand. Traveling, of course, to any of the selected points and working in ceremony, in song, or in meditation would allow an infusion of such to come to you for your use and for your daily application. To live in such an area would bring about the same result. You see, Dear ones, Dear chelas, the infusion of these energies through and around you will only bring you into greater harmony with the Divine Will. Each of these locations is connected to the apex of other Golden City locations. Therefore, when you meditate in such a location, the energy travels quite quickly as a network of consciousness. The Golden Cities are comprised primarily of a purity of consciousness. As I have stated before, Beloved Babajaren has also offered herself to serve in harmony with these grids of pure consciousness. But this is given again, as Saint Germain has said, as an opportunity for you to grow and to learn at this time. These locations are very important, for many will travel to them during the Time of Great Change. There have been those who have asked, "When is this Time of Change?" We reply, the *Time is Now*, Dear ones. The changes are upon the Earth Plane and Planet. The changes are happening now within you. As above, so below. This Template of Consciousness is also the first template of the consciousness of Unana.

And it is the Blue Ray, as held by myself, Beloved Archangel MIchael, and Hercules the Elohim, comes forth to bless humanity to understand that the work of harmony must come first in all of its creations. In the Jurisdiction, Harmony was brought forward first. For harmony must be contained in all creations and Beloved Saint Germain has lectured upon the use of the Violet Flame.

Now, let us continue with the lesson of harmony. Harmony is the only way that this New Time can be understood. If you feel even the slightest tinge of dissension, the slightest tinge of disharmony, then move yourself back, set yourself away. Take time in silence and address your intention. Anything that does not align to Divine Harmony must now have its place in

A QUICKENING

purification. Bring yourself forward, Dear chelas, ready to face the New Times, restored unto yourself. You see, beloveds, this is how harmony moves forward. It is through that simple intention of harmony. Questions?

Question: "Harmony seems to be a very illusive thing for most of us on the planet, for those of us who choose to be of service with you. I understand the use of the Violet Flame as a focus to create the harmony if that is the intention. However, I would ask that you would also share to create more of the harmony here in all that we do, and participate with us and join us."

It is as simple as focus. For you see, Dear ones, focus aligns. Focus brings all into the clarity that is required to bring the union of harmony. You see, Dear ones, harmony is indeed a union. One would think that harmony is a simple, single focus, but not so, beloveds. Harmony is indeed a union of focus coming together, focus coalescing from one to the next: one simple thought and one simple thought, one plus one equals two. That two is harmony. One plus one does not equal four. One plus one does not equal eight, but one plus one equals two. It is that simple. It is the coalescing of the harmony. It is this union that is contained within the self, this union that is then contained throughout the being, this union that then is expressed in Beloved Gobean. But what are we really speaking about...one plus one? It is left plus right. It is dark plus light. It is hot plus cold. It is the knowledge that the dual forces work together at all times to bring forth a greater wisdom. And yet there is such dissension that is felt through this process, such chaos as it is judged as, such disorder as it is judged as, such disharmony as it is judged as. This Point of Perception is indeed choice, the way you are willing to see such a thing. Seek the higher level through your intention, understand your intention, understand the power of your creative force. It is this creative force that moves throughout you. It is known as ONE. This Divine Source is the center of Unana. In the same way that the Violet Flame moves forth from the Eight-Sided Cell of Perfection, the consciousness of Unana runs forth through you. It is part of you. It is you. It is connected to this earth. It is connected to us. You see, Dear ones, it is the force that brings us to you. It is the force that brings you to us. It is the seeking of this ONE, the seeking of this unity, the seeking of this harmony that brings us together. Why deny such a thing?

Harmony is a natural Law of Nature. It is mirrored throughout your world. Harmony exists to bring you peace. Questions?

Question: "So the path of harmony is the Violet Flame?"

They are interconnected as ONE. They are known as ONE. Divinity exists all around you, but you must see it. You must perceive it. Divine Intervention is but a glance away, a moment away. To bring it into your experience of now, to your Time of Now, you must choose for it to be so, to choose such Divinity, to choose such Grace, to choose such harmony. Are these not the qualities of the Co-creator? Beloveds, Dear ones, this time has been brought forward so that you could understand that which is within yourself without

A QUICKENING

judgment and without shame. It is the Light that is within you that will bring you now to the greater harmony. It is when you engage in such judgment. It is not judgment of another. It is judgment of the Light within yourself, the Light that you deny yourself, the unity that you deny yourself. Do you understand?

Answer: "Yes, then it is truly my choice for this harmony. I choose for the Divine Intervention of this moment to be sustained always. So be it."

So be it, Beloved.

These Strategic Points that exist now within the Beloved Star of Gobean can assist you in understanding this. Travel to such a point and spend just a day reflecting upon the intention within yourself, the intention of your soul to bring it into greater unity, and into greater harmony. Take this, Dear one, as your first step, a small step into creating a New Day.

Answer: "So be it."

And now I shall open the floor for questions.

Question: "Beloved Master, these polarities that we perceive, or that we seem to perceive and seem to experience, are they ultimately not real when we choose to be non-judgmental?"

They become as ONE within yourself, Dear one, and that unrealness becomes the reality of Oneness. It is the reality of Oneness where all fear is brought to the side, where all sense of injustice is brought to the side. It is discarded as an unused garment, something that no longer serves the consciousness. You see, when one understands unity, that all forces work together as ONE, there is purpose in all things. Do you understand?

Question: "Yes, I do. Therefore, if you were to address all humanity, what would you say are the three most important things that we must endeavor to do?"

Choose, choose and then choose again for yourself. Find within yourself the Divinity that you are, that is of all things. Choose, choose, choose for the ONE, for the ONE that is contained within All. Choose, choose, choose for love. As Dear Brother Sananda has said, "Love one another." These are the three that I would choose.

Question: "Is there any additional information, Beloved Master, that you would like to share with us at this time?"

Light of Awakening

A QUICKENING

Prepare yourself, beloveds, prepare yourself, for the time is at hand. A quickening is amongst humanity. As we have said so many times before, those who have the eyes to see and the ears to hear, now bring your hands into action. Join as ONE in that choosing of the new qualities: these qualities of harmony, of cooperation. Bring forth this transformation within yourself, assisted through the work of Beloved Saint Germain's Mighty Violet Flame. Beloveds, Dear ones, this time has been brought forth again as an opportunity, an opportunity for your growth, an opportunity for your understanding. If you are feeling disharmony within your life, it is important now to choose. If you are feeling disharmony in your life, use the Violet Flame. If you are feeling disharmony within your life, see all things working together as ONE. These are the simple lessons, the simple understandings. But this is where we must start to create a New Time and a New Day.

Now, I shall proceed upon more of the Vortex structures. (Now, he's also drawing a diagram. He's circling the Stars, and now he's pointing to the Northern Door of the Vortex.)

The Northern door as you have understood it is indeed an area of fruition and growth. If you seek the growth and understanding of harmony within yourself to bring things together to the unity of causes, this is a simple place to travel to, to ingest and take in such energies, for this will bring a fruition and an understanding. (Now, he's drawing the Southern Door.)

If you perceive yourself to be ill at ease, the disharmony has brought dis-ease within your physical body, travel to this area and ingest such energies to bring about harmony, to bring about miraculous healing. These areas are infused with the waters of miracle healing. We have stated before that air, water and food that are contained within certain areas of the Golden Cities are indeed infused with energies to bring about such qualities. Travel, Dear ones, to this area, if you feel you need to bring about healing of the body (Now, he's drawing the Western Door.)

To bring about higher understanding, higher knowledge of harmony, higher knowledge of unity, higher knowledge of peace, higher knowledge of cooperation, move to this Western area, stay for several days, ingest such energies. They will bring about a greater and higher clarity, knowledge that can be utilized, knowledge that is known as wisdom. (Now, he's drawing the Eastern Door of the Vortex.)

To this Eastern door, travel when you seek harmony among friends, harmony among groups, harmony with one another. If there is dissension within your family, travel to this area, spend but a few days, or a few hours, whatever it takes to infuse yourself with these energies until you feel the energies complete within.

A QUICKENING

You see, Dear ones, this is a great opportunity that is given to humanity at this time. It is brought forward to create collective healing on our planet so that we may move much more swiftly into the New Times. Questions?

Question: "You are making these references to the Star locations of the points on the compass. Correct?"

I'm making these references to the entire Vortex, and now for the Star.

The Star is the perfect harmony of all energies coming together, coalescing with one another, infusing and working together. This is where you travel to if you seek transformation, if you seek new knowledge, if you seek new understanding through the path of harmony or through the path of transformation. Travel there to seek your new intention, to seek your new understanding. Do you understand?

Answer: "Yes, thank you."

The Star of Knowledge is brought forward as a ceremonial ground. This ceremony exists only within yourself, but can be shared with others as a celebration of the ONE. So you see, Dear ones, the work and the purpose at hand. You see, Dear ones, the work of the Golden Cities, their great service to humanity, and what they now afford for All. Share this information with many others so that they, too, may come to know and to understand the great time. I shall now turn the floor back to Beloved Saint Germain.

Response: "Thank you, El Morya."

(Saint Germain steps forward.)

Greetings, Dear ones. In that Mighty Violet Ray I now conclude this discourse. And I ask that Grace impart within all of your hearts. May Grace be the final Law that binds us all into the New Time. Hitaka.

Response: "Hitaka."

6

Golden City Rays
Saint Germain on Ray Forces and the Golden Cities

GREETINGS, BELOVEDS, IN THAT MIGHTY CHRIST, I AM SAINT GERMAIN, AND I STREAM FORTH ON THAT MIGHTY VIOLET RAY OF MERCY AND FORGIVENESS.

As usual Dear hearts, I request permission to come forward.

"Please, Saint Germain, come forward. You're most welcome."

Today, Dear ones, we shall focus on a teaching of the Rays and Ray Forces and their interaction with the Golden Cities, how they work through the Golden Cities, and how this information may be used to move humanity forward into the New Times

The Rays, as you see, Dear ones, are a coalescing of life force, a singular focus of light and sound that come forward to lift humanity in evolution. In this sense, a Ray can allow a person to move forward to become a new being clothed with a new body.

Ray Forces work in such a manner, prodding and moving the person along the path of evolution, spiritual evolution, and begin to move that person onward into greater understanding, knowledge, intuition, and Mastery of the force of his life.

As I have said before, it is important for you to know thyself first, and to know thyself is to understand how the Rays work within the being, the aura and the electromagnetic field.

The Human Aura is comprised of many such Ray Forces coming together and working, coalescing, one arcing among the other. The Chakra System is also influenced by the different Ray Forces, each of them coming forward and moving each chakra in a different vibration and through a different sound. It is indeed true that a Ray Force influences each of the chakras, even though there may be a coalescing of the various life forces.

The chakras work alongside the light forces, and alongside each light force is also a sound; these work together, Dear ones. The light forces are determined at the moment of birth, and, as you have studied, it is the Astral Body that determines the predominance of a Ray Force or

---

For more information and study topics on *Golden City Rays*, see Appendix F, page 179.

GOLDEN CITY RAYS

the predominance of a sound force. The two work together, as an Elohim of light and sound, in an Absolute Harmony and absolute cooperation, moving the individual to greater understanding and to greater evolution.

As we understand that there is a predominant light force and a predominant Ray Force, a predominant sound force within the individual, there is also a predominant light force or Ray Force and a predominant sound force in each of the Golden Cities. As you have known, Gobean is known as the Blue City. It is working toward the qualities of harmony and cooperation. The Blue Ray brings one toward this. First, it holds one's consciousness steadfast unto the idea of a unifying force of cooperation of the Oneship of all things, so steadfastly one holds to this Blue Ray. It is known as Will, or Power, or Force. This, of course, then aligns the Vertical Power Current, which you know as the Kundalini of the spine. It works with many of the chakras in different combinations, but, of course, it is most identified with the Throat Chakra and upon occasion with the Third Eye, or pineal gland. This allows one to make the choice in an expression and allows the choice to be expressed through the Will, for the Blue Ray is also at times known as a Ray of Will. This, of course, must be developed within the being to allow evolution. It is only through choices that one begins to evolve in a greater understanding, knowledge, and power of their own Godship.

You see, Dear ones, the Blue Ray is of vast importance and, of course, is always known as the First Ray. For it is only through Will and the development of choice, and the expression of those choices that one is able to understand one's *own* cause and effect. Cause and effect, of course, has been known as Karma, but it is only through Karma, or cause and effect, that one begins to learn and to grow through one's choices. So, you see, Dear ones, the Blue Ray is of vast importance. And it is, of course, the first Blue Ray that serves in the Golden City of Gobean.

The Ray Force enters through the apex of each Golden City. It is directed through the Great Central Sun. The Great Central Sun is a source of order in your Universe of collective thought, feeling, and action. Each Ray Force enters into the apex and radiates out in a circular motion, and when one is working toward integration of a Ray Force, it is important to move closer to the apex of a Golden City. And as one is there physically enjoying the energies, one becomes aligned in assimilating the Ray Force into one's being and purifying that Ray Force within one's being. In the beginning of understanding a Ray Force, such as the Blue Ray, one would feel a bit of purification, a bit of disharmony, in the same sense as when a body enters into disease, which sometimes has the same effect. When the Ray strikes the body, the purity of the Ray Force causes one to begin to discard all which does not align to the force and the working of the Ray. In the same way, when the body enters into disease, it is dispelling what the body will not cooperate with. So, it is in the same manner. When one is closer to the purity of a Ray Force when entering into a Golden City, and in this instance I AM referring to the locations of the Stars, there will first be some discomfort. The body may require larger amounts of rest. There could be disharmony in relationships with others, and there may be some purifying process that the body must go through in order to begin to assimilate the pu-

GOLDEN CITY RAYS

rity of the Ray Force. This you will notice in any Golden City when you are working to align with the Ray Force.

It is the same for all of the other Golden Cities. In Malton, you would be working to align with the Ruby and the Gold Ray. The Ruby and the Gold Ray are Rays of Devotion. This Ray may create desires into manifestation, for it has been stated that in Golden City Vortices desires are instantly manifested. So one begins to understand, through one's choices, the desires that they choose, the desires that they wish to attain and bring to fruition. It is also understood that the Ruby and Gold Rays play important roles at this time in assisting and helping the Elemental Kingdoms of the earth. For many of the Elemental Kingdoms, the Devas and the little fairies, the gnomes and all those who are there and *do exist*, are also going through their own type of purification. You see, humanity has created an earth out of balance through the use of many pollutants, which are affecting the Kingdoms and causing an imbalance in many of the Nature Kingdoms. So, it is through the use of the Ruby and the Gold Rays that these are brought back into a balance.

The Gold Ray also rules the ability to take action, and the ability to take action with *force*. Sometimes it is only through force that things are achieved. Through the Ruby and the Gold Ray rules such actions that exist on the planet as volcanic eruptions, tidal wave motion, tectonic plates moving. This is the Elemental Force at work, working to bring balance to remove that which has brought about disharmony. In the recent tidal wave that you have had upon the planet, humanity must understand that even though great sorrow was brought for the many who have now crossed over into New Dimensions, a great balance was also achieved. This balance allowed the Elemental Kingdoms to achieve a greater sense of their own harmony. You see, Dear ones, it is Absolute Harmony and balance that is sought at this time upon the Earth Plane and Planet. It is balance that must be held in order for humanity to move into the consciousness of Unana. It is only through balance that this is achieved in the great Oneship.

The Ruby and the Gold Rays enter into the Vortex of Malton at the apex, and it is the alignment to this Ray that, if one is seeking fruition of desires to bring their thoughts into instant manifestation, one may travel to align one's energies and Chakra System to this. The chakra that aligns most evenly with the Ruby and the Gold Rays, even though I would also like to add that all chakras are affected by all Rays, is the lowest chakra (base chakra). The lowest chakra is an action chakra. It is the chakra that allows things to move and to be birthed into existence. When one moves to Malton and allows the activation of these energies into one's being, they will begin to experience a movement of the Kundalini forces. Of course, in the beginning, they will notice an increase in sexuality, the creative ability and the desire capacity. It is important to understand when you are integrating a Ray Force from a Golden City into the being, that you must use a type of breathwork to move the energy through the chakras, to keep the body in balance. Any type of breath-work is recommended, any that the chela finds to bring balance.

GOLDEN CITY RAYS

Of course, Energy Balancing is also recommended, and we have spent much time upon these techniques, have we not? So, Dear hearts, I would suggest that any technique that balances the energy throughout the system will help.

Of course, in the beginning, as in Gobean and the assimilation of the Blue Ray, you will note that nothing seems to go right, that the desires that serve your Divine Purpose seem to not work or manifest correctly. But this is all the process of purification, of bringing this forward into alignment to your plan of the best and the highest good.

So, this beloved Ruby and Gold Ray of Ministration and Service begins to serve in its highest way. There will be those souls that will be attracted in the times to come, in the New Times, the Golden Age, to the different Golden City locations that will align to the Ray Force that is most predominant within their being, their soul force, their Star Seed. You see, Dear ones, different Star Seeds serve along different Ray Forces. Of course, there has been such an intermingling of Ray Forces and genetic mix that it is difficult to say that one is strictly of this Star Seed or that Star Seed. But, you see, there will be one (genetic) that becomes more predominant. This domination comes, through the choice of where you wish to serve. So, you see, the Ray Forces serve and work together to bring a greater harmony and a greater self-knowledge. Questions?

Question: "So, what you are saying about the different Star Seeds is the multiplicity of genetic tribes on the planet was for the integration of the individual or the group for each of the Rays, so we have all had our turn, in a sense, through embodiment after embodiment?"

This is so. It brings about a greater orchestration of self-knowledge, a greater orchestration of knowledge of the Rays and their greater working with light and sound forces.

I shall continue. In the Golden City of Wahanee is the Ray Force of the Violet Ray. The Ray Force enters into the apex of the Golden City. The apex is located in Augusta, as we have enacted a certain amount of inpouring into that area in terms of consciousness and intention. The Ray Force of the Violet Ray brings forth compassion, mercy and forgiveness, but another value of the Violet Ray is its ability to transmute any situation that is holding you back from your achieving the internal union of the ONE.

In working with the Violet Ray, one first begins to understand the purifying and transmuting fires. As I have always stated, "Down with death, God I AM. Conscious immortality arise." It is only through the use of the Violet Ray that one begins to understand that one is indeed immortal. The Violet Ray allows one to release the consciousness of death. It is through the Violet Ray that one can begin to regenerate. When you live in a Star area that is near the apex of Wahanee, you can begin to regenerate yourself. You see, there is such a condensation of the Violet Ray energies now entering into that area that the orgone, or prana, is tightly condensed, and for those chelas who wish to drop the consciousness of death and begin to accept their immortal destiny, this is the place toward which they will gravitate.

GOLDEN CITY RAYS

There are many other uses of the Violet Ray. Of course, this is one that we are releasing at this time so that humanity may begin to understand the great service that the Golden Cities have to offer. So, healing clinics would be a wonderful location in the Golden City of Wahanee for those who wish to regenerate their perspective. You see, *mind is the builder,* and one must begin with mind if one is to have the new body. We must start first with the thoughts that we hold. We must transmute the old thoughts to bring in the new thoughts. So, Dear hearts, it is through the use of the Violet Ray that Divine Intervention, grace and mercy are imparted to humanity. At a higher level, these energies will be used for Brotherhood, for bringing all to a greater understanding of the unity of all of consciousness. Once we drop the energies of Cellular Fear, we can begin to move into a greater understanding of love and compassion, but first things first. And let us start with regeneration and purification. It is here in this Vortex where one will, in the beginning, notice harder effects upon the physical body: flu-like symptoms, intestinal upsets. You see, the Violet Ray works, not only with the Heart Chakra, but also with the Solar Plexus. It is a transmutation of the Solar Plexus energies that are needed in order to drop the idea of death.

Down with death. Conscious immortality arise.

At the higher levels, the Violet Ray works with the Crown Chakra and moves the Kundalini energies to the top of understanding. Are there questions?

Answer: "Not at this time."

I shall move on to the Vortex of Shalahah. Shalahah is known as the Green City. It is only through the Green Ray that one begins to harmonize the body, mind and spirit. You see, healing is not just repairing the body; it is repairing the mind. It is repairing the spirit; it is repairing the soul. All of these must come into balance in order for total healing to be sustained. The Ray Force, which is the Green Healing Ray, enters into the apex, located near Lolo Pass. This also has a certain coalescing of energies of Blue Rays and Gold Rays. You see, Dear ones, they work together, bringing forth a greater understanding and a greater harmony. Healing is about accepting the Divinity within yourself. These healing forces will bring such about. Healing, also, is understanding that you are not separated, that you are ONE with all things. When one has accepted healing within oneself, he is ready to move to the New Dimensions.

There are two Vortices that have been outlined, sub-vortices that exist within the Shalahah Vortex. One is known as *Ascension Valley,* which is a Vortex area where one may go to integrate one's Oneship, one's divinity within, to prepare the body, mind and spirit to move into the New Dimensions.

Also, there is that which is known as the *Transportation Vortex*. The Transportation Vortex is a Vortex that will be developed more as we move into the New Times. This is an interdimensional portal, a place where Mother Earth has allowed her energies to commingle with

GOLDEN CITY RAYS

the energies needed, and the heavenly energies of the other dimensions. More will be understood on the Transportation Vortex as we move on and are attuned with the Ray Forces and how they work. You see, Dear ones, when you enter into Shalahah, because of the commingling of the Blue Ray and the Gold Ray, there are other anomalies that exist. This allows for interdimensional travel that is achieved, of course, through the projection of the mind, but as the body becomes fine-tuned, bi-location is indeed a possibility. In the New Times, this will be an accepted form and mode of travel, but only until the body, mind and spirit are honed and able to accept this type of acceleration. It is suggested that many health retreats be built in this area in the New Times, but the health retreats should focus primarily upon mind as a builder, and body will follow. Do you understand?

Answer: "Yes, so far."

Now, let us return. When chelas travel, or gravitate, to these areas in Shalahah to bring forth the healing forces, they will notice that abundance and prosperity will enter into their lives. When the body, mind and spirit are brought into balance in complete and Absolute Harmony, the next result is abundance. Natural prosperity comes forward. We have taught this in the Jurisdictions, and Shalahah will be the physical demonstration of this. So, chelas who are working to bring abundance and prosperity into their lives travel to Shalahah, to the apexes, to align themselves to the Green energy. But, Dear hearts, you must understand that in the integration of such a force there is an unraveling effect in the beginning. This will affect not only Heart Chakra energies, but also the Solar Plexus energies. You see, one begins to feel unsafe, for there is over identification with physical materiality. When one begins to understand that it is the coalescing of all the energies that brings about balance within the body, safety is truly a matter of the heart. Abundance, then, can stream forth with clarity and with beauty.

Now, I shall move on to the last and final Golden City and the Ray Force of Klehma. The White Ray of Purity is a Ray of Cooperation. It is also a Ray of Attainment, for it allows one to enter into the New Dimensions that exist beyond where physical embodiment is not required. In the Golden City of Klehma one of the first Crystal Cities will etherealize in the New Times.

It has been said that this will be the new capitol of the United States, and indeed it is so, for the rulership and the guidance of the United States in the New Times will come from this ethereal city, where those who have gone before, leaders such as Abraham Lincoln, John F. Kennedy, Martin Luther King, George Washington, Thomas Jefferson. And those you have known as Native American leaders, Mayan leaders, who have known the Christ as Quetzalcoatl will also serve in this City of Cooperation in Klehma.

You see, Dear ones, vibration to the White Ray is a vibration to all the Venusian energies. The Venusian energies are a vibration to a White and Crystal Purity, a purity of intention, a purity of heart and mind united in service. So you see, beloveds, when leadership comes from the highest of intention, it leads the country into a New Time, into a new vision.

GOLDEN CITY RAYS

Klehma, itself, is aligned to the Golden Cities that existed at one time in South America and in Mexico. These were the Golden Cities that held the ethereal Crystal Cities that guided the Mayan culture into its dimensional leap. You see, Dear one, there is a purpose and a timing to all things. Klehma, as the White Ray, brings about a purity and a cleansing of intention. As we have said before, scrutinize your intentions, for they are powerful Creators. This creation can move one into greater understanding of community and into greater understanding of cooperation. And those who are seeking to learn of unity through cooperation and community, service to humanity, and the united Brotherhoods and Sisterhoods of this earth can travel and absorb the energies at the Star of Klehma.

This energy also develops the energies of Ascension, which will have similar effect on body as in Shalahah, but it is the quality of White Fire. You see, the White Fire is *purity*, and the body releases the final death urges. The work that is initiated in Wahanee is completed in Klehma. I have given you a brief outline of how the Golden Cities work along with Ray Forces.

Now, let us talk about sound, for each of the Ray Forces also vibrates to a sound quality, which is important to understand.

Om Shanti vibrates to the Golden City of Gobean. Om Shanti brings about a sense of peace and a sense of harmony, so chelas who wish to chant this as a sound vibration may do so.

Om Eandra is the mantra vibration to be chanted for Malton. Om Eandra is the Vibration of the Elemental Kingdoms. It creates a harmony and a balance. It is also the mantra, or the sound vibration, that can be chanted to bring something into fruition, into attainment, so that you may own it as a Master of your desires.

Om Hue is the chant for Wahanee. You see, Dear ones, Hue aligns all chakras along that Vertical Core Axis, and allows the Violet Flame to work its Mighty Miracle! Om Hue is a Vibration of the Violet Flame Angels and brings about it the most purifying and healing effects to the body.

In Shalahah, the vibration to be chanted is *Om Sheahah*. Om Sheahah for Shalahah means *I AM as ONE*. You see, Dear ones, in Shalahah one must become as ONE to find healing. One must become as ONE to find true prosperity.

And the final mantra that is chanted for Klehma is again Om Eandra. Om Eandra is the final capstone placed upon the Golden Cities, Om Eandra. You see, Dear ones, through sound vibration and light Ray Forces, all is brought together in a glory and a conclusion. Are there questions?

Question: "I see, so that's how it's qualified. So, for Gobean, when you say Om Shanti, that's the qualification of the Ray specifically for the use of the Blue Ray in Gobean?"

GOLDEN CITY RAYS

This is so, Dear one.

Question: "Are each of these specific chants the activating phrases for each of the Rays?"

Indeed they are. The activating phrases for the Rays as they work in a Golden City. Remember, it is the energy of your own electromagnetic field, your own aura, working with that of the Golden City Ray Force.

Question: "Okay, and when we utilize these mantras and chants, are you saying that we can apply them in the same way as the Violet Flame in creating, you know, our intention or bringing something into fruition?"

Yes. This is the purpose. This is the intention of the Golden City forces and the way in which they work with your own electromagnetic force-field. You see, Dear ones, the Golden Cities are indeed force-fields that exist for you to access. These are some of the keys of how you may access them and the results that you may get.

Question: "I see, so its effectiveness is better located within the Star?"

This is so, Dear one. It brings forth the intention, the fruition, the qualification of the energy of the Golden City.

Question: "I see. So even if someone wishes to move to a Golden City and they find it difficult to get to the specific one that they have chosen, this chant would help them to expedite that?"

This is so. However, it is preferred that these chants be used within the Golden City, as they are sound vibrations that work with the centrifugal force of that Ray Force in the Star. It can be used throughout the whole Golden City, but the pull of it, as you can see, will work most strongly in the apexes. It can be used, of course, throughout the Golden City.

Question: "Hmm. So, by knowing the qualities of each of the Golden Cities, as stated in this discourse and in previous discourses that show up in the books and the tapes and the maps, and utilizing these specific mantras, the purpose intended by you in your life in a Golden City can then be brought into manifestation more easily?"

This is so, Dear one, for those who feel aligned to move to the Golden Cities, can go forward in alignment, knowledge and the force that they may bring into their lives.

Answer: "I see. Well, this sounds like an extremely valuable tool. Thank you."

Now, Dear one, unless if there are other questions, I shall depart.

GOLDEN CITY RAYS

Response: "Not at this time. This is more than enough to think about and to put into application."

In that Mighty Christ, I AM!

Response: "Thank you."

Blue Illumination
Teachings on the Golden Cities of Gobean, Gobi, and Shamballa

GREETINGS, BELOVEDS, IN THAT MIGHTY CHRIST, I AM SAINT GERMAIN, AND, AS USUAL DEAR HEARTS, I ASK PERMISSION TO COME FORTH.

"Please, Saint Germain, come forward."

Today, we will discourse more upon the Gobean Vortex, and I have brought with me Beloved Brother El Morya. He is coming forward. (El Morya steps forward, besides Saint Germain.)

Greetings, Dear one, in that Mighty Blue Flame, I AM El Morya. I ask permission to come forward.

Answer: "Please do, Brother and Teacher, come forward."

Today, I shall bring forth further discourse on the Vortex of Gobean. We have discussed all the Strategic Points, the doorways and the Star of Knowledge. Now, we shall move forward so that you may understand a bit of the ancient history that surrounds the network of the Golden Cities.

Dear hearts, we have spoken about the idea that many of these Golden City Vortices are aligned to other Vortices throughout the planet. As we have explained before, Gobean aligns to energy in Gobi, which is now the Vortex that covers the ancient City of Shamballa. You see, Dear ones, all of these are connected to the idea of emanation, how energy is built. This enables the (Golden Cities') demonstration or the physical manifestation. When energy is built according to the principal of emanation, you can begin to understand how manifestation, or physical desire, can manifest. Saint Germain has given you continued discourse upon this principal, and it is important to understand, when studying a Golden City Vortex, its doorways, its points, and how it functions. Each of the Golden Cities that are given in the complete network of Vortices are all connected to other cities, but for now we shall place our emphasis upon Gobean and the work of the Blue Ray.

For more information and study topics on *Blue Illumination*, see Appendix G, page 211.

BLUE ILLUMINATION

It is the work of the Blue Ray that brought Shamballa into its physical manifestation. You see, Dear ones, some of the original inhabitants of Shamballa were not only from Venus but from other planets. Mercury played a very large role in its inhabitation, along with other planets that are not in your present star system. These people were known as the Blue Race. Many of you have known them the Vedic traditions. There they built the ethereal city and manifested it into your Earth Plane. Many of those who lived in Shamballa knew perfection and also understood the work of the Blue Ray as representing truth, harmony, and cooperation as a manifestation upon the earth.

The first city, when it was built, held many Crystal Castles. The Crystal Castles were encrusted with rubies, emeralds, pearls and gems that today would be deemed of great value. It was there that the first Unfed Flame of Love, Wisdom, and Power was kept enshrined, and many celebrations and ceremonies were held in honor of this flame. Many of the people understood the idea that they were indeed beyond physical incarnation; and death, as you now understand, did not exist. The great immortals, those who were the great teachers whom your history has now honored, existed in that first City of Shamballa. However, as the earth was populated from other Star Seeds, that is from other planets, a warring force, or a warring energy of non-cooperation and disharmony, was generated. This brought about a dissent within the city. You see, there were those who would enter into the city and their vibration not able to handle the perfection, and the emanation, or the energy, that was built in Shamballa deteriorated. It was then decided that this city shall be moved, and indeed it was, and rebuilt. This time, it was kept hidden, so that those, who at that time upon the earth sought to find it, but could not. This city held again the same energies of perfection, of longevity, of perfect health, and perfect harmony. Music played throughout the day. The night-time was sweet, and the scent of jasmine filled the air. You see, Dear ones, perfection is indeed an emanation. It is an energy that is built and held within the body. When you seek your own perfection, you must idealize it as a perfect crystalline thought in your mind first, and then build the energy through the Principle of Emanation. The Principle of Conductivity then comes into play, and it was through conductivity that the second City of Shamballa began to radiate throughout the earth. The second City of Shamballa grew in such a manner that it affected all the earth for greater harmony and greater perfection. But materiality began to obsess the population. Materiality was the demise of the second City of Shamballa, and this time the deterioration came from within the city. Many long-term residents, the immortals who first held the focus of Shamballa, also fell in consciousness, and for the most part, required rebirth. But the few remaining, who held the purity of consciousness, rebuilt the city for the third time. Upon the request of Sanat Kamara, it was decided that this city would not manifest in the physcial planes, or to plainly speak: seek physical incarnation. This time, the city was held in the finer ethreal qualities and the emanation would be detected only by those who had developed the finer subtle bodies (qualities) within the Astral Body. So, those who were trained in different ashrams throughout Eastern Asia were also trained to seek, through higher consciousness, entry into the Golden City of Shamballa. It remains in this same location today.

At one time, the consciousness of humanity was raised to such a peak that within the Gobi Desert, directly beneath the ethereal Crystal City of Shamballa, another civilization was built. *As above, so below.* The law was mirrored, and many traveled to this city seeking healing

BLUE ILLUMINATION

and the ancient teachings. However, as humanity moved into the time period now known as Kali, the gates of Shamballa were tightly shut to but a few; now, this time period is over, and the New Time period moves earth forward and humanity develops into a new understanding and into a new evolution.

Before I proceed with more information, are there any questions?

Answer: "Yes, there are."

Proceed.

Question: "You spoke of conductivity, and prior to that you spoke of focus in creating perfection. In that step-by-step manner, is there an exercise, or is there a tangible way to take this and utilize it for everyday use for humanity?"

To build your energy fields through the Principle of Conductivity, it is important to understand the ONE, the Oneship, unity of all things. Conductivity is based upon this idea. Through the course of emanation and conductivity all energies basically function as ONE. To build this within your own energy fields, practice again the meditation which I gave you years ago of the candle. You must have the singular focus that you and the candle become as ONE. Do you understand?

Answer: "Yes, I do."

This prepares the mind for a greater understanding, a greater illumination. Are there more questions?

Question: "So, the practice of the candle meditation, you would say, is the first step in developing the focus what may be sustained through any distraction or any time period that would allow the conductivity to also be sustained?"

This is true, Dear one. You will receive great results if you practice this in earnest.

Response: "Thank you. Please continue."

So, the third and final City of Shamballa, which it was decided should remain in its ethereal state, has kept its position over the Gobi Desert. Of course, of the ancient civilization that existed in a physical state, there are still remnants of it, and those who search for the City of Shamballa may find it if they so choose. The energies of Gobean align to this ancient Golden City, known as Gobi. You see, Dear ones, as above, so below. When Shamballa and the City of Gobi intertwined, it created a force-field. The force-field then created a Vortex. This is how

BLUE ILLUMINATION

all Vortices come into being, through a relationship of ethereal consciousness and emanation and conductivity. Do you understand?

Question: "I see. It's the basic structure of how the Rays of Light and Sound go together."

It is indeed as such, a Co-creation of Heaven and Earth. The two exist simultaneously, exist together. It takes the two for such to exist, built upon, as I have explained and Master Saint Germain has explained, through the elements of conductivity and emanation.

Now, I shall proceed, Dear ones. There is yet another city that aligns its energy to the energies of Shamballa, or the City of Gobi, the Golden City of Gobean. These two Vortices are connected as ONE. So, when you meditate upon the perfection of Shamballa in the City of Gobean, you can be instantly transported there. You see, Dear ones, as the perfection streams forth into your own bodies, your own minds, your own hearts, as you are accelerated in the times to come, the times of the Golden Perfections, you shall then be able to transport your body, through the process of bi-location, to the City of Gobi. You shall also be able to take in the perfected energies of the ancient City of Shamballa. This ancient City of Shamballa is the city where many of the Master Teachers meet on a yearly basis. This I'm sure you are familiar with.

Response: "Yes, absolutely."

As you integrate these perfected energies, as we have instructed you, as time progresses, or as time compacts, in this grand opportunity that is being offered to humanity, you will note further perfections within your own bodies. As you see, the water and air in a Golden City is of a higher and finer quality. The principal of prahna or orgone, as you have been taught, is much more condensed, It rotates at a higher millisecond. This higher rotation within your body brings about an acceleration. We have spoken of the Cellular Awakening. This acceleration brings you closer and closer to the idea of a deathless body of physical immortality, of Ascension into new realms of understanding. This acceleration is most essential to access the energies that are inherent in a Golden City Vortex.

Of course, there are other energies that are apparent. I have spoken already of the ability for miraculous healing in the Southern Doors. I have also spoken of the abilities of Instant-Thought-Manifestations of the Northern Doors. You see, there are other qualities and other gifts that the Cities are here to bring to humanity as the course of Divine Intervention proceeds. This alignment of energy with the ancient City of Shamballa is most important, Dear hearts and Dear ones, for Gobean is the perfect location to extract the ancient records through Thought Projection. I have taught you before about this principle; do you not recall?

Answer: "Yes, I recall."

Light of Awakening

BLUE ILLUMINATION

To project your thoughts, or your mental body, into another realm to receive information, in Gobean one may travel to receive the ancient knowledge of other times. In meditation, you can access this information much more readily than in any other Golden City. You see, Dear ones, through the Blue Ray of Truth, the *truth of the history of the planet* comes forward for you now to view. It is not a truth that is given through another one's perspective. It is a truth that is infused directly to you so that each is given his or her own individual understanding of the history of this earth, the history of this schoolroom and your own individual participation. You see, in truth, it must be received at an individual level, so through the individual experiences of each they can receive. When it is imparted only as knowledge or as belief, it carries less importance. You see, Dear hearts, Dear ones, this is the importance of Gobean for its alignment to the ancient knowledge.

Historically, Gobean also aligns to another ancient city. In your history, this is known as Giza. Why is this so? The teacher Serapis Bey, who was known as Akhenaten, traveled to the location of Gobean, and there he gave forth his teachings. Many did not understand them at the time, for you see he was able to project through his consciousness a perfect form of himself, ethereally, and there the teachings were brought to the cultures that existed in the ancient areas that are now known as Gobean. This is why you will see there are similarities in the cultures. He was known as a great teacher among many, and yet this was a projection of the (his) consciousness. So, you see, again, as above, so below.

Serapis Bey became one of the first teachers of the Continuity of Consciousness. He taught about the opening of the Third Eye and the Crown chakra, the Star of Knowledge. This was passed down, you see, Dear ones, and the energy and the focus that were held through these teachings created a force-field that is in the location of Gobean. In later years, I was to come under the tutelage of this same teacher, and I, too, was taught the technique so that I could project my consciousness, and there became a series of teachings in Gobean, and many of the cultures gravitated toward this. These appearances had a tendency to raise the energies, and you see now how this has come to be. Do you have questions?

Question: "Yes. Question one: Was the center of Gobean at that time, when you were projecting into it, in the same exact location that it is in now?"

It was more to the North, and assisted many of the different tribes of people that are now known as Native Americans.

Question: "Would these tribes be the Hopi?"

Some of the Hopi were affected by this emanation, as well as Anasazi and Mayan cultures. The work that Akhenaten began was a long-held tradition. Before Akhenaten had begun this type of bi-location projection, there were those from the City of Shamballa who were doing such work. I hope this brings a greater understanding to the location. The reason Egyptian teachings now fill the area of Gobean is because of the work of Akhenaten to bring the energy of the Christ forward. This energy of the Christ was known as Quetzalcoatl. Quetzalcoatl was the first to actually anchor this energy into human consciousness in the geophysical area that is now known as Gobean. Do you understand?

Question: "What you're saying is that if we go back to the City of Shamballa, that is in essence the portal for the upliftment of all of humanity, which is a collection of many Star Seeds?"

This is true, Dear ones. This is also known as the Hall of Wisdom. For this earth, it is an entry point for many souls who come here to gain higher knowledge. Of course, there are those souls who try to come to schoolroom earth to disrupt the knowledge process, the learning process that is imparted. But now you can understand that, through Thought Projection and bi-location, the evolution of humanity has largely been brought forward through the work of Shamballa. Do you understand?

Question: "Yes, I understand. One more question."

Proceed.

Question: "Then all the Golden Cities are, in essence, stepping stones at one level on the path of the upliftment, and, on another level, they are also energy points that energize the consciousness of humanity in the upliftment process?"

They serve as Divine Intervention, to bring about higher knowledge, higher understanding. They are indeed a pivotal point of evolution.

The Light of a Thousand Suns
Saint Germain and Kuthumi Reveal Prophecies and Teachings

GREETINGS, BELOVEDS, IN THAT MIGHTY VIOLET FLAME, I AM SAINT GERMAIN, AND I REQUEST PERMISSION TO COME FORTH.

"Saint Germain, come forward. You are most welcome."

Today, Dear ones, we have much to talk about, not only a brief discourse from myself, but today Master Kuthumi, or Brother Kuthumi, as he is known by us, will bring a discourse about the attributes of the Golden City of Malton.

I must continue to remind you, Dear ones, that along the path of what you have been assigned to do, to bring forward the Earth Changes Prophecies, that you will encounter many along the path who, while connected to the work of the Brotherhood, may not have the same connection to the type of work that you are bringing forward. This is important to understand, Dear ones, that while all are united in a consciousness of Unana, a Unity Consciousness, that there are still the individual paths that one may take. As Beloved El Morya has said, "Choose. Choose. Choose." It is in the choosing that the individual becomes strong and is strengthened by the spiritual fires that temper the Will and show the individual the power of choice.

You see, Dear ones, to raise the consciousness—the animal consciousness—into the human consciousness requires the development of the Will. And it is only through tempering the spirit, that the Will is strengthened. When you encounter those whose paths are somewhat different than yours, you must understand that not one has more power than another. The power is equal. This is important, Dear ones, that you gain this concept. "Equal to" is of vast importance. However, it is also important that you stay entirely focused on the work at hand. Each of these pieces must be strong if they are to fit into the mosaic.

It is also important for you to know that within the next three months there will be an earthquake that will strike the coast of California. While we hope this can be averted or lessened in some small way through the work of your consciousness, it is important that you know this, so that the work at hand can now solve the problem. There have been many other changes that have been happening on your world or global scene. There have been several activations of the Ring of Fire and volcanic eruptions that may soon happen. Understand,

---

For more information and study topics on *The Light of a Thousand Suns*, see Appendix H, page 233.

THE LIGHT OF A THOUSAND SUNS

Dear ones, Dear hearts, that each of these changes birth a New Time, and while they may be frightening at first to understand, when you understand them in a greater scope and in the greater unity you will see that they birth the New Time, the Golden Age.

The Golden Age is the fruit of the out-picturing, as you understand from the Point of Perception. It is in the grand out-picturing that creation comes forward into a greater harmony, into a greater knowledge. The seed that is engendered in you as a Co-creator is, of course, of the most importance. You are not a puppet of predestination. Instead, you are a purveyor of your own Will. It is important that you understand the power of choice and how, through your own Point of Perception, you perceive, how you bring the seed of thought forward and carefully grow it into your Creative Will; then create the world that you live within.

As usual, Dear hearts, I still remind you that it is the use of the Violet Flame that will bring an ease within your life. When you feel the stress and turmoil about you of others, their energy projecting its creation upon you, it is only through the use of the Violet Flame that you can clear the air; so use it in the same way in which you would light a stick of incense or that you would shift the energy through music. In the same way, with each chant of the Violet Flame excess Karma is wiped away from your path. The agendas and the creations of others are wiped away from your path. The Violet Flame is a way to pave the pathway clear for you so that you may again take each step upon your own path.

As I have said so many times, it is important to know thyself, and to know thyself first. It is very difficult to bring two together until they understand the value of this lesson. When you know yourself clearly and have identified your path so clearly, then it is always much easier to unite two into the consciousness of the ONE. Then, there is a natural harmony, and the consequence of that harmony is always a good action. It is important, Dear ones, that you not judge your Brothers and Sisters, but that you discern. As dear Sananda has said, "By their fruits you shall know them." But it is important that you not cast a final judgment upon one, and that you understand that indeed a grander harmony, a grander symphony will someday play. Today, you are simply tuning the instrument, preparing ALL and ONE for the grand conduction, but indeed, you are ALL still united as ONE. Indeed, you are all upon individual paths. Today, the work at hand is to stay focused upon your path. Stay focused upon the work at hand.

Before I turn the floor over to Beloved Brother Kuthumi, do you have questions?

Question: "I have only one question."

Proceed.

Question: "You have just alluded that at a level of harmony it is much easier for two to join the ONE. Is this so?"

Light of Awakening

THE LIGHT OF A THOUSAND SUNS

It is always so, Dear one. Have you not noted the instruments in a grand symphony? They are all playing one piece of composed music, and yet all are playing a different part. It is only through knowing the part they play, the role they serve, that they unite in a greater union. Know thyself first, and harmony is then assured.

Answer: "I understand. Thank you."

And now, Dear ones, I turn the floor over to Beloved Brother Kuthumi. (Master Kuthumi steps forward.)

Greetings, Beloved Brothers and Sisters of the Golden Sun. I AM Kuthumi of the Ruby and Gold Ray, and I request permission to come forward.

Answer: "Please, Kuthumi, you are most welcome."

Dear hearts, the time is at hand. You see the earth in its changing glory. You see the stars predict it as so. You also know that the earth is beginning its process of purification. Beloved Saint Germain and Beloved El Morya have brought forward information that is to assist humanity at this time, and I, too, now join as a group in their Oneness. I, too, bring my service. This service is to lend yet a deeper understanding of why such change would come and why such change is needed. There are many who hope that the change may not be filled with the fury they demand. There are many who hope that through their prayer they may hold such change back. It is not the idea of holding such a change back, but the idea of praying that humanity will change itself inside.

There is much that is happening now upon the Earth Plane and Planet, much that is happening now in terms of change and the Times of Change. It is rare that we bring this type of information forward, but there are several things that are important for you to know and to understand. The economy of your nation is in grave danger. And while you may look at this time and ask how this could possibly happen, it is true that manipulation is happening behind the scenes, and world politics will ever play out its web of deceit. But this is important for you to know, to understand and to plan for.

The Elemental, Vegetable, and Mineral Kingdoms are now within a change. Their evolution must move forward. You see, Dear hearts, Dear ones, our beloved Brothers and Sisters of these Kingdoms are an evolving consciousness and part of the total system of your evolution. They have offered themselves to be of service to you. Have you not seen how your own special animals have become as pets and dear companions to you? Each of them offers a special form of consciousness that allows you to develop and to understand your own path. It is the same with the Vegetable and the Mineral Kingdom. The very crystal qualities of every mineral, arcs the qualities of a Ray Force to serve you. The Vegetable Kingdom, with fruits, nuts, berries and vegetables offer their own life force, their own prana, so that you may continue to grow and to learn in this planetary scheme. All is now moving forward in a greater evolution. It is important that this change not be held back, but that it be assisted, as in a gentle birth.

THE LIGHT OF A THOUSAND SUNS

We have spoken of this birth in previous discourses, but it is important to teach others the value of the great birth, the value of the New Time. A greater harmony awaits mankind. This is the harmony of the Vegetable and the Mineral Kingdom. Do you realize, Dear ones, Dear hearts, that if you were to bring your own spirit into total harmony with the earth and its various Kingdoms, that open telepathic communication between plants, animals, and minerals would be totally possible? It is through the lack of harmony, as my Brother El Morya has brought forward, that there is separateness and a separation. In the same way in which I come forward and bring this telepathic information to you, there is an opening, a bridge. The time will now come to all humanity when an opening and a bridge will be formed. This *Bridge of Awakening* will allow a telepathic connection to occur between animals, plants, and minerals from each human. As this opens in a greater awareness and a greater knowledge of all of consciousness, it is equal to the amount of harmony and peace that is created among yourselves. Are there questions?

Answer: "Not at this time. Please continue."

I would like to give further information concerning these Kingdoms and the purpose of Malton. You see, Beloveds, Dear hearts, it is indeed the Ruby Ray that opens this bridge as an awakening so that the desire can come into fruition. There are many wants among humanity: wants for money, for particular things that the world can give you, but let me assure you that sometimes the desires are trappings within themselves. What is at the core of all of it, but an urge to know God.

God dwells within each of us. God is part of all of us: your neighbor, your political leaders, your family members, the little pets in your household, the trees that grow among you. Everything contains God in some form and is part of God. This quest or thirst to know God is the greatest of all desires. To bring this into fruition is also of vast importance. The path of knowing God is also the path of desire. To bring a desire into fruition is the path of completion. How does one complete himself through all that he or she wants, through all that one yearns for? It is through the Ruby Ray that this bridge is formed.

When one begins to see the unity of all cause united as ONE, he can desire no more, for Divinity is indeed within ALL. When one realizes that at any moment one can touch the desire that he craves, that he can be part of the unity of ALL, then completion may come to order. But you see, among humanity, while this has been presented in its most simple form, humanity is not yet evolved enough to understand it in its most simplistic manner.

Humanity craves demonstration, wanting to create everything to be much bigger and better. The peace of God that is in front of people is not enough. The peace of God that they contain and hold is not enough, so more must come forward, until the soul tires. Part of the purpose of Malton is to bring desire into fruition, but for the cause only, and I must emphasize this to bring completion to the soul.

While one may want to judge such desire as futile, it is not.

THE LIGHT OF A THOUSAND SUNS

In the same way that a child craves candy or a continuous display of colorful toys, eventually they tire of such and grow out of such things. Yet, the innocence and the wonder of the thirst, the innocence and the wonder of the desire bring one to this completion. The energies of Malton are present to bring such desire to completion. It has always been said that before one leaves the schoolhouse known as earth, one must complete all that they want, all they desire. Malton's purpose, as a Golden City in this New Time, is to bring this forward.

Think of all the little desires you yourself have that have not been fulfilled. Think of those who see themselves as less because of that long list that has been written lifetime after lifetime that has never been fulfilled. What a gift the Nature Kingdoms bring you! It is through their cooperation, the Elemental Forces, that this can now be so.

The great gift of the New Time is to demonstrate to humanity that, in their sojourn upon the earth, heaven does indeed exist, that the world of spirit and the principles which create it indeed exist. Truth is indeed supreme. Along with these forces from the beloved Elemental Kingdoms is also the work of the Gold Ray.

The work of the Gold Ray for the New Time will help birth the earth into its new vibration. I use this word although, while it is not entirely accurate, it is the best to understand. You see, the earth, during this Time of Great Change, is raising its vibratory rate. It is the difference between entering a room where there are many angry and frustrated people, and moving on to the next room where there is peace and cooperation. This, I know, many of you, Dear ones, Dear chelas, have felt, and the best word to describe the New Time is that a total vibratory rate will heighten upon the earth. This is due to the new energies that are being utilized by the Elemental, Vegetable, Mineral and Animal Kingdoms. It is important that we assist them, too; that humanity may understand the new vibration, so that it may assist in this great unity and great rising of consciousness.

Consciousness is at the core of all of this.

As it has been taught before, it is your Point of Perception that will determine the outcome. Consciousness and its qualification—the way in which it is utilized—will again be of great assistance in this New Time. As you see that water is comprised of the Elemental Kingdoms, it, in itself, is raised in consciousness.

As you see that the Plant Kingdoms are raised in vibrational content, they are raised, too, in consciousness. So, do you see this greater working that is coming through the Gold Ray?

This plan was long determined about the year 2000 for humanity, that a greater consciousness, a *Ray of Light*, would flood the earth. Now, it is humanity's choice of how it will utilize this new Ray Force. In the beginning of this, there may be discomfort and there may be disharmony, but to prepare for this and its greater working is to continue your work in consciousness.

THE LIGHT OF A THOUSAND SUNS

Remain stalwart and stay focused, Dear ones.

Keep in vigilance your prayers for your Sisters and your Brothers.

When there is disharmony among you, pray simply, "Bring harmony forth to my Brothers and Sisters. Let us be united as ONE, for we truly are." When you confirm this great law and truth, it is recognized and, therefore, acted upon. The Gold Ray, as it beams forward in its greater illumination and its greater understanding, will bring the *Light of a Thousand Suns* to those whose hearts are open and willing. Do you have questions?

Question: "Yes, Dear one. Does the Gold Ray come about in an overall Divine Plan for the forward movement of humanity?"

Yes, as it was determined long ago that there would be those as the Lords of Venus to out-picture such a Ray and, in its Divine Order and Divine Timing, would come forward.

Question: "So, we have now come to this time?"

As Sananda has said, "The time is at hand; the awakening is now." The Ruby Ray has built this bridge to allow the Gold Ray to come forward in its greater working. Do you understand?

Answer: "Yes, I understand that things work in a sequence and one must be laid down before the other can come forward, so the Ruby Ray has played this part. And so it would seem as though humanity is now faced with the great potential of this harmony, or the great potential of discord. Once again, it is choice."

Vibration, you see, Dear ones, is the key to understanding. The Mineral Kingdom is also growing in its vibratory rate. The Vegetable Kingdom, plants, flowers, herbs and trees, are all growing in a vibratory rate, as has been taught in other discourses by my beloved Brothers. These vibratory rates are enhanced in the Golden City Vortices. That is why we have requested for many to move to such areas to live because of the increase in vibration. It is through this increase in vibration that greater understanding and the bond of telepathy is established—not only telepathy with us as your Teachers and Guides into this New Time, but a telepathic bond with all of nature, a telepathic bond with the Elemental Kingdoms. You see, Dear ones, this is important to understand in totality. In Malton, not only will there be fruition of desire, but a greater harmony will exist for the Mineral and Vegetable Kingdoms. This greater harmony will then arc itself to the Sister City of Denasha and fulfill, in a greater plan, a harmony to all Elemental Kingdoms. Do you have questions?

Question: "What is your definition of vibration?"

Light of Awakening

THE LIGHT OF A THOUSAND SUNS

I use that term sparingly, for vibration is not perhaps the most accurate way to understand what I AM speaking about. However, it is the closest in terms of your understanding. It has to do with movement, movement of light within the cells of your physical body— a physical demonstration of light movement. However, as you know, that it is the Point of Perception; light uses as its seed the vehicle of consciousness, so it is only in perception that vibration can be *as it is*. Vibration is, of course, movement to see something move or to vibrate. It is a vibration that may not be perceived by the physical eye or even through various tests. However, it is a movement that is in the *Eye of Consciousness*. Do you understand?

Question: "The Eye of Consciousness—so that would mean that the light movement is going to be proportionate to the openness of someone's perception, perspective or attitude?"

It was once said that beauty is in the eye of the beholder, and so is the *vibration within the eye of the perceiver*. In order for a heightened consciousness or vibration to be understood, it must be perceived first in the one who recognizes it. So, when I use the word vibration I must qualify such a statement. However, we have out-pictured that a greater time shall come to the earth, a greater time when suffering and misery shall be lessened. However, one must then be ready to let go of one's perception of misery, the perception of suffering. Do you understand?

Question: "I see, so if we can perceive it, then it can be created?"

This is so. This is the tool of consciousness, as it must be honed. That is why desire must not be denied or judged. It must be allowed its total fruition, for, through this process, consciousness is exercised and brought into its greater working, where the perception of peace may be attained.

Question: "So if we were to choose to perceive a world of harmony and telepathy with the Nature Kingdoms and each other and the planet on a whole and the spiritual hierarchy, those who would choose that perception would move into this Golden Age?"

This is the idea, to bring such a teaching into a Unity of Consciousness. The desire is that to bring unity to ALL, to bring harmony to ALL, but until that desire is fueled with the fire of Co-creation, it cannot be attained. *Where two or more are gathered, there I AM*; the universal consciousness of peace is exactly that. It is universal. It is for ALL.

Question: "So it really comes down to a matter of desire of the individual and groups?"

It is, Dear ones, Dear hearts. Now I ask of you that within the next year, if you have the opportunity to travel to the Vortex of Malton, to feel these energies, to understand exactly what we have just spoken about. Is this possible, Dear heart?

Answer: "I have great desire for this."

THE LIGHT OF A THOUSAND SUNS

Then, let us bring this into fruition, together as your Brother, so that these energies may be understood and taught. Bringing desire into fruition is a good thing, for there is a greater understanding that lies behind it.

Now, unless, of course, there are no other questions, I shall take my leave.

Response: "At this time, I have no more other than a request that you return more frequently."

So be it.

In the Light of a Thousand Suns, I AM. (Master Kuthumi steps back, and Saint Germain comes forward.)

Greetings, Beloveds, and again I must remind you that it is in the work of the Violet Flame that I hold you ever sincere and dear. Hitaka.

Answer: "Hitaka. Thank you."

Spiritual Lineage of the Violet Flame

The teachings of the Violet Flame, as taught in the work of I AM America, come through the Goddess of Compassion and Mercy Kuan Yin. She holds the feminine aspects of the flame, which are Compassion, Mercy, Forgiveness, and Peace. Her work with the Violet Flame is well documented in the history of Ascended Master teachings, and it is said that the altar of the etheric Temple of Mercy holds the flame in a Lotus Cup. She became Saint Germain's teacher of the Sacred Fire in the inner realms, and he carried the masculine aspect of the flame into human activity through Purification, Alchemy, and Transmutation. One of the best means to attract the beneficent activities of the Violet Flame is through the use of decrees and invocation. However, you can meditate on the flame, visualize the flame, and receive its transmuting energies like "the light of a thousand suns," radiant and vibrant as the first day that the Elohim Arcturus and Diana drew it forth from our solar sun at the creation of the earth. Whatever form, each time you use the Violet Flame these two Master Teachers hold you in the loving arms of its action and power.

The following is an invocation for the Violet Flame to be used at sunrise or sunset. It is utilized while experiencing the visible change of night to day, and day to night. In fact, if you observe the horizon at these times, you will witness light transitioning from pinks to blues, and then a subtle violet strip adorning the sky. We have used this invocation for years in varying scenes and circumstances, overlooking lakes, rivers, mountaintops, deserts, and prairies; in huddled traffic and busy streets; with groups of students or sitting with a friend, but more commonly alone in our home or office, with a glint of soft light streaming from a window. The result is always the same: a calm, centering force of stillness. We call it the Space.

Invocation of the Violet Flame for Sunrise and Sunset
I invoke the Violet Flame to come forth in the name of I AM that I AM,
To the Creative Force of all the realms of all the Universes, the Alpha, the Omega, the Beginning, and the End,
To the Great Cosmic Beings and Torch Bearers of all the realms of all the Universes,
And the Brotherhoods and Sisterhoods of Breath, Sound, and Light, who honor this Violet Flame that comes forth from the Ray of Divine Love—the Pink Ray, and the Ray of Divine Will—the Blue Ray of all Eternal Truths.

I invoke the Violet Flame to come forth in the name of I AM that I AM!
Mighty Violet Flame, stream forth from the Heart of the Central Logos, the Mighty Great Central Sun! Stream in, through, and around me.

(Then insert other prayers and/or decrees for the Violet Flame.)

Glossary

Abundance: The second of the Twelve Jurisdictions is the principle of overflowing fullness in all situations, based upon the Law of Choice. In Divine Destiny, Abundance, as a Meta-need, is defined as richness and complexity. Abundance, perceived as an Evolution Point, is synonymous with the Law of Choice, and develops the individual will; hence, the spiritual recognition of Universal Bounty and Manifestation leads the spiritual student to the discernment and the acknowledgement of the Hermetic principles of Cause and Effect through the Law of Attraction.

Aryan: The fifth Root Race of humanity is identified primarily with Active Intelligence, and the development of the prefrontal lobes of the brain (prefrontal cortex). This is the dominant Root Race currently incarnated on earth.

Akashic Records: The recorded history of all created things from time immemorial, and constructed with the fifth cosmic element: ether.

Akhenaten: The ancient king of Egypt (1388 BC) embraced the unfolding consciousness of the ONE, which culturally replaced the polytheistic religion of his Kingdom. A pioneer of monotheistic religion, Akhenaten embraced the Christ Consciousness and some esoteric historians view him as a spiritual forerunner who led the way for the incarnation of Jesus Christ. According to the Master Teachers, Akhenaten is one of the prior lifetimes attributed to Ascended Master Serapis Bey.

Ascended Master Consciousness: A higher frequency of thought, feeling, and action which embraces the unity of humanity through the principle of the Oneship

Ascension: A process of Mastering thoughts, feelings, and actions that balance positive and negative Karmas in the physical planes. Once engaged, the soul's Ascension Process often involves successive lifetimes, and engages the transmutation of Karma (actions), and the conscious achievement of spiritual immortality. Ascension allows entry to a higher state of consciousness and frees a person from the need to reincarnate on the lower earthly planes, or lokas of experience. Ascension is also known as the process of spiritual liberation, moksha, or spiritual transcendence. The attainment of physical immortality is also associated with Ascension; however, an Ascended Being is not limited by form of any kind, and may take any shape or outward appearance necessary for the task at hand.

GLOSSARY

Ascension Valley: According to the I AM America Prophecies, Ascended Masters appear in physical form in the Golden City Vortices during and after a prophesied twenty-year period. At that time, Mass Ascensions occur in the Golden Cities, at the Golden City Star locations, and in select geophysical locations around the world, which are hosted by the complimentary energies of Mother Earth. A model of this geophysical location is Ascension Valley, located in the Shalahah Vortex. The energy of Ascension Valley prepares students to integrate their light bodies and spiritual consciousness into the Oneship, the divinity within, and further prepares the body, mind, and spirit to experience and travel into the New Dimensions.

Ashram: A secluded community or retreat, especially of spiritual students and seekers

Aspirant: A newly awakened spiritual student, whose ambitions create aspiration; the student has yet to find or acquire a guru—a teacher who can assist their evolutionary journey on the spiritual path. The aspirant is the first level of HU-man development, and occupies the fifth of the Thirteen Evolutionary Pyramids of the Eight-Sided Cell of Perfection: Spiritual Awakening.

Astral Body: This subtle light body contains our feelings, desires, and emotions and exists as an intermediate light body between the physical body and the Causal Body (Mental Body). According to the Master Teachers we enter the Astral Plane through our Astral Body when we sleep, and many dreams and visions are experiences in this Plane of vibrant color and sensation. Through spiritual development the Astral Body strengthens, and the luminosity of its light is often detected in the physical plane. A spiritual adept may have the ability to consciously leave their physical body while traveling in their Astral Body. The Astral Body or Astral Plane has various levels of evolution, and is the heavenly abode where the soul resides after the disintegration of the physical body. The Astral Body is also known to esoteric scholars as the Body Double, the Desire Body, and the Emotional Body.

Atlantis: An ancient civilization of earth, whose mythological genesis was the last Puranic Dvapara Yuga—the Bronze Age of the Yugas, and its demise occurred around the year 9,628 BC. The legends of Atlantis claim the great empire co-existed with Ameru, Lemuria, and the Lands of Rama. According to Theosophical thought, Atlantis' evolving humanity brought about an evolutionary epoch of the Pink Ray on the earth, and the development of the Astral-Emotional bodies and the Heart Chakra. Ascended Master provenance claims the Els—now the Mighty Elohim of the Seven Rays—were the original Master Teachers to the spiritual seekers of Atlantis. Esoteric historians suggest three phases of political and geophysical boundaries best describe its ancient record: the Toltec Nation of Atlantis (Ameru); the Turian Nation of Atlantis (the invaders of the Land of Rama); and Poseid, the Island Nation of the present-day Atlantic Ocean. The early civilizations of Atlantis were ruled by the spiritually evolved Toltec and their spiritual teachings, ceremonies, and temples were dedicated to the worship of the sun. Atlantean culture later deteriorated into the use of nuclear weapons and cruelty towards other nations, including the use of genetic engineering. The demise of Atlantis was inevitable; however, modern-day geologists, archaeologists, and occultists all disagree to its factual timing. Ascended Master teachings affirm that Atlantis—a

GLOSSARY

continent whose geo-physical and political existence probably spanned well over 100,000 years—experienced several phases of traumatic Earth Change. This same belief is held by occult historians who allege the earth repeatedly cycles through periods of massive Earth Change and cataclysmic pole-shifts that activate tectonic plates which subsequently submerge whole continents and create vital new lands for earth's successors.

Awaken: To rouse from the sleep of illusion and become spiritually aware and attentive to one's internal truth. This first level of spiritual evolution is often identified as the Spiritual Aspirant. It can also indicate a new level of spiritual wakefulness or growth, sometimes known as the restorative and vibrant Quickening.

Avatar: The Divine Manifestation of a perfected spiritual consciousness in human form has several meanings. The Siddha is a perfected being; the Jivanmukta is freed while living; and the Paramukta, similar to an Ascended Master, is supremely free, with full power over death. A Paramukta or Ascended Being purposely creates a physical body and descends to earth to either assist humanity or to spiritually bless or balance a disordered world. The perfected, death-free body of a Paramukta does not cast a shadow or leave footprints. Such Masters never appear in the gross public, and have the ability to become invisible. There are, however, Living Avatars who incarnate in a human body to help the masses to spiritually awake and transform at critical times in earth's history. According to Ascended Master teachings there are twelve Living Avatars present on earth at any time. This insures specific levels of vibration, radiance, and spiritual energy to foster humanity's growth and evolutionary requirements.

Bija-Seed Mantra: A one-syllable word spoken aloud to produce spiritual healing and intervention, alongside spiritual growth and insight. Bija-Seed Mantras are said to contain the spiritual laws and patterns of the underlying energy of creation, and their sound vibration recalibrates the energy bodies and light-fields of the Human Aura which affects the physical world of the individual.

Bi-locate: The ability to consciously move the physical body through the spiritual development of the light-bodies. Some spiritual Masters use bi-location to be physically present in two or more locations simultaneously.

Binary Intellect: Dual, human intelligence, based upon the difference of the left brain and the right brain

Blue Flame: The activity of the Blue Ray, based upon the activation of the individual will, manifests the qualities of truth, power, determination, and diligence in human endeavors. The Blue Flame is associated with the transformation of our individual choices, and its inherent processes align the individual will to the Divine Will through the HU-man qualities of detachment, steadiness, calm, harmony, and God-protection.

GLOSSARY

Blue Ray: A Ray is a perceptible light and sound frequency, and the Blue Ray not only resonates with the color blue, but is identified with the qualities of steadiness, calm, perseverance, transformation, harmony, diligence, determination, austerity, protection, humility, truthfulness, and self-negation. It forms one-third of the Unfed Flame within the heart—the Blue Ray of God Power, which nourishes the spiritual unfoldment of the human into the HU-man. Use of the Violet Flame evokes the Blue Ray into action throughout the light bodies, where the Blue Ray clarifies intentions and assists the alignment of the Will. In Ascended Master teachings the Blue Ray is alleged to have played a major role in the physical manifestation of the earth's first Golden City—Shamballa and six of fifty-one Golden Cities emanate the Blue Ray's peaceful, yet piercing frequencies. The Blue Ray is esoterically linked to the planet Saturn, the development of the Will, the ancient Lemurian Civilization, the Archangel Michael, the Elohim Hercules, the Master Teacher El Morya, and the Eastern Doors of all Golden Cities.

Breathwork: The conscious, spiritual application of breath, often accompanied by visualization and meditation forms the nexus of Breathwork. Ascended Master teachings often incorporate various breathing techniques to activate and integrate Ray Forces in the Human Aura and light bodies.

Cellular Awakening: A spiritual initiation activated by the Master Teachers Saint Germain and Kuthumi. Through this process the physical body is accelerated at the cellular level, preparing consciousness to recognize and receive instruction from the Fourth Dimension. Supplemental teachings on the Cellular Awakening claim this process assists the spiritual student to assimilate the higher frequencies and energies now available on earth. Realizing the Cellular Awakening can ameliorate catastrophic Earth Change and initiate consciousness into the ONE through the realization of devotion, compassion, Brotherhood and the Universal Heart.

Cellular Fear: The cumulative emotion of fear held in the light bodies which simultaneously affects human DNA. This energetic build up is carried by the individual to the astral plane after physical death and passed to the next lifetime until it is released by the soul.

Chakra(s): Sanskrit for wheel. Seven spinning wheels of human-bioenergy centers stacked from the base of the spine to top of the head.

Chela: Disciple

Christ, the, or Christ Consciousness: The highest energy or frequency attainable on earth. The Christ or the Christ Consciousness is a Step-down Transformer of the I AM energies, which enlighten, heal, and transform all human conditions of degradation and death.

Closure of Understanding: The completion and release of a Karmic lesson

Co-creation: Creating with the God-Source

Compassion: An attribute of the Violet Flame is the sympathetic understanding of the suffering of another.

GLOSSARY

Conductivity: The transmission of vital energy

Dark Side: The energy and force of the common man that draws power from raw human emotions like: pain, hatred, passion, and attachment

Denasha: The Golden City of Denasha is primarily located over Scotland, and the Ascended Masters assert this Vortex holds the energies of Divine Justice for all of humanity. Denasha is also the Sister Golden City to Malton (Illinois and Indiana, USA) and both Vortices mutually distribute energies to the Nature and Elemental Kingdoms during the New Times. The Master Teacher is Lady Nada; the Ray Force is Yellow; and Denasha's translation means, "Mountain of Zeus."

Dharma: Purpose

Divineship: The essence and presence of the Divine is present within the individual.

Divine Will: The idea of God's plan for humanity; however, from the perspective of the HU-man, the Divine Will is choice.

Divinity: The creative energy of the Source is in all things created, and this philosophy includes ideas, thoughts, emotions, and feelings. As our comprehension of innate divinity evolves, our beliefs often shift and we experience equanimity, harmony, and cooperation.

Earth Plane: The dual aspect of life on earth

Eastern Door: The East side of a Golden City gateway, also known as the Blue Door

Eight-Sided Cell of Perfection: An atomic cell located in the human heart. It is associated with all aspects of perfection, and contains and maintains a visceral connection with the Godhead.

Elemental: A nature-being

El Morya: Ascended Master of the Blue Ray, associated with the development of the Will.

Elohim: Creative beings of love and light that helped manifest the Divine idea of our solar system. Seven Elohim (the Seven Rays) exist on earth. They organize and draw forward Archangels, the Four Elements, Devas, Seraphim, Cherubim, Angels, Nature Guardians, and the Elementals. In Ascended Master teaching, the Silent Watcher—the Great Mystery—gives them direction. It is also claimed the Elohim magnetize the Unfed Flame at the center of the earth. Some esoteric historians perceive the Elohim—also referred to as the Els—as the Ancient Gods, or the Master Teachers of Lemuria and Atlantis.

Emanation: To flow out, issue, or proceed as from a source or origin

GLOSSARY

E-motion: The harmonizing Vibration of Sound, sometimes defined as feeling plays a critical role in the Co-creation process by melding and harmonizing thought and feeling. The E-motion is a charge which ignites and inflames the kernel of thought-feeling into action.

Energy Balancing: Also known as Energy Work, Energy Balancing is a healing technique applied by a trained practitioner who balances the Chakra System of an individual through hands-on-healing and energetic adjustment of the energy fields and light bodies.

Fire Triplicity: Energies from the Great Central Sun, or Galactic Center triangulate to our Solar System through these three planets: the sun, Mars, and Jupiter. These three planets are known as the Fire Triplicity and represent three forms of spiritual fire: the sun is the spiritual leader; Mars is the spiritual pioneer; and Jupiter is the spiritual teacher.

Focus: The point where the Seven Rays of Light and Sound radiate and meet

Galactic Light: Energy streams from the Great Central Sun, or Galactic Center, as the Seven Rays of Light and Sound to earth. Galactic Light calibrates the level of intelligence on earth through memory function; the ability to absorb, recognize, and respect spiritual knowledge; the length of lifespans; and our ability to access the Akashic Records. The amount of Galactic Light streaming to earth at any given time is classically measured through the Hindu Puranic timing of the Yugas, and through a contemporary method—the Electric Cycle—advocated by the Eastern Indian guru Sri Yuteswar.

Gobean: The first United States Golden City located in the states of Arizona and New Mexico. Its qualities are cooperation, harmony, and peace; its Ray Force is blue; and its Master Teacher is El Morya.

Gobi, Golden City of: Steps-down the energies of Shamballa into the entire Golden City Network. This Golden City is located in the Gobi Desert. It is known as the City of Balance, and means Across the Star; its Master Teachers are Lord Meru and Archangel Uriel.

Godhead: The I AM

God-state: The attainment of Unity Consciousness

Golden Perfection: A spiritual acceleration in the physical body, mind, and light-bodies which enables an individual to bi-locate and achieve physical immortality.

Golden Thread Axis: Also known as the Vertical Power Current, the Golden Thread Axis is physically comprised of the Medullar Shushumna, a life-giving nadi physically comprising one-third of the human Kundalini system. Two vital currents intertwine around the Golden Thread Axis: the lunar Ida Current, and the solar Pingala Current. According to the Master Teachers the flow of the Golden Thread Axis begins with the I AM Presence, enters the Crown Chakra, and descends through the spinal system. It descends beyond the Base Chakra and travels to the core of the earth. Esoteric scholars often refer to the axis as the Rod of Power, and it is symbolized by two spheres connected by an elongated rod. Ascended Master students and chelas frequently draw upon the energy of the earth through the Golden Thread Axis for healing and renewal with meditation, visualization, and breath.

GLOSSARY

Gold Ray: The Ray of Brotherhood, Cooperation, and Peace. The Gold Ray produces the qualities of perception, honesty, confidence, courage, and responsibility. It is also associated with leadership, independence, authority, ministration, and justice. The Gold Ray vibrates the energies of Divine Father on earth. Its attributes are: warm; perceptive; honest; confident; positive; independent; courageous; enduring; vital; leadership; responsible; ministration; authority; justice. The Gold Ray is also associated with the Great Central Sun, the Solar Logos, of which our Solar Sun is a Step-down Transformer of its energies. According to the Master Teachers, the Gold Ray is the epitome of change for the New Times. The Gold Ray is the ultimate authority of Cosmic Law, and carries both our personal and worldwide Karma and Dharma (purpose). Its presence is designed to instigate responsible spiritual growth and planetary evolution as a shimmering light for humanity's aspirations and the development of the HU-man. The Gold Ray, however, is also associated with Karmic justice, and will instigate change: constructive and destructive. The extent of catastrophe or transformation is contingent on humanity's personal and collective spiritual growth and evolutionary process as we progress into the New Times.

Great Central Sun: The great sun of our galaxy, of which all of its solar systems rotate. The Great Central Sun is also known as the Galactic Center, which is the origin of the Seven Rays of Light and Sound on earth.

Greater Mind: An outgrowth of the Ascension Process, this mind differs from the deductive and inductive reason of the Rational Mind, and the sporadic, yet instant insights gleaned from the Intuitive Mind. The Greater Mind is activated by self-revealed wisdom versus acquired knowledge.

Great Law, the: The Law of Peace

Great Mystery: The source of creation; all elements of life contain the sacred and are aspects of the Divine.

Great Silence: The Master Teachings encourage a contemplative period of quiet and stillness to intensely apply spiritual energies in certain circumstances and situations. This period of tranquil power is often referred to as the Great Silence.

Green Ray: The Ray of Active Intelligence is associated with education, thoughtfulness, communication, organization, the intellect, science, objectivity, and discrimination. It is also adaptable, rational, healing, and awakened. The Green Ray is affiliated with the planet Mercury. In the I AM America teachings the Green Ray is served by the Archangel Raphael and Archeia Mother Mary; the Elohim of Truth, Vista—also known as Cyclopea, and Virginia; the Ascended Masters Hilarion, Lord Sananda, Lady Viseria, Soltec, and Lady Master Meta.

GLOSSARY

Group Mind: A conscious intelligent force, formed by members of distinguished cultures, societal organizations, and more prominently by religious church members; the Group Mind is held together by the rituals and customs that are peculiar to its members; newcomers instantly sense the energies of the atmosphere, and will either accept or reject its influence. The physics of the Group Mind are important to comprehend, as this collective intelligence is purposely formed to aid the Aspirant to raise human consciousness beyond present limitations.

Harmony: The first virtue of the Twelve Jurisdictions based on the principle of the Law of Agreement.

Harmony of the Spheres: A superior form of music, founded on beauty and harmonious combination, heard by those who have developed the ears to hear—clairaudience.

Heart of the Dove: Also known as the Center of Fire, this energy anomaly is prophesied to exist Northwest of Saint Louis, Missouri. It is here that Master Teachings claim an umbilicus connection between earth and the Galactic Center exists, creating time anomalies and the potential for time travel in the New Times. The Heart of the Dove is also prophesied to become a spiritual center for learning and self-actualizing the consciousness of Quetzalcoatl—the Christ.

Heart's Desire: This Ascended Master teaching recommends by identifying activities that yield personal joy and happiness, one may discover their Heart's Desire. The Heart's Desire is the wellspring of abundance, love, and creativity. Eastern philosophy often refers to this principle as the soul's specific duty or purpose in a lifetime—Dharma. The Heart's Desire is analogous to the principle of desire—the Ninth Jurisdiction. This evolved perception of desire is based on the true etymology of the word. De, is a French word that means of, and the English word sire, means forefather, ancestry, or source. From this context, Sanat Kumara teaches, "The Heart's Desire is the source of creation." Since the Heart's Desire is one of the most influential principles underlying humanity's spiritual development and unfoldment, Ascended Master teachings give it utmost importance. It is considered a physical, emotional, mental, and spiritual presence that raises the un-awakened animal consciousness into the human, and onward to the awakened aspirant and the devoted chela. The Ascended Masters claim that the physical presence of the Flame of Desire lies within the heart nestled inside the Eight-Sided Cell of Perfection. As students and chelas perfect the Co-creation process, some teachings suggest the Flame of Desire evolves alongside the Three-Fold or Unfed Flame of Love, Wisdom, and Power into the Four-Fold Flame. In this physical, progressed state it develops as the fourth White Flame of Creation.

Higher Self: The Atma or Atman. This is the true identity of the soul which resides in the spiritual planes of consciousness, and although it is energetically connected to each individual in the physical plane, the Higher Self is free from the Karmas of the earth plane and identification with the material world.

GLOSSARY

HU, the: In Tibetan dialects, the word hue or hu means breath; however, the HU is a sacred sound and when chanted or meditated upon is said to represent the entire spectrum of the Seven Rays. Because of this, the HU powerfully invokes the presence of the Violet Flame, which is the activity of the Violet Ray and its inherent ability to transform and transmit energies to the next octave. HU is also considered an ancient name for God, and it is sung for spiritual enlightenment.

Initiation: Admission, especially into secret, advanced spiritual knowledge

Instant-Thought-Manifestation: The clear and concise use of thought to Co-create desires. The Master Teachers often refer to this process as Manifest Destiny. Experiences with Instant-Thought-Manifestation are said to prepare our consciousness to enter into the ONE.

Intention: Acts, thoughts, or conceptions earnestly fixed on something, or steadfastly directed. Intentions often reflect the state of an individual's mind which directs their specific actions towards an object or goal.

Interplay: Reciprocal action and reaction

Kali-Yuga: The Age of Iron, or Age of Quarrel, when earth receives twenty-five percent or less galactic light from the Great Central Sun.

Kama: Desire

Klehma: The fifth United States Golden City located primarily in the states of Colorado and Kansas. Its qualities are continuity, balance, and harmony; its Ray Force is white; and its Master Teacher is Serapis Bey.

Kundalini: In Sanskrit, Kundalini literally means coiled, and represents the coiled energy located at the base of the spine, often established in the lower Base and Sacral Chakras. Kundalini Shatki (shatki means energy) is claimed to initiate spiritual development, wisdom, knowledge, and enlightenment.

Law of Love: Perhaps every religion on earth is founded upon the Law of Love, as the notion to "treat others as you would like to be treated." The Law of Love, however, from the Ascended Master tradition is simply understood as consciously living without fear, or inflicting fear on others. The Fourth of the Twelve Jurisdictions instructs Love is the Law of Allowing, Maintaining, and Sustainability. All of these precepts distinguishes love from an emotion or feeling, and observes Love as action, will, or choice. The Ascended Masters affirm, "If you live love, you will create love." This premise is fundamental to understand the esoteric underpinnings of the Law of Love. The Master Teachers declare that through practicing the Law of Love one experiences acceptance and understanding; tolerance, alongside detachment. Metaphysically, the Law of Love allows different and varied perceptions of ONE experience, situation, or circumstance to exist simultaneously. From this viewpoint the Law of Love is the practice of tolerance.

GLOSSARY

Lemuria: According to Ascended Master Teachings, Lemuria primarily existed in the present Pacific Ocean and esoteric historians theorize the oceanic tectonic Pacific Plate, through periodic geologic upheaval and Earth Changes forms the submerged lost continent of Lemuria. Spiritual teachings claim the evolutionary purpose of the ancient civilization developed humanity's Will (the Blue Ray of Power), and Lemurian culture venerated the Golden Disk of the Sun and the Right-hand Path. Lemuria, while claimed to be one the earliest cultures of humanity, ultimately integrated with the Lands of Rama, and Sri Lanka is alleged to have been one of the empire's capital cities. Asuramaya is one of the great Manus of Lemuria's Root Race. According to Theosophical history the Lemurian and Atlantean epochs overlap and it is alleged the lands of Lemuria, also known as Shalmali, existed in the Indian and Southern Pacific Oceans, and included the continent of Australia. Lemuria is the remaining culture and civilization of Mu—an expansive continent that once spanned the entire present-day Pacific Ocean. Some esoteric writers place the destruction of Mu around the year 30,000 BCE; others place its demise millions of years ago. The apparent discrepancy of these timelines is likely due to two different interpretations of the Cycle of the Yugas. It is claimed the venerated Elders of Lemuria escaped the global tragedy by moving to an uninhabited plateau in central Asia. This account mirrors Ascended Master teachings and Lord Himalaya's founding of the Retreat of the Blue Lotus. The Lemurian elders re-established their spiritual teachings and massive library as the Thirteenth School. It is claimed these teachings and spiritual records became foundational teachings in the Great White Brotherhood of the mystical lands of Hsi Wang Mu (the Abode of the Immortals), and the Kuan Yin Lineage of Gurus. Today, present-day Australia once known by Egyptian gold-miners as the ancient Land of Punt is the remainder of the once great continent of Mu and Lemuria which likely existed in the time period of Dvapara-Yuga, over 800,000 years ago.

Light of Awakening: A prophesied wave of cosmic light, originating from the Galactic Center, is destined to evolve humanity into the Golden Age by altering our human genetics and transforming our sensation of fear.

Light Side: Evolves the human to the HU-man, and the HU-man to the ONE, and is aligned with honesty, compassion, mercy, love, and self-sacrifice

Lineage of Gurus: The venerated ancestral root of certain spiritual teachings. Kuan Yin and Lord Apollo are two of Saint Germain's spiritual teachers; therefore, they compose his Lineage of Gurus.

Lord Meru or Lord Machah: An Ascended Master of the Ruby and Gold Ray is also known as the great Sage of Ancient Mu. Lord Meru is a teacher of the ancient civilizations of the earth and considered a spiritual historian of their mythological records. Lord Meru is also known as Lord Machah—the parrot—a symbol of beauty, wisdom, and spiritual knowledge. Lord Machah's dark skin is contrasted by a colorful headdress filled with parrot, trogon, and quetzal bird feathers, a symbol of Quetzalcoatl—the Christ Consciousness. In the New Times, Lord Meru is prophesied to steward the Golden City of Gobi.

GLOSSARY

Malton: The second United States Golden City located in the states of Illinois and Indiana. Its qualities are fruition and attainment; its Ray Force is Ruby and Gold; and its Master Teacher is Kuthumi.

Mantra: Certain sounds, syllables, and sets of words are deemed sacred and often carry the ability to transmute Karma, spiritually purify, and transform an individual and are known as mantras.

New Age: Prophesied by Utopian Francis Bacon, the New Age would herald a United Brotherhood of the Earth. This Brotherhood and Sisterhood would be built as Solomon's Temple, and supported by the Four Pillars of history, science, philosophy, and religion. These four teachings would synergize the consciousness of humanity to Universal Fellowship and Peace.

New Day: The spiritual ideal of positive energy and a fresh start

New Dimensions: As humanity enters the New Times, subtle elements and aspects physically appear and spiritually and simultaneously enable HU-man consciousness to embrace allowing, alignment, transformation, and self-knowledge. The Ascended Masters claim this spiritual growth is the result of New Dimensions.

North Door: The North side of a Golden City gateway, also known as the Black Door

Oral Tradition: According to the Master Teachers and many indigenous teachers, the Oral Tradition, or learning through oral instruction, is the preferred medium to receive spiritual knowledge. This method requires the use of memory and memorization and also instigates the recognition of vital, yet subtle nuances that engender spiritual comprehension and may include the Master Teacher's use of telepathy, clairaudience, and clairvoyance.

Pink Ray: The Pink Ray is the energy of the Divine Mother and associated with the moon. It is affiliated with these qualities: loving; nurturing; hopeful; heartfelt; compassionate; considerate; communicative; intuitive; friendly; humane; tolerant; adoring. In the I AM America teachings the Pink Ray is served by the Archangel Chamuel and Archeia Charity; the Elohim of Divine Love Orion and Angelica; and the Ascended Masters Kuan Yin, Mother Mary, Goddess Meru, and Paul the Venetian.

Point of Perception: A Co-creation teaching of the Ascended Masters and its processes pivot on the fulcrum of choice. By carefully choosing certain actions, a Master of Choice opens the world of possibility through honing carefully cultivated perceptions, attitudes, beliefs, thoughts, and feelings. This allows the development of outcome through various scenarios and opens the multi-dimensional door to multiple realities and simultaneous experiences that dissolve linear timeframes into the Ever-present Now.

Portals of Entry: These geological locations on earth are prophesied locations where energy anomalies occur. Portals of Entry are also prophesied sites where new energies will enter the earth and affect her evolution physically, emotionally, mentally, and spiritually.

GLOSSARY

Prana or Prahna: Vital, life-sustaining energy. The Masters Teachers often refer to earth as Prahna.

Projection of Consciousness: The ability acquired through a Mastery of meditation and enables the individual to split their consciousness (existence, sensations, and cognitions) to another physical location or plane, while retaining the physical body in the physical dimension.

Prophecy: A spiritual teaching given simultaneously with a warning. It's designed to change, alter, lessen, or mitigate the prophesied warning. This caveat may be literal or metaphoric; the outcome of these events are contingent on the choices and the consciousness of those willing to apply the teachings.

Prosperity: Comfort and ease, the result of spiritual growth and development

Purification: A clearing process, especially in spiritual practice, which frees consciousness from encumbering or objectionable elements

Quetzalcoatl: The Quetzalcoatl Energies, as explained and taught by Lord Meru, are akin to the Christ energies when applied in the esoteric Western Christian tradition. This ancient spiritual teacher, however, predates Christianity and likely has its roots in alchemic Atlantean (Toltec) teaching. Quetzalcoatl, in contemporary terms, is the Incan Christ.

Radiation: The emission and diffusion of Rays of heat, light, electricity, or sounds

Ruby Ray: The Ruby Ray is the energy of the Divine Masculine and Spiritual Warrior. It is associated with these qualities: energetic; passionate; devoted; determination; dutiful; dependable; direct; insightful; inventive; technical; skilled; forceful. This Ray Force is astrologically affiliated with the planet Mars and the Archangel Uriel, Lord Sananda, and Master Kuthumi. The Ruby Ray is often paired with the Gold Ray, which symbolizes Divine Father. The Ruby Ray is the evolutionary Ray Force of both the base and solar chakras of the HU-man; and the Gold and Ruby Rays step-down and radiate sublime energies into six Golden Cities.

Sacred Fire: The Unfed Flame of Divine Consciousness within the human heart. Also, the term Sacred Fire is synonymous to the Violet Flame.

Sacred Geometry: Esoteric scholars suggest diverse universal patterns, geometrical shapes, and geometric proportions symbolize spiritual balance and perfection.

Sanat Kumara: Sanat Kumara is a Venusian Ascended Master and the venerated leader of the Ascended Masters, best known as the founder of Shamballa, the first Golden City on earth. He is also known in the teachings of the Great White Brotherhood as the Lord of the World, and is regarded as a savior and eminent spiritual teacher. Sanat Kumara is the guru of four of the Twelve Jurisdictions: Cooperation, Charity, Desire, and Stillness. These spiritual precepts are based on the principles of Co-creation, and are prophesied to guide human consciousness into the New Times. These four Jurisdictions reiterate the symbolic revelation of Sanat Kumara's four-fold identity as the Cosmic Christ, which assist human-

GLOSSARY

ity's evolutionary process into the New Times. As Kartikkeya, the commander of God's Army, Sanat Kumara teaches Cooperation to overcome the lower mind; as Kumar the holy youth, Sanat Kumara imparts Charity to conquer the darkness of disease and poverty; as Skanda, the son of Shiva and the spiritual warrior, Sanat Kumara offers Desire as the hopeful seed of God's transformation; and as Guha, the Jurisdiction Stillness restores the cave of all hearts.

Serapis Bey: An Ascended Master from Venus who works on the White Ray. He is the great disciplinarian—essential for Ascension; and works closely with all unascended humanity who remain focused for its attainment.

Seven Rays: The traditional Seven Rays of Light and Sound are: the Blue Ray of Truth; the Yellow Ray of Wisdom; the Pink Ray of Love; the White Ray of Purity; the Green Ray of Healing; the Gold and Ruby Ray of Ministration; and the Violet Ray of Transmutation.

Shalahah: The fourth United States Golden City located primarily in the states of Montana and Idaho. Its qualities are abundance, prosperity, and healing; its Ray Force is Green; and its Master Teacher is Sananda.

Shamballa: Venusian volunteers, who arrived 900 years before their leader Sanat Kumara, built the earth's first Golden City. Known as the City of White, located in the present-day Gobi Desert, its purpose was to hold conscious light for the earth and to sustain her evolutionary place in the solar system.

Southern Door: The South side of a Golden City gateway, also known as the Red Door

Spiritual Migration: The intentional use of the Golden City Vortices to transmute personal Karmas and initiate the Ascension Process through physically accessing Golden City energies is known as Spiritual Migration. This spiritual process involves the metaphysical knowledge of the four doorways—the four directions—of a Golden City.

Star: The apex, or center of each Golden City.

Star Seed Consciousness: The Star Seed is a family or soul group whose members have evolved to Fifth-Dimensional awareness. Star Seeds can also contain members who have not yet evolved to this level and are still incarnating on earth. Ascended Master teachings also refer to a Star Seed as an indication of a soul group or Ray Family of origin of which the individual possesses a natural aptitude of its qualities and characteristics.

Strategic Points: Strategic Points exist throughout the Golden Cities and are prophesied to physically manifest the energies necessary to move earth and humanity into the New Times. Adjutant Points are perhaps the most powerful Strategic Points one may access for interaction with Golden City energies.

Telepathy: According to the Master Teachings, telepathy is the result of human consciousness rising in vibration and is considered one of the Super-senses. The incidence of telepathy, or the ability to non-verbally communicate from one mind to another, develops Oneness—also known as Unity Consciousness.

GLOSSARY

Time Compaction: An anomaly produced as we enter into the prophesied Time of Change. Our perception of time compresses; time seems to speed by. The unfolding of events accelerates, and situations are jammed into a short period of time. This experience of time will become more prevalent as we get closer to the period of cataclysmic Earth Changes.

Time of Change: The period of time currently underway. Tremendous changes in our society, cultures, and politics in tandem with individual and collective spiritual awakenings and transformations will abound. These events occur simultaneously with the possibilities of massive global warming, climactic changes, and seismic and volcanic activity—Earth Changes. The Time of Change guides the earth to a New Time, the Golden Age.

Time of Tribulation: Humanity is currently experiencing the Time of Tribulation, as prophesied by Jesus Christ, in Matthew 24:21. The prophesied tribulation of the Bible is reference to signs that mark the return of Christ—as the Christ Consciousness—and the end of the current age. The Ascended Masters refer to this prophesied Time of Tribulation as the Time of Testing.

Transmutation: Alchemy and the transformation of a lower energy into a higher energy, nature, or form

Transportation Vortex: Prophesied to develop as we enter the New Times, a model of this energy anomaly will exist in the Golden City of Shalahah hear Coeur d'Alene, Idaho (USA). This inter-dimensional portal functions through the developed projection of the mind. As our understanding of Ray Forces evolves, our bodies take on a finer quality in light and substance and we are able to bi-locate through these energy Vortices. In the New Times this becomes an accepted form of travel.

Unana: Unity Consciousness

Vertical Power Current: The Ascended Masters often refer to the Vertical Power Current as the Golden Thread Axis or the Vibral-Core. A portion of this major energy current links the soul to the higher mind and is known as the Hindu Antahkarana. According to the I AM America teachings, the Vertical Power Current connects to our solar sun and its resident deities Helios and Vesta. Its energies travel to the I AM Presence and stream from the Presence through the Crown Chakra, and flow through the physical spine of the individual (Kundalini), and the current grounds into the center of earth's core—itself considered a latent, fiery sun. In Hinduism, the portion of the Antahkarana that enters the physical planes and the earth's core is known as the Sutratma, or Silver Cord. [See Golden Thread Axis]

Vibration: In common English, vibration comes from the word vibrate, which means to move, swing, or oscillate. In Ascended Master teaching, vibration is associated with light's movement in both physical and spiritual presence.

GLOSSARY

Violet Flame: The Violet Flame is the practice of balancing Karmas of the past through transmutation, forgiveness, and mercy. The result is an opening of the Spiritual Heart and the development of bhakti—unconditional love and compassion. It came into existence when the Lords of Venus first transmitted the Violet Flame, also known as the Violet Fire, at the end of Lemuria to clear the earth's etheric and psychic realms, and the lower physical atmosphere of negative forces and energies. This paved the way for the Atlanteans, who used it during religious ceremonies and as a visible marker of temples. The Violet Flame also induces Alchemy. Violet light emits the shortest wavelength and the highest frequency in the spectrum, so it induces a point of transition to the next octave of light.

Violet Flame Angels: Legions of Violet Flame Angels are claimed to carry the energies of the transmuting Violet Flame whenever they are called upon. The Angels of the Violet Flame protect the flame in its purity and dispense its transforming vibration.

Violet Ray: The Seventh Ray is primarily associated with Freedom and Ordered Service alongside Transmutation, Alchemy, Mercy, Compassion, and Forgiveness. It is served by the Archangel Zadkiel, the Elohim Arcturus, the Ascended Master Saint Germain and Goddess Portia.

Wahanee: The third United States Golden City located primarily in the states of South Carolina and Georgia. Its qualities are justice, liberty, and freedom; its Ray Force is violet; and its Master Teacher is Saint Germain.

Western Door: The West side of a Golden City gateway, also known as the Yellow Door

White Ray: The Ray of the Divine Feminine is primarily associated with the planet Venus. It is affiliated with beauty, balance, purity, and cooperation. In the I AM America teachings the White Ray is served by the Archangel Gabriel and Archeia Hope; the Elohim Astrea and Claire; and the Ascended Masters Serapis Bey, Paul the Devoted, Reya, the Lady Masters Venus and Se Ray, and the Group of Twelve.

Write and Burn Technique: An esoteric technique venerated by Ascended Master students and chelas to transmute any unwanted situation or circumstance, primarily dysfunctional life patterns. This technique involves hand-writing and then burning a letter—a petition—to the I AM Presence for Healing and Divine Intervention.

Yellow Ray: The Ray of the Divine Wisdom is primarily associated with the planet Jupiter and is also known as the Divine Guru. It is affiliated with expansion, optimism, joy, and spiritual enlightenment. In the I AM America teachings the Yellow Ray is served by the Archangel Jophiel and Archeia Christine; the Elohim of Illumination Cassiopeia and Lumina; and the Ascended Masters Lady Nada, Peter the Everlasting, Confucius, Lanto, Laura, Minerva, and Mighty Victory.

Yuga: Large recurring periods of time employed in the Hindu timekeeping system

APPENDIX A

Topics and Terms for Light a Candle

The Great Silence
Energies of Light and Peace
Transmuting the Energy Behind War
The Power of Prayer

Prophecies of Change
1. Today, many of our world leaders are in conflict and turmoil, due in part to the time we are experiencing—Kali Yuga. The world's political imbalance and the continued political misuse of earth's spiritual energy may escalate humanity toward another world war.
2. Our challenge at this time is to continue ever-vigilant prayer and meditation for our world leaders, while utilizing the higher energies of the Rays for worldwide harmony and peace.
3. We are experiencing a tipping point in our world political scene: we can either create world wars or world peace. The outcome is contingent upon our ability to drive out the lower energies of competition, greed, avarice, and fear. The individual ability to integrate the subtle energies of the ever-evolving Ray forces leads one to the *Path of Light*.
4. The combined effect of the collective will of mankind and the rhythm of cycles as the *forces of nature*—positions the world on the precipice of war and peace, bounty and famine, poverty and prosperity.

The Great Silence
Periods of tranquil power are referred to as the *Great Silence*. This Ascended Master spiritual principle encourages contemplative periods of quiet and stillness, which create intense spiritual energies in certain circumstances and situations.

Use of Ray Forces
The foundation of Ascended Master education is rooted in the spiritual teachings of the Seven Rays of Light and Sound. The Rays expand esoteric power; the utilization of their energies guides students to the fascinating world of Co-creation. A restorative and sacred journey, where the soul encounters the inherent blueprint of perfection, begins with this venerated science. Knowledge and application of the Seven Rays can emancipate an individual from third-dimensional restraints and transform consciousness into the expanded

APPENDIX A

experiences of the super senses: telepathy, clairvoyance, clairaudience, spontaneous healing, and Unity Consciousness.

A Ray is a perceptible energy, though its presence is often subtle. Only individuals whose attention is tuned to the nuances of the Fourth and Fifth Dimensions may readily detect the esoteric existence of a Ray. Through personal experience, conscious understanding, and various states of awareness and manifestation students refine their ability to recognize the presence of Ray Forces. According to Ascended Master teachings, Ray Forces are present in every aspect of human endeavor; these energies influence the physical, psychological, emotional, and psychic essence of mankind. Rays are said to dispense Karma and direct spiritual evolution—individually and collectively.

The Definition of a Ray

A Ray, simply stated, divides its efforts into two measurable and discernable powers: light and sound. Alice Bailey, author of many spiritual and esoteric works, wrote in *A Treatise on the Seven Rays*, "A Ray is but a name for a particular force or type of energy, with the emphasis upon the quality which that force exhibits, and not upon the form aspect which it creates. This is a true definition of a Ray."[1] Bailey's work underscores the abstract elements of a Ray but omits its tangible importance. The presence of a Ray also creates many physical attributes, which are significant in Ascended Master teachings.

Light and sound are the building blocks of our universe; therefore, the Rays permeate everything in our world of thought, feeling, and action. A developed psychic may perceive the twin matrix powers of light and sound as specific colors and sound frequencies in the energy fields of an individual—the aura. Nature mimics a similar pattern: a plant blooms a variety of colorful flowers, a common mineral becomes a precious gem, a songbird's melody is distinct and characteristic to its species. Each color and sound contains an undeniable unique vibration.

Light and sound evoke attributes and properties that carry specific cultural meaning as well. In the Western world, black is often associated with darkness and evil; it is the hue of mourning and death. Yet in some Native American traditions, black represents the Great Mystery and is linked to the cardinal direction north on the medicine wheel. Though white is traditional attire for a Western wedding, white is often worn at funerals in Eastern cultures. Sound is no exception to cultural identity. Western music reflects the spectral experience of human emotion; Eastern music mimics the sounds of nature and its tranquil effect on human consciousness.

A person's culture will influence his or her experience of the Rays, creating a diverse spiritual interpretation. This cultural filter can cause misunderstandings, discrepancies, and confusion. That's why the esoteric translation of the Rays is often lost to the novice.

Ray Systems

Most teachings of the Ascended Masters offer various analyses of the Rays, their assigned qualities, and the accompanying Master Teachers and Archangels whose work resonates with various Rays. A variety of books also exist that explain Ascended Master Ray Systems. I recommend any book written by Alice Bailey. However, my favorite source book on the Rays is *Law of Life, Volume Two* by A.D.K. Luk. This series—known by many as the *Yellow*

APPENDIX A

Books—was written by Luk, the former secretary to Guy Ballard, founder of the I AM Activity. This volume features a pullout Rayschematic on page 382, detailing various attributes and features.

Though some Ray Systems include up to forty singular Rays, it is best to stick with and memorize the basic seven Rays. Also, discard confusing numbering systems. Instead, focus on the color of the Ray to grasp its core meaning.

Below is a Ray System based on Ascended Master teachings and Vedic or Hindu astrology—*Jyotish*. In Sanskrit, Jyotish coincidentally means *science of light*. I have incorporated the Vedic system with the Ascended Master teachings for several reasons. First, it is perhaps the oldest astrology system on earth (Jyotish traces back to 4,000 BC), and it articulates information on the Rays. Second, Jyotish and the Seven Ray System are uniquely compatible. It is likely the Vedic system is the same arrangement once studied by many of our contemporary Master Teachers.

Please note, the following two levels of attributes are given for each Ray: common qualities and cosmic qualities. The understanding of astrological planets is vital to grasping how Ray forces work in our solar system.

- **Blue Ray**

Common Attributes: steady, calm, persevering, transforming, harmonizing, diligent, determined, austere, protective, humble, truthful, self-negating, stern
Cosmic Attribute: Divine Will or Choice
Planet: Saturn

- **Yellow Ray**

Common Attributes: studious, learned, expansive, optimistic, joyful, fun-loving, generous, proper, formal
Cosmic Attribute: Spiritual Enlightenment
Planet: Jupiter

- **Pink Ray**

Common Attributes: loving, nurturing, hopeful, heartfelt, compassionate, considerate, communicative, intuitive, friendly, humane, tolerant, adoring
Cosmic Attribute: Divine Mother
Planet: Moon

- **White Ray**

Common Attributes: beautiful, pure, elegant, refined, sensitive, charming, graceful, creative, artistic, cooperative, uplifting, strong, piercing, blissful
Cosmic Attribute: Divine Feminine
Planet: Venus

- **Green Ray**

Common Attributes: educated, thoughtful, communicative, organized, intellectual, objective, scientific, discriminating, practical, discerning, adaptable, rational, healing, awakened
Cosmic Attribute: Active Intelligence
Planet: Mercury

APPENDIX A

The Seven Rays

BLUE	YELLOW	PINK	WHITE
Saturn	Jupiter	Moon	Venus
Divine Will Divine Power	Divine Teacher Divine Wisdom Guru	Divine Mother Divine Heart Divine Creatrix	Divine Feminine Divine Beauty Divine Love
Steady; calm; persevering; transforming; harmonizing; diligent; disciplined; determined; austere; protective; humble; truthful; self-negating; stern.	Studious; learned; expansive; optimistic; joyful; fun-loving; generous; proper; formal.	Loving; nurturing; hopeful; heartfelt; compassionate; considerate; communicative; intuitive; friendly; humane; tolerant; adoring.	Beautiful; pure; elegant; refined; sensitive; charming; graceful; creative; artistic; cooperative; uplifting; strong; piercing; blissful.
Blue Sapphire *Blue Topaz* *Lapis Lazuli*	*Yellow Sapphire* *Yellow Topaz* *Citrine*	*Pearl* *Moonstone* *Pink Tourmaline*	*Diamond* *White Sapphire* *Clear Quartz Crystal*
Myrrh, Frankincense, Cedar, Juniper	*Sandalwood, Lotus*	*Jasmine, Gardenia*	*Rose, Nag Champa*

FIGURE 1-A
Rays Blue through White
The first four Rays and their Planetary Force, Archetype, qualities, gemstone, and scent.

Light of Awakening

APPENDIX A

The Seven Rays

GREEN	RUBY GOLD	VIOLET	AQUAMARINE GOLD
Mercury	Mars Sun	Saturn Uranus	Neptune Great Central Sun
Divine Child Divine Intelligence Divine Messenger	*Mars:* Divine Warrior Divine Masculine *Sun:* Divine Father Divine Creator	*Saturn:* Divine Grace *Uranus:* Divine Alchemy	*Neptune:* Divine Heaven *Great Central Sun:* Divine Man
Educated; thoughtful; communicative; organized; intellectual; objective; scientific; discriminating; practical; discerning; adaptable; rational; healing; awakened.	(Ruby): Energetic; passionate; devoted; determination; dutiful; dependable; direct; insightful; inventive; forceful. (Gold): Warm; honest; confident; positive; independent; courageous; leadership; responsible; ministration; authority; justice.	Forgiving; transmuting; alchemizing; electric; intervening; diplomatic; magical; merciful; graceful; original; freedom; ordered service.	Unifying; perceptive; intuitive; sensitive; cooperative; creative; integrative; spiritual; idealistic; self-realized.
Emerald *Green Tourmaline* *Peridot* *Jade*	***Mars*** *(Ruby or Red Ray):* *Red Coral, Carnelian* ***Sun*** *(Gold Ray):* *Ruby, Red Garnet*	*Amethyst* *Purple Sugilite*	*Aquamarine* *Tourquoise*
Mint, Wintergreen	*Ruby Ray: Musk, Camphor* *Gold Ray: Ginger, Cinnamon*	*Lavendar, Lilac*	*Hydrangea, Bayberry, Sage*

FIGURE 2-A
Rays Green through Aquamarine-Gold
The second four Rays and their Planetary Force,
Archetype, qualities, gemstone, and scent.

APPENDIX A

- **Ruby (Red) and Gold Ray**

Common Attributes (Ruby): energetic, passionate, devoted, determination, dutiful, dependable, direct, insightful, inventive, technical, skilled, forceful
Cosmic Attribute (Ruby): Divine Masculine
Planet (Ruby): Mars
Common Attributes (Gold): warm, perceptive, honest, confident, positive, independent, courageous, enduring, vital, leadership, responsible, ministration, authority, justice
Cosmic Attribute (Gold): Divine Father
Planet (Gold): Sun

- **Violet Ray**

Common Attributes: forgiving, transmuting, alchemizing, electric, intervening, diplomatic, magical, merciful, graceful, freedom, ordered service
Cosmic Attribute: Divine Grace
Planet: Currently undetermined, but some systems place Uranus, the higher vibration of Saturn, or both under this Ray force.

Co-creation through the Rays: Mantras, Decrees, Gemstone, and Aromatherapy

As one begins to access the pure, restorative energy of each Ray force, changes will occur in all aspects of an individual's life. When a person calls upon the Rays, the soul becomes receptive to the process of Co-creation, thus spiritual growth and evolution are the outcomes. These changes are often subtle and require patience, diligence, and perseverance, but the results can also be immediate. The perfected support inherent in the power of a Ray encourages healing in many aspects of a person's life, including relationships, career, finances, and health. Spiritual healing through the Rays also improves and sharpens the super senses. Many people report enhanced psychic and telepathic links with Master Teachers after chanting mantras, decrees, or both. The healing energy of the Rays aren't just limited to individuals; groups and societies can benefit as well. Ray-oriented mantras and decrees when performed by a group of people often generate an exponential super-sensory experience and increase the collective consciousness, thereby creating a Group Mind. Fifth-dimensional energies are bridged to the physical plane by the collective consciousness of the Group Mind. The Ascended Masters refer to this anomaly as *Oneship* or *Unana*.

Sound is indeed the twin sibling of light. This esoteric aspect of the Rays cannot be overlooked or understated as El Morya, Master Teacher of the Blue Ray articulates: "Now understand, Dear Ones … even sound itself works as a Ray. It is through this circular vibration, which we have explained as the spiral…. Light and Sound join to one another."[2] Mantras invoke the energy of a Ray with scientific precision. Dr. David Frawley, an authority on Vedic and Hindu spiritual tradition, writes, "Mantras are seed sounds (the foremost of which is Om) that contain the laws and the archetypes behind all the workings of energy in the universe. Applying this mantric knowledge on different levels, any domain of existence can be comprehended in its inner truth. Through the mantra, the Rishis were able to be adept in all fields of knowledge, including Yoga, Philosophy, Astrology, Geomancy, Medicine, Poetry, Art and Music. This

APPENDIX A

root knowledge of the mantra is thus an instrument on which all knowledge can be revealed by a shifting of scales."[3]

Try this experiment with the Bija-seed mantra, *Om*. Bija, by the way, means one—a one-syllable mantra. While slowly chanting Om, place your forefinger and thumb on your cheekbones. You will feel a vibration through your cheeks and a resonation in your skull, which will inevitably reach your spine. This same vibration affects your entire Chakra System. Some scholars claim that the sound vibration of a Bija-seed mantra simultaneously creates light frequencies in the human aura. I recommended a Ruby Ray Bija-seed mantra for a client, and she ardently chanted this mantra prior to a Kirlian photograph. [Editor's Note: Kirlian photography is alleged to capture the light energy surrounding a subject or object.] The photograph depicted her aura with shades and tones of red and ruby light. The Sanskrit Bija-seed mantras for each of the Rays are listed below.

> **Blue Ray:** Om Sham or Om Shanti (Saturn)
> **Yellow Ray:** Om Güm (Jupiter)
> **Pink Ray:** Om Som (Moon)
> **White Ray:** Om Shüm (Venus)
> **Green Ray:** Om Büm (Mercury)
> **Ruby Ray:** Om Ung (Mars)
> **Gold Ray:** Om Süm (Sun)
> **Violet Ray:** Om Hue (Higher aspect of Saturn; Uranus)

Decrees, similar to mantras, are yet another form of verbal prayer; however, decrees differ because of the added element of visualization, the spoken word, and the spiritual stillness of meditation. Some claim that decrees are one of the most powerful forms of prayer because they unite four chakras: prayer (Heart Chakra); spoken word (throat chakra); visualization (third eye chakra); meditation (crown chakra).[4] Violet Flame decrees are used worldwide by thousands of Ascended Master students. They can be spoken individually or used in groups to generate the benefic qualities of the Violet Ray: mercy, compassion, and forgiveness. One of my favorites is the simple Violet Fire decree by Mark Prophet, "I AM a being of Violet Fire! I AM the purity God desires!"

Decrees or mantras are often said rhythmically, in groups of seven, or in rounds of 108—the traditional Mala. [Editor's Note: A Mala is a prayer or rosary bead typically used in Hinduism and Buddhism, and a full Mala contains 108 beads with one final large bead often referred to as the *guru* bead.] Decrees and mantras are also repeated silently in the mind, similar to prayer, in preparation for meditation. El Morya lends further insight: "... it is when this (decree) is consciously applied by the chela, through the work of the Violet Flame, or other mantra work they may engage ... light is then bonded to sound. Ultimately, this is the intertwining of consciousness with action." Simply stated, sound activates light, and light and sound together command the Ray into a force of conscious activity.

APPENDIX A

Gemstones are perhaps one of the most simple and powerful ways to correct Ray deficiencies or enhance and intensify the attributes of a Ray. Our aura, inner spiritual light, and overall vibration reflect the numerous lifetimes, experiences, and evolutionary journeys of our soul with the Seven Rays. Ray deficiencies appear as the under-developed aspects of the Rays and signify areas in our life that may need more individual effort, attention, and personal refinement. Chronic disease, relationship problems, financial setbacks, and personal suffering are often the result of Ray deficiencies. The qualified concentration of the Ray through specific, remedial gemstones can treat the undersupplied Ray by infusing the aura with its light. This supportive healing light can alter the trajectory of life's events and transform spiritual consciousness; corrective gemstones can ameliorate certain Karmic difficulties. Wear the gemstone so its facets touch the skin (this is classic in Jyotish), or hold a cluster of crystals to intensify a Ray force during meditation. Gem elixir—a liquid infused with the energies and essence of certain gemstones according to Vedic traditions—is also effective. Remember, never use a gemstone that is chemically dyed, heat-treated, or irradiated; unfortunately, today, many are. Vedic-quality gemstones are best for spiritual purposes. The list below identifies certain Ray forces contained in precious and semi-precious gemstones.

> **Blue Ray:** blue sapphire and blue topaz; lapis lazuli and turquoise
> **Yellow Ray:** yellow sapphire, yellow topaz, and citrine
> **Pink Ray:** Pearl and moonstone. Pink tourmaline can give good results. The best metal to enhance energies of the moon—the Divine Mother—is silver.
> **White Ray:** Diamond and white sapphire. Very clear, high-quality quartz crystal works well. I have seen good results from large, high-quality, clear pieces of cubic zirconia.
> **Green Ray:** Emerald and green tourmaline; green peridot and green jade work well too.
> **Ruby and Gold Ray:** Ruby Ray: red coral. Gold Ray: Red ruby and red garnet are good gemstones for the energies of the sun—the Divine Father. Red and raspberry rhodolite (a type of garnet) also work well. Good metals are yellow and white gold.
> **Violet Ray:** Amethyst is best; however, I have seen good results with purple sugilite.

The Scent of a Ray

Certain scents contain the essence of a Ray. Often, before the appearance of an ascended being or angel, a fragrance will imbue the area about to be occupied. Since these spiritual beings have focused their energies upon a specific Ray, their scent carries the same vibration of the Ray. This aroma often contains a healing power, or it intentionally heightens the energies of the space for the materialization of a Master Teacher and their ensuing teachings. Manifestations of Mother Mary are often accompanied by the faint perfume of rose, while Kuan Yin's scent is Neroli—or-

APPENDIX A

ange blossom. Lavender or lilac most often heralds the presence of Saint Germain.

The practice of burning certain incenses and smudging a room with sage for purification has become increasingly popular. These religious and shamanic traditions enhance and reinforce certain Rays. The scents listed below are commonly associated with the following Rays:

Blue Ray: myrrh, frankincense, cedar, and juniper
Yellow Ray: sandalwood and lotus
Pink Ray: jasmine and gardenia
White Ray: rose and nag champa
Green Ray: Mint and wintergreen. Sage is good for the Green Ray ; it also vibrates to the Gold (Sun) Ray.
Ruby Ray: musk and camphor
Gold Ray: ginger and cinnamon
Violet Ray: lavender and lilac

The Great Central Sun and Movement of the Rays

In Ascended Master teachings, the energies of the Rays originate from the Great Central Sun. This mythic sun is said to exist a great distance from our own solar system; it is perceived as a master intelligence. From its benevolent presence, the Rays of Light and Sound are sent to earth, and humanity is educated and perfected through their influence. This same principle is present in Vedic astrology; however, this great sun is known as the *Galactic Center*. The Galactic Center is renowned as *Brahma*, which means *creative force or the navel of Vishnu*. Dr. Frawley writes, "From the Galactic Sun emanates the light which determines life and intelligence on Earth and which direct the play of the Seven Rays of creation and the distribution of Karma."[5]

In the Vedic tradition, the planet Jupiter transmits the energies of the Galactic Center to our solar system. Mars initiates the Ray-force energy while the sun stabilizes the Rays. This planetary trinity comprising the sun, Jupiter, and Mars is commonly known as the *Fire Triplicity*.

Ray forces move by two scientific principles: emanation and radiation. Emanation means to flow out, as from a source or origin; radiation is defined as the emission and diffusion of Rays of heat, light, electricity, or sounds. According to Ascended Master teachings, Rays enter our solar system from the emanations of our sun—hence, the use of Om before each Bija-seed mantra. From our sun, a Ray completes its celestial journey at the core of the earth; Ray forces then emanate from the center of the earth to its surface. When we personally apply the energies of the Rays through gemstones, mantras, and scents, we are utilizing the second principle of Ray movement: radiation.

APPENDIX A

Ascended Masters, Archangels, and Ray Forces

Ascended beings and archetypes of evolution apply the Rays to receive and achieve higher states of perfection and knowledge. Through this profound diligence and submission to the grand interplay of the Rays, they have overcome Karmic reaction and retribution; they have opened the doors to liberation, higher states of consciousness, and enlightenment. Each Ascended Master individualizes his or her conscious energy upon a Ray force, especially while serving students and chelas as Master Teacher. The qualities and attributes of a Master's teaching clearly reflect the distinct energy of a Ray. You will note that before Saint Germain presents a lesson, he consistently qualifies each session through a Ray force by announcing, "I AM Saint Germain, and I stream forth on the Mighty Violet Ray of Mercy, Compassion, and Forgiveness."

Similarly, Archangels work on a specific Ray. Master Teachers and angels occasionally employ the energies of all of the Seven Rays to achieve a specific goal or mission. Certain Master Teachers, however, are best known for their work with specific Rays, which are listed below.

> **Blue Ray:** Archangel Michael and Master Teacher El Morya
> **Yellow Ray:** Archangel Jophiel, Master Teachers Confucius and Lanto, and Peter the Everlasting
> **Pink Ray:** Archangel Chamuel, Beloved Mother Mary, and Paul the Venetian [Editor's Notes: Mother Mary is often identified with the Green Ray as well.]
> **Green Ray:** Archangel Raphael and Master Teachers Hilarion and Soltec
> **White Ray:** Archangel Gabriel and Master Teachers Serapis Bey and Paul the Devoted. [Editor's Note: Paul the Devoted also serves the Pink Ray.]
> **Ruby and Gold Ray:** Archangel Uriel, Lord Sananda, and Master Teacher Kuthumi [Editor's Note: Lord Sananda is often identified with the Green Ray as well.]
> **Violet Ray:** Archangel Zadkiel, Master Teacher Saint Germain, and Kuan Yin [Editor's Note: Kuan Yin is often identified with the Pink Ray as well.]

History of the Rays in World Religions

H. P. Blavatsky, the founder of theosophy, introduced the Seven Rays in her first book *The Secret Doctrine* as the "primeval Seven Rays ... found and recognized in every religion," as a type of "light substance conveying Divine Qualities." She later wrote that the symbolism of the Seven Rays was adopted by Christianity as the "Seven Angels of the Presence."[6] The concept of the Seven Rays dates back to ancient religions and occult philosophies, as early as the sixth century BCE of Western culture, Egypt, and India. Esoteric historians note the presence of the Rays as both the Seven Rays of the ancient Chaldaean Mithra and the Seven Days of Genesis. In 1894 Harvard scholar S.F. Dunlap wrote, "The other planets which circling around the Sun lead the dance as round the King of heaven receive from him with the light also their powers; while as the light comes to them from the Sun, so from him they receive their powers that he pours out into the Seven Spheres of the Seven

APPENDIX A

Planets, of which the Sun is the centre." Dunlap maintained the Seven Rays were the religious base for the ancient Chaldeans, Jews, Persians, Syrian, Phoenicians, and Egyptians. Nineteenth-century Egyptologist Gerald Massey theorized the unity of the Seven Rays as "the seven souls of the Pharaoh; the seven arms of the Hindu God Agni; the seven-rayed Sun-God of the Gnostic-stones; and, the seven stars in the hand of the Christ in Revelation."[7]

Symbolic art of early Christianity depicts the emanation of the Seven Rays in union with the image of Mother Mary. The dove, symbolizing the Holy Spirit, is frequently accompanied by the golden ethereal Seven Rays of heaven. Of all the Seven Rays, perhaps the seventh—the Violet Ray—is distinct. Art historian and philosopher, Ananda Coomaraswamy, noted the complex iconology of the Seventh Ray that appears in Indian, Islamic, Chinese, Hellenic, and Christian symbolism. "(It) corresponds to the distinction of transcendent from immanent and infinite from finite ... the Seventh Ray alone passes through the Sun to the suprasolar Brahma worlds, where no Sun shines ... all that is under the Sun being in the power of death, and all beyond immortal."[8]

Point of Perception

Point of Perception is a Co-creation teaching of the Ascended Masters. This process pivots on the fulcrum of choice. A Master of Choice carefully selects specific actions, which opens a world of possibility by cultivating perceptions, attitudes, beliefs, thoughts, and feelings. This allows the development of outcome by creating various scenarios and opening the dimensional doors to multiple realities and simultaneous experiences that dissolve linear timeframes into the *Ever-present Now*.

Spiritual Teachings

In *Light a Candle* the Ascended Masters convey spiritual instruction regarding the dangerous polarizing effects of war on the human consciousness; they encourage students to learn the art of impartiality. This is developed by offering prayerful respect for *both* sides involved in conflict and keeping a vigilant awareness of individual thoughts, feelings, and actions that may become collectively engaged in blind patriotism and religious fanaticism, which create the incentive for war. The absurdity of fervent nationalism is presented in Mark Twain's well-known short story, *The War Prayer*. Twain feared the work would be seen as sacrilegious and asked that it be published after his death. The aged messenger of its verses averred, "O Lord our God, help us to tear their soldiers to bloody shreds with our shells; help us to cover their smiling fields with the pale forms of their patriot dead; help us to drown the thunder of the guns with shrieks of their wounded, writhing in pain; help us to lay waste their humble homes with hurricanes of fire; help us to wring the heart of their unoffending widows with unavailing grief; help us to turn them out roofless with their little children to wander unfriended the wastes of their desolated land in rags and hunger and thirst...."[9] *The War Prayer* was published six years after Twain's death.

APPENDIX A

Greater Mind

The Greater Mind, an outgrowth of the Ascension Process, differs from the deductive and inductive reasoning of the rational mind, and the sporadic yet instant insights gleaned from the intuitive mind. The Greater Mind is activated by self-revealed wisdom versus acquired knowledge. According to spiritual philosopher, Sri Aurobindo, this mind is said to be an aspect of the developing will: "whole being with a new and superior consciousness," which is the foundation of personal growth and transformation.[10] [Editor's Note: See Points of Perception, page 254, *The Eight-Sided Cell of Perfection Energy Map.*]

White Candle Meditation and Prayer for Peace

According to the Master Teachers, the lighting and burning of white candles invokes the assistance of the Great White Brotherhood. This practice also helps sustain their mission for world peace. The white candle is a symbol of unity, peace, and the ONE spiritual light shared by all nations of the world. Master Teachers recommend directing prayer, meditation, and the lighting of the candle toward world leaders in particular. They often state, "May Divine Grace empower the little wills of man!" Lighting of white candles, along with meditation and prayer for peace, is reportedly more intense when it is physically done in Golden City Stars (apexes) and in the Heart of the Dove—also known as the Center of Fire, located northwest of Saint Louis, Missouri. The list below delineates the towns and cities located in the Stars of the five Golden Cities of the United States. [Editor's Note: for more information see the I AM America Map and New World Atlas, Volume One.]

1. Golden City of Gobean
    Pinetop, Ariz.
    Lakeside, Ariz.
    Springerville, Ariz.
    Eagar, Ariz.

2. Golden City of Malton
    Mattoon, Ill.
    Charleston, Ill.
    Shelbyville, Ill.
    Sullivan, Ill.
    Humboldt, Ill.

Light of Awakening

APPENDIX A

3. Golden City of Wahanee
    Augusta, Ga.
    Grovetown, Ga.
    Appling, Ga.
    Harlem, Ga.
    Gracewood, Ga.
    Thompson, Ga.
    Modeo, Ga.
    North Augusta, S.C.
    Trenton, S.C.
    Eureka, S.C.
    Parksville, S.C.
    Kitchings Mill, S.C.
    Williston, S.C.

4. Golden City of Shalahah
    Lolo Pass, Mont.
    Lolo, Mont.
    Missoula, Mont.
    Stevensville, Mont.

5. Golden City of Klehma
    Cope, Colo.

When it comes to studying the Ascended Masters, a Ray chart is an invaluable and fundamental learning tool. It initiates the mind to archetypal thinking—the ability to perceive and recognize the ancient Gods and myths as part of our everyday experiences. This clarity helps the student connect and synthesize the theosophic concepts, characters, and characteristics so vital to understanding the Ascended Masters. But, thanks to cultural ambiguities and pedagogic differences, Ray charts do have imperfections.

For one, until recently little was known about the Mithraic mysteries. According to Franz Cumont, an authority on the subject, the genesis of Mithraism can be traced to a time when India and Persia shared a common language, as far back as 2,000 BCE. Time, cultural movement, and the shifting of political boundaries helped spread the practice of Mithraism throughout the Roman Empire later on. Its central character—a deity of light—shows up in Avestan and Vedic texts as Mithra and Mitra, respectively. Mitra represents the Divine Friend, a savior, and Lord of Mercy and Compassion. The story of Mitra, a benevolent Vedic sun god, is one of creation. The deity is born from a sacred rock and sacrifices a bull (a likely symbol from the Age of Taurus), from which flows life-sustaining flora and fauna. Mitra also creates the archetypal energies of the Christ; while Maitreya, the prophesied future Buddha, derives his name from this ancient immortal. Mitra, the god of friendship and partnership, wears the sun's crown of

APPENDIX A

Divine Rays, comprising compassion, devotion, love, and cooperation. Many Mithraic doctrines were rooted in celestial and astrological references, which serve as a link to the ambiguous light of the Seven Rays. These teachings were reportedly well known in culturally cloistered India and the Middle East but virtually unheard of in the Western world.

Second, and probably even more importantly, the didactic underpinnings of Ray charts are riddled with confusing discrepancies, which are due, in part, to the wide-ranging interpretations of innumerable messengers, channels, and mediums who follow various spiritual leaders and divergent philosophies.

The source of these disparities comes from the venerated esoteric giants of theosophical thought themselves—H.P. Blavatsky, Annie Besant, Alice Bailey, Dion Fortune, and Nicolas and Helena Roerich. Naturally, their backgrounds and cultural experiences colored their perceptions and subsequent presentation of the subject matter. The Roeriches and Blavatsky were born in nineteenth-century imperial Russia amid social upheaval and political reformation, while Besant, Bailey and Fortune grew up in disparate regions of the United Kingdom during different times. Their seminal work has morphed into a vast and diverse body of spiritual education, which includes the I AM Activity (Guy and Edna Ballard); the Bridge to Freedom (Geraldine Innocente); White Eagle Lodge (Ivan and Grace Cooke); and the Summit Lighthouse (Mark and Elizabeth Prophet). The Seven Rays are, of course, a component of these teachings, but the resulting information is inconsistent for the reasons mentioned above.

The key to these irregularities lies in ideological differences. Consider the various Christian denominations—Catholicism, Baptism, Lutheranism, Methodism, and so on. The common denominator is Christianity: a monotheistic religion rooted in the teachings and life of Jesus Christ. The differences, however, are doctrinal. For instance, Catholics have seven sacraments; Protestants recognize only two. Often the greatest truths hold dichotomy and paradox.

The Ray Chart's Correlation to the Seven Traditional Planets

In 1996 I began to study the traditional astrology of India—Jyotish—the Science of Light. It is a complex, multifaceted, and comprehensive system of astrology. Not only does it incorporate the traditional zodiac of Western astrology, it embraces the twenty-seven goddesses, which serve as the foundation of Vedic and Chinese esoteric arts. The lunar mansions, or houses of the moon, encompass the feminine-based astrology long forgotten by the West. The twelve houses of astrology were likely derived from the twenty-seven signs of the goddesses, who in Vedic and Celtic lore are the wives of the moon. Chandra, the Vedic God of the moon, visits each Sister-wife every day of the month. This rotation ends in twenty-eight days, the length of the female menstrual cycle.

As my understanding and practice of Jyotish deepened, the obscure and vague teachings of the Seven Rays were clearly revealed as the seven traditional astrological planets: Jupiter, Saturn, Venus, Mercury, Mars, and the sun and the moon—the earth's luminaries. This information filled in blanks, answered long-asked questions, and of course, satisfied an occultist's greatest desire—the discovery of layer upon layer of

APPENDIX A

FIGURE 3-A
Mithra and King Antiochus

King Antiochus (left) and Mithra (right) note the Rays streaming from Mithra's crown chakra. The depiction of Mithra is a relief from a Temple built by Antiochus I of Commagne, 69-31 BCE. Commagne was an ancient kingdom of the Hellenistic Age, located in south-central Turkey.

[Franz Cumot, *The Mysteries of Mithra*, http://www.sacred-texts.com/cla/mom/mom7.htm, (2010)]

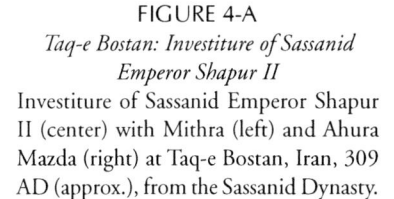

FIGURE 4-A
Taq-e Bostan: Investiture of Sassanid Emperor Shapur II

Investiture of Sassanid Emperor Shapur II (center) with Mithra (left) and Ahura Mazda (right) at Taq-e Bostan, Iran, 309 AD (approx.), from the Sassanid Dynasty.

[Photo by Phillipe Chavez, with permission Creative Commons, WikiMedia, 2010.]

FIGURE 5-A
Mithra, the Sun God

Mithra as Sol, the Sun God. (Roman) Mithra holds the globe of power and Seven Rays stream from his crown chakra. According to Franz Cumot this is a representation of "Graeco-Roman Paganism" amd "Solar Pantheism."

[Franz Cumot, *Mithraism and the Religions of the Empire*, http://www.sacred-texts.com/cla/mom/mom7.htm, (2010)]

APPENDIX A

correlated information regarding the Seven Rays. Vedic astrology tracks an individual's relationship with the Seven Rays through thoughts, feelings, and actions, which are distilled from the following Hindu philosophical principles:

1. Vedic aims of life—kama (desire), artha (wealth), dharma (purpose), and moksha (liberation)
2. Gunas or qualities one may experience—sattvic (spiritual), rajasic (agitated), and tamasic (dark)
3. Elements of physical life—earth, water, fire, air, ether

The Seven Rays become conspicuous in the body by our level of health or disease; our foods and diet reflect the type of energy we receive and emit. Herbs, colors, flowers, scents, gemstones, and sounds resonate with specific Ray forces. In fact, prayers, mantras, and ceremonies dedicated to the planets—disguised as the Rays—are the cornerstones of Hinduism.

Unfortunately, the ancient Vedic principles that constitute Jyotish are rarely included in the construction of Ray charts. When the original data were assembled—in the late nineteenth and early twentieth centuries—it just wasn't available. In particular, esoteric scholars did not have access to the astrological knowledge of India, which according to some authorities dates back more than 5,000 years, and in my opinion, is an integral element of esoteric teaching. Vedic astrology is a vast, complex, and arcane area of study. The ability of one human being to grasp and distill this information is simply impossible, especially without the modern conveniences of technology and air travel. To give you an idea of the expansiveness of Vedic astrology, Jyotish comprises a mere one-sixth of the knowledge contained in the Vedanga—the six disciplines developed by Indian culture to understand the Vedas. The Vedas form the Sanskrit basis of Hinduism and were written by Rishis, the spiritual Masters from a time of greater light on earth—likely Dvapara Yuga. Inaccessibility and inundation led to misinformation, especially in the theosophical interpretation of occult history. These mistakes were passed on to the lineages of Ascended Master teaching.

Archetypes of Evolution

Ideally the language of the Seven Rays is the language of the Gods. The Greeks and Romans recognized the polarity between their deities: the folly and the grandeur, the corruption and the honesty, the immorality and the morality—akin to the human and *HU-man* of the Ascended Masters. The Seven Rays live a mortal life within us, manifested in ignorance, fear, and ego. Simultaneously, they inspire immortality expressed as love, wisdom, and truth. This Ray chart incorporates Ascended Masters, Archangels, and Elohim. In Ascended Master teaching the Elohim are often depicted as the gods and goddesses of nature, typified by the Seven Rays and the deities that likely inspired their evolutionary journeys thousands of years ago.

APPENDIX A

The Mighty Elohim

Some esoteric historians perceive the Elohim—also referred to as *the Els*—as the ancient gods or Master Teachers of Lemuria and Atlantis. This area of the Ray chart seems logical but, again, filled with discrepancy, depending on the school of Ascended Master teaching you are studying. For my purposes, I have included the Elohim as described in the I AM America material—evolved nature gods. Some of the ancient deities actually make more sense to me than their contemporary counterparts, and I wanted to share these interesting tidbits.

1. The Titans are fierce elder gods overthrown by a race of younger deities. They represent the mature yet fierce experience of Saturn and the Blue Ray.
2. The White Ray through its affiliation with Divine Beauty represents literature and the arts, similar to the nine Muses of Greek mythology.
3. Kukulkan—the plumed serpent of the Mayan—is also known as Quetzalcoatl to the Aztecs. The astrology of ancient America was based on Venus.
4. According to some scholars, the compassionate centaur Chiron was the Master Teacher of young Apollo and Artemis. His renown as an astrologer and healer secures his placement on the Green Ray, which is associated with the ability to teach.
5. The Romans portrayed Jesus Christ as a sun deity; his ardent devotion—the spiritual warrior—places him on the Ruby and Gold Ray.
6. The Greek cup-bearer of the Gods Ganymede represents the human ascent to spiritual liberation and perfection, qualities of the Aquamarine and Gold Ray.

Defining the Difference

This Ray chart also has its own inconsistencies, and I would like to point out that the Blue Ray is traditionally associated with Saturn. However, in Vedic teaching Saturn is the son of the Sun; and *Surya*—the Sanskrit name for the sun—by ancestral lineage is related to the Blue Ray. While studying other Ray charts to corroborate this compilation, I noticed confusion and lack of clarity regarding the Pink and White Rays. Some esoteric scholars identify the Pink Ray as the Divine Feminine and the White Ray as the Divine Mother. Again, the baseline for this chart relies on the Vedic knowledge of the moon and Venus. The moon is the Divine Mother, the Divine Creatrix, and the heart of our emotions—the Pink Ray. Venus is the White Ray of the Divine Feminine, Divine Love, and the balance we achieve in our thoughts, feelings, and actions—beauty.

Please note that Ascended Masters can simultaneously serve on several Rays, and while archetypically identified with a particular Ray, he or she may temporarily give aid and service to humanity by serving on another Ray. Geraldine Innocente's work, *Bridge to Freedom*, often comments on this unusual but not uncommon occurrence. Sananda said he was "not limited by form of any kind" and would "take on any form or appearance for the task at hand."

APPENDIX A
The Seven Rays

BLUE	YELLOW	PINK	WHITE
EVOLUTIONARY ARCHETYPES			
Archangel Michael	Archangel Jophiel	Archangel Chamuel	Archangel Gabriel
Archeia Faith	Archeia Christine	Archeia Charity	Archeia Hope
El Morya	Lady Nada	Kuan Yin	Serapis Bey
Lady Miriam	Confucius	Mother Mary	Lady Master Se Ray
Lord Himalaya	Lanto	Goddess Meru	Paul the Devoted
Lady Master Desiree	Peter the Everlasting	Great Divine Mother	Lady Master Venus
Goddess of Light	Minerva	Paul the Ventian*	Reya
ELOHIM			
Elohim of Power	Elohim of Illumination	Elohim of Divine Love	Elohim of Purity
Hercules	Cassiopea	Orion	Claire
Amazonia	Lumina	Angelica	Astrea
DEITIES			
Shiva (Kala)	Brihaspati	Isis	Laksmi
Kali	Ganesh	Parvati	Venus
Yama	Saraswati	Chandra	Aphrodite
Durga	Lord Siddhartha-	Demeter	Hathor
Titans	Guatama Buddha	Ceres	Dionysus
Cronus		Luna	Kulkulcan
		Artemis	Tlahuizcalpantecuhtli
		Ix Chel (Mayan)	(Aztec)
		Sin (Sumerian)	
CHINESE ELEMENT / GUA			
Earth	Wood	Water	Metal
2,8	3, 4	1	6, 7
VEDIC ELEMENT			
Air	Ether	Water	Water
DAY OF WEEK			
Saturday	Thursday	Monday	Friday
MAHAPURUSHA YOGA			
Shasha Yoga	Hamsa Yoga	None	Malavya Yoga

*Serve on more than one Ray

FIGURE 6-A
The Deities of the Rays, Blue through White
Deities and Associated Qualities of the Rays

Light of Awakening

APPENDIX A

The Seven Rays

GREEN	RUBY GOLD	VIOLET	AQUAMARINE GOLD
EVOLUTIONARY ARCHETYPES			
Archangel Raphael Archeia Mother Mary* Hilarion Soltec Lady Viseria Lord Sananda Lady Master Meta	Archangel Uriel Archeia Aurora Kuthumi* Lord Meru Amaryllis Lady Nada* Sanat Kumara*	Archangel Zadkiel Archeia Holy Amethyst Saint Germain Kuan Yin* Portia Zarathustra Omri-Tas	Archangel Crystiel Archeia Clarity Casimir Poseidon Master Kona Djwal Khul Lady Master Leto Helios and Vesta
ELOHIM			
Elohim of Truth Vista (Cyclopea) Virginia	Elohim of Peace Tranquility Pacifica	Elohim of Freedom Arcturus Diana	Elohim of Unity Rainbow Iris
DEITIES			
Vishnu Hermes Thoth The Christ Child Krishna Pallas Athena Fortuna The Muses Chiron	*Sun:* Apollo Indra Agni Shiva Maha Deva *Mars:* Skanda Horus God Ares Kartikeyya Jesus Christ Archangel Michael *(Leader of the Heavenly Hosts)*	Rama Krittika Radha Osiris Hebe Zoraster	Brahma Narada Asclepius Wadjet Leto Ganymede
CHINESE ELEMENT / GUA			
Water 1	Fire 9	Earth-Metal 2, 6, 7, 8	Water-Wood 1, 3, 4 Fire 9
VEDIC ELEMENT			
Earth	Fire	N/A	N/A
DAY OF WEEK			
Wednesday	Sunday *(Sun)* Tuesday *(Mars)*	Saturday	Everpresent Now
MAHAPURUSHA YOGA			
Bhadra Yoga	Ruchaka Yoga *(Mars)* None *(Sun)*	Shasha Yoga	N/A

*Serve on more than one Ray

FIGURE 7-A
The Deities of the Rays, Green through Aquamarine-Gold
Deities and Associated Qualities of the Rays

APPENDIX A

The Elements: Chinese and Vedic

Chinese and Vedic astrology are both based on the planet Jupiter, however, Vedic astrology operates on sidereal or star-based calculations. It is interesting to compare the Chinese planetary interpretation of the elements—one of the foundations of Feng Shui—with the elements of Vastu Shastra, the Hindu science of architecture and construction. Remember that the Violet Ray is ruled by the two planets Saturn and Uranus, so this Ray's elements are both earth and metal. Uranus does not specifically rule the element of metal; however, metal rules the *hsiu* constellations that include Uranus.[11]

Planetary Yogas (Unions)

According to the study of Jyotish, yogas are planetary unions that create and define certain astral conditions. Raja Yoga is the metaphysical union of Heaven and Earth, and it assures positive, evolutionary movement in our lives. A Sanskrit term meaning *kingmaker*, Raja Yogas give rise to positions of political or social status. Theosophic scholar, Alice Bailey, took this concept a step further and linked Raja Yogas with specific Ray forces to further refine and clarify the connection between theosophy and Vedic thinking. This type of yoga, or union, merges two astrological houses—a trine and a quadrant—and almost every chart contains one or two of each. A trinal house (Astrological Houses One, Five, and Nine) are houses of dharma, purpose, and blessing; a quadrant house—also referred to as a kendra (Astrological Houses One, Four, and Ten) manifests earthly results. Vedic astrologers study the houses involved in Raja Yoga unions to determine how this energy will shape a person's life.

Mahapurusha Yogas comprise a powerful subset of Raja Yogas. Known in Sanskrit as *combinations of a great being*, these five unions increase the energy of a specific planet and its accompanying Ray. Mahapurusha Yoga planets are Saturn, Jupiter, Venus, Mercury, and Mars. The luminaries—the sun and moon—are not included. When the energy of a particular planet is imprinted and magnified by one of these benefic yogas, the recipient of its energy tends to express planet-specific qualities and characteristics, which is incorporated in the Ray chart and explained below.

1. Mahapurusha Yoga for Jupiter is *Hamsa Yoga*. Supports the strong qualities of Jupiter and the Yellow Ray ; expressed as an ethical, honest, and moral nature. Philosophical, religious, good teacher, fair disposition, optimistic, joyful, and spiritual. The Dark Side of this yoga produces self-promotion and self-righteousness.
2. Mahapurusha Yoga for Saturn is *Shasha Yoga*. This yoga endows power over people; it manifests in positions of authority and administration, control over material resources, and the creation of model workers. Vedic texts claim this person will become the leader of the village. This yoga may sustain detachment, happiness, and spiritual perception. The Dark Side of this yoga may foster cruelty, selfishness, ruthless, and the usurpation of another's wealth.
3. Mahapurusha Yoga for Venus is *Malavya Yoga*: Provides comfort and prosperity in life, including children, marriage and good fortune; is a common yoga for artists, beautiful women, and the wealthy and the affluent. This yoga also

APPENDIX A

bestows charm, grace, culture, beauty, artistic talents, fame, and social influence. The higher side of Malavya Yoga inspires devotion, kindness, and compassion; the darker side emphasizes hedonistic tendencies, including the excessive pursuit of sex, glamour, and sensuality

4. Mahapurusha Yoga for Mercury is *Bhadra Yoga*: Also known as the *auspicious combination*, this yoga blesses an individual with positive mercurial qualities, including good speech and communication, commerce, keen intellect, wit, humor, humanism, and a balanced psychology. This yoga is often seen in the charts of business people, writers, and intellectuals. The Dark Side of Bhadra Yoga creates an overly commercial orientation and a one-dimensional, intellectual experience of life.

5. Mahapurusha Yoga for Mars is *Ruchaka Yoga*: This yoga is also known as the *radiant combination*; it creates strong martial tendencies, including courage, force of will, decisiveness, independence, leadership, achievement, and the ability to take actions and achieve victory at any cost. Ruchaka Yoga overcomes enemies and emerges victorious. Many athletes, military leaders, generals, lawyers, and executives have this yoga. The Dark Side of this yoga creates aggression and violence; this person can be accident prone and fond of confrontation.

[Editor's Note: The above information was compiled from two Western classics written on the subject of Jyotish: Dr. David Frawley's *The Astrology of the Seers, a Guide to Vedic (Hindu) Astrology*, and Hart DeFouw's *Light on Life, an Introduction to the Astrology of India*.]

Aquamarine and Gold Ray

The Aquamarine and Gold Ray is a new addition to this chart. According to the Ascended Masters it began to influence humanity in the twentieth century. The influence of this Ray is destined to develop the higher spiritual qualities of humanity and guide earth's entrance into the New Times—the Golden Age. This Ray is also associated with Unity Consciousness and is said to originate from the Galactic Center: the Great Central Sun.

APPENDIX A

The Rays of Golden Cities

Each of the fifty-one prophesied Golden Cities is said to represent and qualify certain Ray forces, which are broken down into the following categories:

Ray	Number of Golden Cities
Blue	Six
Yellow	Eight
Pink	Nine
White	Six
Green	Seven
Ruby and Gold	Six
Violet	Eight
Gold (only)	Three
Aquamarine and Gold	Three

Heart, Wisdom, Grace

As we enter the Golden Age, three Rays dominate the evolution of humanity and earth: The Yellow Ray of Divine Wisdom; the Pink Ray of the Divine Mother and the Divine Heart; and the Violet Ray of Divine Grace. This suggests a transformation from the Unfed Flame's symbology of Love, Wisdom, and Power to Heart, Wisdom, and Grace.

---

[1] Alice Bailey, *Esoteric Psychology* (Lucis Publishing Co., 1962, New York, N.Y.), page 316.

[2] Lori Toye, *Blue Flame of Gobean*, (Seventh Ray Publishing, 1998, Payson, Ariz.), transcript pg. 5.

[3] David Frawley, *The Astrology of the Seers: A Guide to Vedic (Hindu) Astrology*, (Passage Press, 1990, Salt Lake City, Utah), page 38.

[4] Craig Donaldson, *How to Get Great Results When You Pray*, http://www.ascension-research.org/prayer.html, (2010)

[5] David Frawley, *The Astrology of the Seers: A Guide to Vedic (Hindu) Astrology*, (Passage Press, 1990, Salt Lake City, Utah), page 48.

[6] Wikipedia, *Seven Rays*, http://en.wikipedia.org/wiki/Seven_Rays, (2010).

[7] Ibid.

[8] Ibid.

[9] *The War Prayer by Mark Twain*, http://www.ntua.gr/lurk/making/warprayer.html, (2010).

[10] M. Alan Kazlev, *The Higher Mind and Transformation*, http://www.kheper.net/Aurobindo/Higher_Mind.html, (2010)

[11] Christopher McIntosh, *A Short History of Astrology*, (Barnes and Noble Books by arrangement with Random House, UK, Ltd., 1994), page 49.

APPENDIX B

Topics and Terms for Emanation

Absorption of Light Forces
Genetic Fear
The Light of Awakening
The Time of Cellular and Genetic Acceleration
Ray Forces and Cellular Awakening
The Ever-present Now
Seven Ray Forces
Chohans and Master Teachers of the Rays
Processes Versus Results
Qualification and Emanation of a Ray
The Principles of Conductivity and Sacred Geometry
The Astral Body
Enhancement of Ray Forces
Harmonizing Ray Forces
Teachings on the Violet Flame

Dharma
　Often confused with the idea of good Karma, this Sanskrit word means duty or purpose.

Emanation
　To flow out, issue, or proceed as from a source or origin; especially the path of a Ray as it travels from the Great Central Sun.

Earth Plane and Planet
　According to the Ascended Masters, the *Earth Plane* includes everything that inhabits and occurs on our planet, including the Third, Fourth, and Fifth Dimensions. *Earth Planet* refers to Babajeran—the earth mother—and it comprises her physical, emotional, and spiritual existence.

The Great Central Sun
　The Great Central Sun is the center of the Cosmos—the sun behind the sun. It also known as the Galactic Center or the Central Galactic Sun. According to the Vedic sidereal (or star) zodiac, the Great Central Sun is located in the sign of Sagittarius and the nakshatra of Mula—which means *root*—and connotes a foundation, a beginning, or a source. A

APPENDIX B

real root is often gnarled and knotted, that's why the meaning of Mula also encompasses the notions of restraint and bondage.[1] Consequently, the Seven Rays travel from the Great Central Sun under a form of cosmic bondage to the Earth Plane, where our personal Karma is dispensed.

Galactic Light

Galactic Light is a non-quasar type of extrasensory light that emanates from the Great Central Sun or the Galactic Center. Galactic Light is said to conduct the esoteric Seven Rays of Light and Sound.

Portals of Entry

Portals of Entry are prophesied geological locations on earth where energy anomalies occur. New energies enter the planet via these locales, affecting her physical, emotional, mental, and spiritual evolution. Models of this type of energy portal include Ascension Valley in Washington and Idaho and the Transportation Vortex, located near Coeur d'Alene, Idaho. According to various prophecies, hundreds of energy portals—each with a distinct and unique power—will emerge and develop as we enter the Golden Age.

Light of Awakening

Light of Awakening is a prophesied wave of cosmic light that originates in the Galactic Center. Its destiny is to evolve humanity into the Golden Age by altering human genetics and transforming our sensation of fear. The appearance of the Light of Awakening will also play an important role in activating individual and worldwide spiritual healing and initiating earth's entrance into the consciousness of the ONE.

Astral Body

An *Astral Body* is a subtle light body that contains the feelings, desires, and emotions of an individual. It exists as an intermediate light body between the physical body and the causal (mental) body. According to the Master Teachers, humans enter the Astral Plane—the transitionary ether between dimensions—during sleep with the help of the Astral Body. Many dreams and visions are experienced in this plane of vibrant color and sensation. Spiritual development increases the strength of one's Astral Body; the luminosity of its light is often detected in the physical plane. Some spiritual adepts can consciously leave their physical bodies and travel in their Astral Bodies. For most people, however, this happens only during sleep and after physical death, when the energies of the soul journey to the Astral Plane. Paramahansa Yogananda, the revered spiritual leader of the Self-Realization Fellowship, questioned the avatar of his Master Teacher Sri Yuteswar after it appeared to him following the sage's death. "Are you wearing a body like the one I buried beneath the cruel Puri sands?" The adept answered, "Yes, I am the same ... though I see it as ethereal; to your sight it is physical. From cosmic atoms I created an entirely new body, which you laid beneath the dream-sands at Puri in your dream-world. I am in truth resurrected—not on earth but on an astral planet. Its inhabitants are better able than earthly humanity to meet my lofty standards. There you and your loved ones shall someday come to be with me."[2]

Light of Awakening

APPENDIX B

The Astral Body is also known to esoteric scholars as Body Double, Desire Body, or Emotional Body.

Location and Movement of the Rays through the Eight-Sided Cell of Perfection

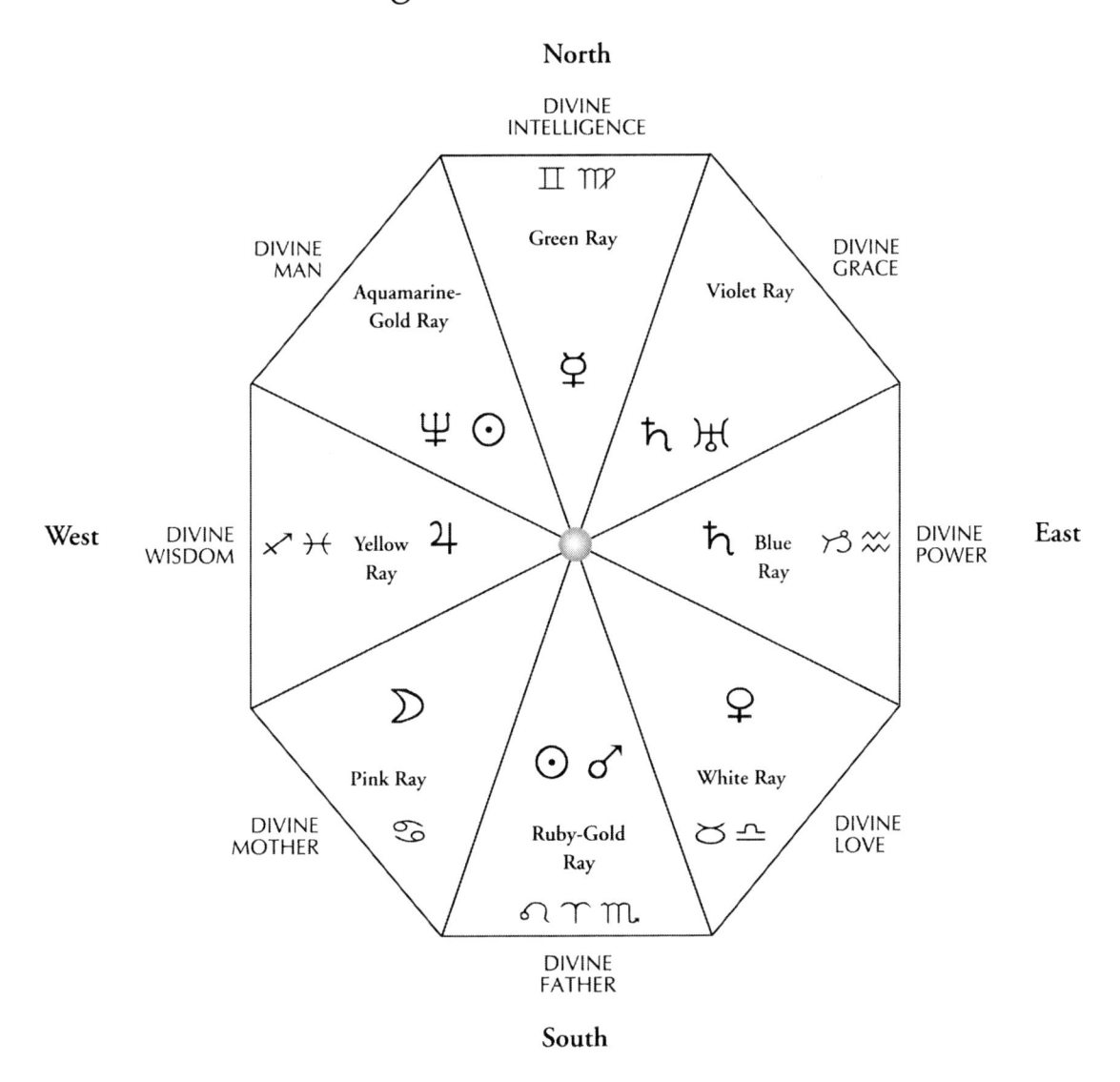

FIGURE 1-B
Eight-Sided Cell of Perfection
Energy Map Depicting the Rays within the Sacred Cell

Movement of the Rays through the Eight-sided Cell of Perfection

The above figure depicts the location of the Ray Forces within the Eight-sided Cell of Perfection. The subsequent figure depicts the Rays' movement within the Sacred Cell.

---

129 The Golden City Series: Book Two

APPENDIX B

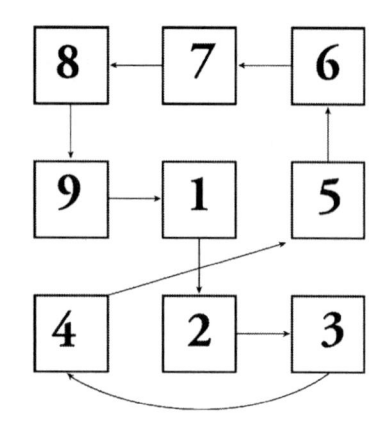

FIGURE 2-B
Directional Movement of Energy through the Eight Palaces of the Eight-Sided Cell of Perfection
This illustration depicts how the Ray Forces move within the Eight-Sided Cell of Perfection.

Rays enter the cell at the center and the Rays begin their movement through the eight sectors, also known as palaces. The flow of energy begins in the center (known as the first movement, or first sector); travels to pure South (the second movement, or second sector); travels to the Southeast (third movement, or third sector); then crosses the South, and travels to the Southwest (fourth movement, or fourth sector); from the Southwest the Ray traverses the upper Southern sector and travels to the East (fifth movement or fifth sector); continues North to the Northeast (sixth movement or sixth sector); to pure North (seventh movement or seventh sector); travels west to Northwest (eighth movement, or the eighth sector); moves Southwest to West (ninth movement, or ninth sector); and completes its journey as it travels back to the center and where yet another circulatory movement initiates through the Eight Palaces.

The Eight Palaces of the Eight-sided Cell of Perfection

The Eighth Sectors, also known as palaces, mansion, or houses, of the Eight-Sided Cell of Perfection are identified with specific Ray Forces. They are (clockwise, starting in the North):

North Sector:	Green Ray
Northeast Sector:	Violet Ray
East Sector:	Blue Ray
Southeast Sector:	White Ray
South Sector:	Ruby-Gold Ray
Southwest Sector:	Pink Ray
West Sector:	Yellow Ray
Northwest Sector:	Aquamarine-Gold Ray
Center:	All of the Rays

Light of Awakening

APPENDIX B

FIGURE 3-B
*Eight-Sided Cell of Perfection
Overlaid the Human Body*
Energy Map and the Human Body

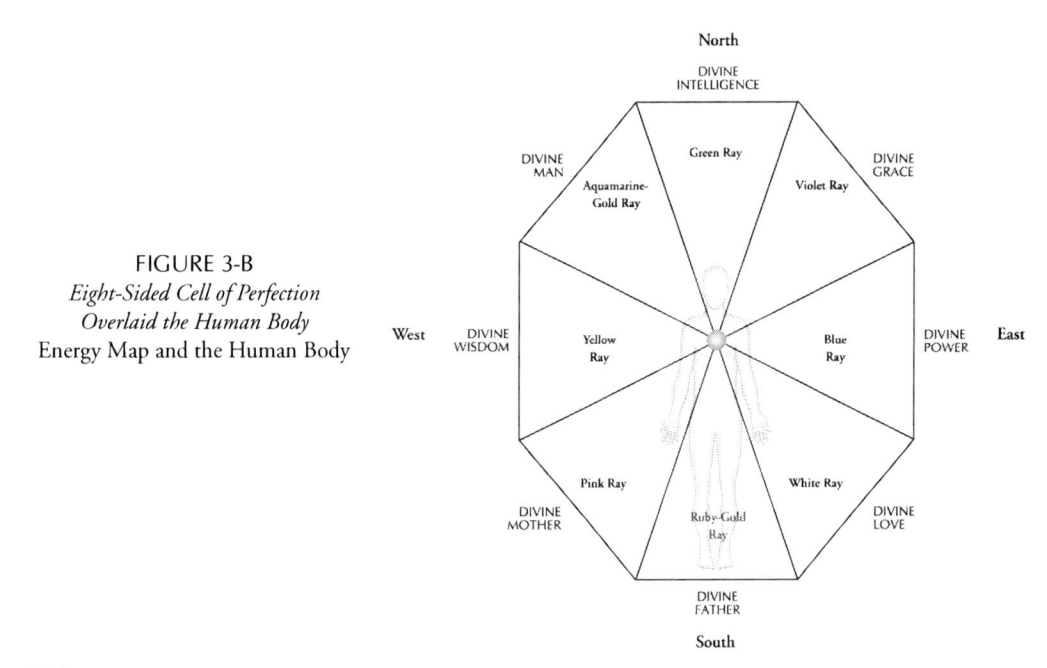

Microcosm and Macrocosm

The Eight-sided cell of Perfection is a small atomic cell, located in the Chamber of the HU-man Heart and represents both the microcosmic and macrocosmic creative movement of the Rays. Overlay this energy map over the human body and the head represents the North; the feet represent the South; the left-side of the body represents the East; and the right side of the body represents the West. The Golden Thread Axis, also known as the Vibral-Core, Antahkarana, and Vertical Power Current, flows from the I AM Presence (North), and grounds itself into the center of the earth's core (South).

The system of the movement of the Rays through the Eight-sided cell of Perfection may be applied to the structure of Golden City Vortices, and the energy of the Rays may be sensed in the many lei-lines, adjutant points, and sub-vortices of the Vortex. Ray Forces are often experienced in a Golden City Vortex; however, the Ray of the presiding Master Teacher, Archangel, or Elohim of the specific Golden City Vortex will likely dominate. During each evolutionary epoch of humanity, one of the Rays and their influence is said to dominate our spiritual growth and development. The following table reflects this theosophical thought:

Lemuria:	Blue Ray	Development of the Will (Power)
Atlantis:	Pink Ray	Development of the Heart (Emotion)
Aryan:	Green Ray	Development of the Intellect (Intelligence)

Currently, humanity is guided by the Divine Presence of the Green Ray, which likely accounts for its presence governing the Crown Chakra. (See Figure 3-B) However, the periodic influence of other Ray Forces is also experienced. Humanity's entrance into the New Times and consequent evolutionary process is inspired by the Aquamarine-Gold Ray.

APPENDIX B

The Ascended Masters prophesy as humanity progresses into the New Times, a feminine orientation in our culture and society will temper the out-of-balance energies of male tyranny. This may explain to some extent, why the energies of the Divine Father (South) are currently surrounded on both the Southwest and Southeast by the White Ray (Divine Feminine) and the Pink Ray (Divine Mother). And please remember that the energies of the Eight-Sided Cell of Perfection are never static and are always moving and evolving to match humanity's development. The above illustration is said to reflect humanity's important passage into the New Times and the individual realization of the HU-man—the Divine Man. As groups and individuals realize the energies of perfection held latent in the Eight-sided Cell of Perfection, it is likely new arrangements of the Rays and their subsequent Energy Maps will emerge.

Prophecies of Change
1. The Ascended Masters increase Galactic Light on the Earth Plane and Planet and among humanity. This suspends cataclysmic geological changes.
2. Intensified Galactic Light, channeled through the Eighth Ray and Cellular Awakening, provides humanity the opportunity to assimilate to the higher energies and frequencies now available on earth.
3. Certain higher energies are dispersed among Golden Cities, Portals of Entry, ancient vortices of earth, and other sensitive geological locations throughout the world.
4. The disbursement of new energies resembles a rising tide. This flow of energy accelerates the higher consciousness of humanity toward the One and Unity Consciousness.
5. The wave of Galactic Light from the Great Central Sun allows individuals to transmute lifetimes of genetically held fear. This cosmic wave of luminescence is known to the Master Teachers as the *Light of Awakening*.
6. Accelerations of Galactic Light intensify the processes of New Energy Light waves and Cellular Awakening. Light of Awakening then blankets humanity, thereby obstructing cataclysmic Earth Changes. Individual and world healing commence instead. The earth's entrance into the consciousness of the ONE has been initiated.
7. The energies of Golden City Vortices grow alongside their emanation of light. This process fortifies the Ray Force of each Golden City Vortex qualifies as we enter the New Times. Golden Cities of the United States are represented by the following Ray Forces:
    a. Gobean: Blue Ray
    b. Malton: Ruby and Gold Ray
    c. Wahanee: Violet Ray
    d. Shalahah: Green Ray
    e. Klehma: White Ray

APPENDIX B

8. The energies of nascent Golden Cities may be difficult to detect at first. That's because the development of its Astral Body is incomplete. As the energy field of an incipient Golden City increases its strength and power to 10 percent, subtle indications of the qualified Ray Force commence. Paradoxical anomalies, however, are often present in the early stages of development.
    a. The lower energies of a qualified Ray may manifest before the maturation of Golden City's Astral Body. Collective and individual characteristics may include:
        i. Blue Ray: Inflation, greed, gambling, weakness, vulnerability.
        ii. Pink Ray: Selfishness, lack of conscience, emotional instability, moodiness, negativity.
        iii. Yellow Ray: Lack of integrity, common sense, enthusiasm, and compassion.
        iv. White Ray: Vanity, compulsion, attention-seeking, vulgarity, insensitivity.
        v. Green Ray: Dependence on technology, disease, poverty, addictions, irrationality.
        vi. Ruby and Gold Ray: Worry, doubt, obsession, lack of confidence, fear, passivity.
        vii. Violet Ray: Competition, violence, manipulation, political corruption.
    b. Master Teachers counsel by developing spiritual perception and choice; chelas and students can qualify energies of Golden Cities beyond their primitive level. "Perception is critical to utilize a Ray Force"—this key understanding is often known as *qualification of a Ray*.
9. During the Golden Age, Golden City Vortices will replicate the energies of their designated Ray Force throughout the planet. This energy will expand and emanate toward its highest achievable level possible on earth. As earth and humanity progress toward the apex of the Golden Age and as further light is received from the Great Central Sun, this synergistic emission of energies will occur sequentially.
10. The light and energy from the Golden Cities evolve individuals into the HU-man—the God Man. This individual evolutionary process moves humanity toward the experience and the understanding of the *Co-creative and Instant-Thought-Manifestation Process*. The Master Teachers refer to this phenomenon as *Manifest Destiny*.

Spiritual Prophecies

The Time of Cellular and Genetic Acceleration, according to many esoteric prophecies, will develop as light energies proliferate on earth and are properly utilized by humanity. The following traits characterize this time of transformation:
1. The purpose of the I AM is revealed to many.
2. This spiritual light is not exclusively for the spiritually initiated; it is for everyone and intended to affect the masses.
3. The overall spiritual consciousness of humanity progresses via the evolving mediums of conscience and choice.

APPENDIX B

Binary Intellect

The intelligence of humanity, according to the Master Teachers, is binary. Rather, it is based on the dual experiences of the left brain and the right brain. These differences are illustrated in the table below. [3]

Left Brain	Right Brain
Logical Sequential	Random
Rational	Intuitive
Analytical	Holistic Synthesizing
Objective	Subjective
Looks at parts	Looks at wholes

Conductivity

Spiritual energies, according to the Master Teachers, are often transmitted the same way metal conducts electricity. Instead of a mass of free-floating electrons being pushed along by an electrical current, however, geometrical shape and geometric movement serve as the conduit of these subtle yet vital energies. Perhaps one of the best illustrations of geometrical conductivity is the sacred geometry of the Golden City Structure.

Kundalini

In Sanskrit, *Kundalini* literally means *coiled*. It represents the coiled energy located at the base of the spine, often established in the lower Base and Sacral Chakras. Some scholars claim that *Kundalini Shakti*—shakti meaning energy—initiates spiritual development, wisdom, knowledge, and enlightenment.

Sacred Geometry

Esoteric scholars suggest that many universal patterns, geometrical shapes, and geometric proportions symbolize spiritual balance and perfection. In other words, a fundamental mathematical order exists in the universe, one that is divinely inspired, because it cannot be explained by conventional means. Nature is rife with examples of Sacred Geometry, including the hexagonal cell of the honeybee, the chambered shell of the nautilus, and the spiral arms of a galaxy. Instances in the arts and sciences are also prevalent: the musical harmonic ratios of Pythagoras, the Spiritual Lokas of Vedic Cosmology, the mathematical beauty of the Golden Ratio, and Leonardo da Vinci's renowned Vitruvian Man. Meanwhile, the Sine Wave, the Sphere, Vesica Piscis, the Torus Tube, the Five Platonic Solids—Tetrahedron, Cube, Octahedron, Dodecahedron, Icosahedron; the Golden Spiral; the Tesseract four-dimensional hypercube; Fractals, the Star Tetrahedron (a Golden City shape); and the spiritually metaphoric Merkabah are just a few mathematical concepts that illustrate the ancient origins of this divine theory.[4]

APPENDIX B

Golden City Vortex Dimensional Symbolism

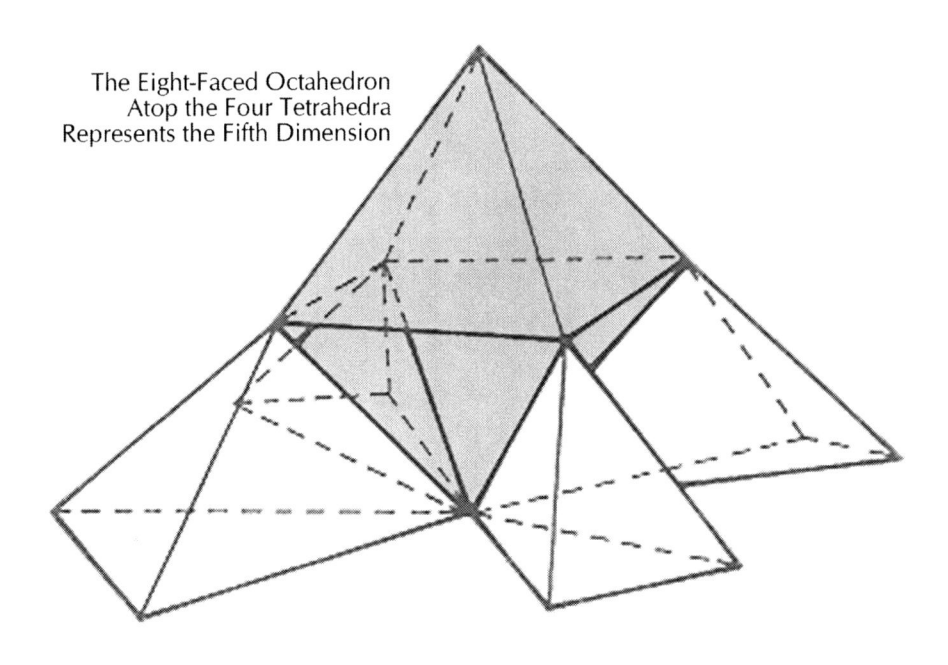

The Eight-Faced Octahedron
Atop the Four Tetrahedra
Represents the Fifth Dimension

FIGURE 4-B
Fifth Dimension: Golden City Vortex
The Fifth Dimension is represented by a Octahedron in the Golden City Structure

Four Tetrahedra Represent the Fourth Dimension

Three Exposed Faces
of the Tetrahedra
Represent the
Third Dimension

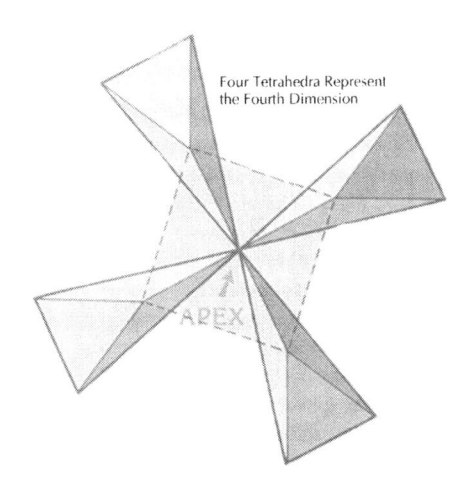

FIGURE 5-B
Fourth Dimension: Golden City Vortex
The Fourth Dimension is represented by four Tetrahedra in the Golden City Structure

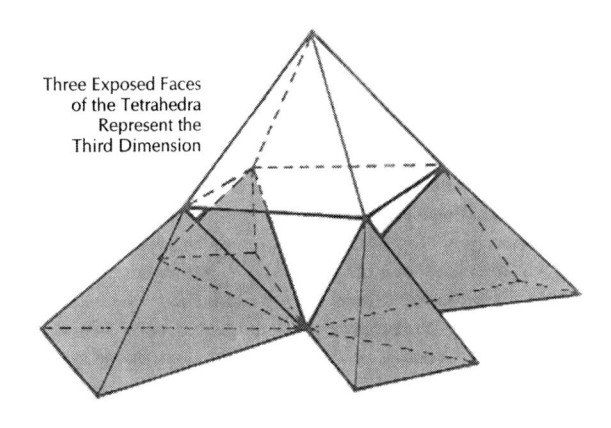

FIGURE 6-B
Third Dimension: Golden City Vortex
The three exposed faces of the Tetrahedra represent Third Dimension in the Golden City Structure

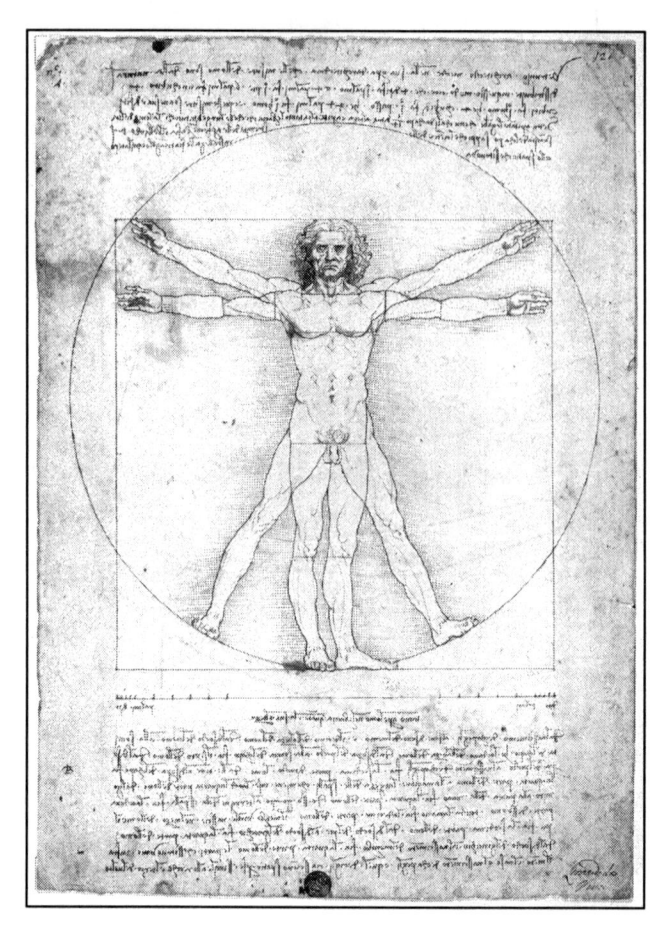

APPENDIX B
Sacred Geometry

FIGURE 7-B
Vitruvian Man
by Leonardo da Vinci, Galleria dell'Accademia, Venice, (1485-90), original drawing 1487.

Leonardo da Vinci's work serves as a compelling framework in which to study esoteric principles. Two of his pieces specifically—*Vitruvian Man* and his interpretation of the Flower of Life—investigate and illustrate the underlying elements of sacred geometry, which is a key concept in understanding Golden City Vortices. *Vitruvian Man* is ubiquitous in modern culture. He's on everything from t-shirts to NASA mission patches to international currency. There's a reason *Virtuvian Man* shows up all over the place—he's iconic, he simple yet complex, and he symbolizes the convergence of art, science, and metaphysics. In fact, Italy's prime minister, Carlo Azeglio Ciampi, said *Vitruvian Man* represents "man as a measure of all things."[5] Da Vinci uses *Vitruvian Man* to express his ideals about human balance, proportion, and symmetry. The rendering itself is of a male body in a square, arms out, feet together, superimposed on the same human form in a circle, legs spread-eagle, arms out but raised to meet the top of the head. *Vitruvian Man* is based on the work of the Roman architect Vitruvius, who postulated that the proportions of the human body were divinely inspired and thus perfect. Several centuries later Da Vinci expanded this notion—he felt the human body served as a microcosmic reflection of the universe. *Vitruvian Man* is a series of mathematical and geometric calculations that correlate measurements of the body using the distance between body parts, such as palms, hands, elbows, legs, and feet. For instance, the length of a man's outstretched arms is equal to his height. Da Vinci also relied on facial elements and dimensions to create his rendering— the distance from the bottom of the chin to the nose, for example, is a third of the face. At first glance, *Vitruvian Man* has two stances, but by combining various arm and leg positions, scholars have actually discovered sixteen poses. *Vitruvian Man* is considered a masterpiece and represents the inherent sacred geometry depicted in nature. Today *Vitruvian Man* represents the essential symmetry of the human body as an extension of the universe as a whole. He is often employed as a contemporary symbol of holistic and alternative medicine.

[Leonardo da Vinci, *Vitruvian Man*, 1487, Wikimedia Commons, Public Domain, (2010).]

APPENDIX B

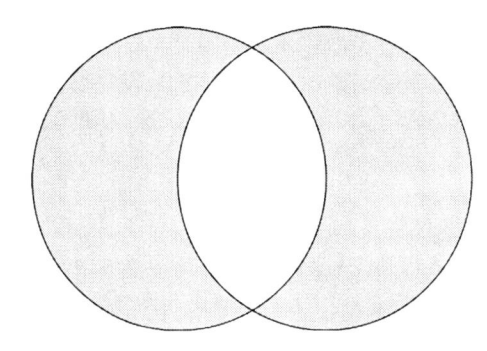

FIGURE 8-B
Vesica Piscis
Vesica Piscis appears in all kinds of religious, metaphysical, spiritual, and mathematical contexts throughout time. The shape itself is based on two interlocking circles of the same radius; the center of each circle lies upon the circumference of the other, forming an eye-shaped oval at its intersection, the Vesica Piscis. The mathematical ratio of the Vesica Piscis (width to height: 265/153) equals the square root of three—a metaphysical reference to the mystical triune, the Holy Trinity. Part of that ratio is also connected to the Gospel of John in the New Testament of the Bible and the number of fish caught in the Sea of Galilee in the teachings of Jesus Christ: 153. This phenomenon often referred to as the "miraculous draught of fish." The abundant iconography of the Vesica Piscis is prevalent throughout the art, architecture, and the symbology of Christianity. Vesica Piscis is also a dominant motif among the Freemason movement and Kabbalism.

FIGURE 9-B
Flower of Life
Though da Vinci did not create the *Flower of Life*, he was fascinated by its mathematical properties, which inspired him to produce his own rendition of this enigmatic spiritual symbol. The *Flower of Life* is considered by many occultists as the foundation of sacred geometry and is associated with multiple spiritual beliefs, including Kabbalism, Judaism, and Wicca, while its geometric figures are noted throughout ancient Assyria, Egypt, India, Europe, the Middle East, Peru, and Mexico. Hermeticists, Kabbalists, and Pythagoreans have adopted it as a sacred symbol, one that represents the diagram of the Universal Seed of Life.

The pattern of the flower depicts the fundamental form of dimensional time and space. Its basis is the rotating or spinning octahedron, consisting of six vertices, eight faces, and twelve edges. Its spiritual influence is said to connect all patterns of life, especially to the Akashic Records, ethereal information that contains the breadth of knowledge of human experience. The *Flower of Life*, which blossoms in the following eight stages, forms the structural bedrock of the Tube Torus—the underlying geometric principle and structure of the Vortices.

1. Rotating Octahedron [Editor's Note: The symbol for the Fifth Dimension of the Golden City Vortices and an integral part of the Golden City's structure.]
2. Spherical Octahedron
3. Vesica Piscis
4. Tripod of Life—the Holy Trinity
5. Four intersecting rings
6. Five intersecting rings
7. Six intersecting rings
8. Seven interlocking rings

The *Flower of Life* is considered the initial structural foundation in the formation of Tube Torus—the underlying geometric principle and structure in Vortices.

[Wikipedia, http://en.wikipedia.org/wiki/Flower_of_Life, (2010).]

APPENDIX B

Closure of Understanding

When an individual completes a specific soul lesson, the Karma affiliated with this educational process is released, and the soul is freed for new and further growth and development. The Ascended Masters often refer to this as *Closure of Understanding*.

Saint Germain's Teachings of Ray Enhancement

To enhance the energies of a Ray Force, an individual must first accomplish a level of esoteric education in regard to the Seven Rays. Second, a student must be able to recognize the presence and the influence of a distinctive Ray in their life. Finally, a student or chela must be able to critically define their intention for augmenting or treating a Ray Force.

According to Saint Germain, various spiritual teachings and techniques can enhance the potency of Ray Forces:

1. Meditation on a Ray establishes the energies of that particular Ray Force in the mind. The purity of a Ray activates the will. The Ray can then be further applied to the development of the conscience and the growth of consciousness.
2. The use of certain gemstones manifests qualities of the Rays.
3. Certain Golden Cities that emanate a corresponding Ray can increase the strength of Ray Forces.
4. The use of sound—specifically mantras—can also enhance Ray Forces. This treats the Astral Body.
5. The Violet Flame drives the energies of a Ray Force into its higher use while releasing the Karma surrounding the lower emanation of a Ray. This liberates a Ray Force. Saint Germain recommends an easy decree for this purpose: *Violet Flame, I AM, come forth! Violet Flame, I AM!*
6. While transmuting Karmas, the Violet Flame expands the Astral Body and the overall light and life of the physical body. This expansion induces spiritual freedom and the individual's liberation from perception.
7. As an Alchemical Ray, the Violet Flame fuses the interplay of the Rays with *sound vibration-ing*. This creates harmony and the ability to apply individual choices, while expanding and evolving spiritual consciousness to achieve personal goals.
8. Saint Germain specifically gives this decree to harmonize the Ray Forces of an individual:

Violet Flame come forth in the Harmony of the Seven Rays!
Transmute the cause and effect, and all records (akashic) that have been genetically inscribed and genetically used by me.
Violet Flame, blaze forth in Great Harmony to the Divine Plan and the Divine Will!

APPENDIX B

Teachings on the Violet Flame

1. The Violet Flame fosters harmony within by fusing together Rays and Ray Forces. Rays work with focused cooperation, affirming inherent divinity and Co-creatorship.
2. Ascended Masters use the Violet Flame as a *Grand Conductor* of Ray Forces; they employ the conductivity, emanation, and qualification of the Rays to achieve contact with the One to ultimately attain Unity Consciousness—Unana.
3. The Ascended Masters do not give an exact amount of prescribed Violet Flame since this quantity is based solely on individual need. Some individuals may need to use the Violet Flame only once a day; others may need to focus on its transformative and transmuting energies minute by minute.
4. As one begins to acquire more experience with the use and the results of the Violet Flame, the vibration and the energy of the Spiritual Fire are not spoken or decreed. Rather, they are carried in light bodies and are in constant activity, influencing personal choices, actions, and interactions with others. According to Saint Germain, this sanctity of the Violet Flame is akin to chanting Violet Flame decrees in temples, "It is possible to carry that Mighty Violet Flame in, through, and around your being *all* the time."
5. The Violet Flame, similar to Ray Forces, operates on the concept of emanation.
6. When one begins to work with the energies of the Violet Flame, Saint Germain suggests chanting a mantra or decree forty-nine times (seven times seven). This creates a momentum of energy that increases the power of each of the seven Ray Forces.
7. In the beginning stages, the use of the Violet Flame mitigates the difficult burdens in a person's life. Continued focus and use of the Violet Flame manifest attributes of the Violet Flame in the physical world. These are:
    a. Acts of Forgiveness
    b. Acts of Compassion
    c. Acts of Mercy
8. Please remember: there is no exact method of calculating the Violet Flame's function and result. Saint Germain states, "…this is about the chela's inner union and harmony with regards to the Seven Forces—the Seven Rays."
9. The ideal use of the Violet Flame moves one beyond egotistical, selfish motives and into the service of the greater good. The intention of the alchemic Spiritual Fire, ideally, is to liberate an individual from the fears that inhibit him or her from uniting with the Light of God.

APPENDIX B

The Human Energy System and the Rays

Perhaps the most distinctive and personal system of the Seven Rays is the Human Energy System. The Seven Rays play a role in the formation of:

1. The Human Aura and its unique layers
2. The Auric Blueprint that maps the major and minor Energy Meridians and the gross and subtle Nadis (energy currents) of the Human Body
3. The Lunar Energy Current (Ida), the Solar Energy Current (Pingala), and the Golden Thread Axis (Medullar Shushumna); these three major Nadis of the physical body are related to the Kundalini. This is the familiar Caduceus, the ancient symbol of Hermes.
4. The Major Chakras—energy centers—located to the front of the Golden Thread Axis; the Crown and Base Chakra, located at the top and bottom of the Golden Thread Axis; and the Four Will Chakras, located at the back of the Golden Thread Axis.

Each of the Rays nourishes and encourages the growth of humanity through their specific qualities and characteristics. Accordingly, as humanity evolves so does the Human Energy System and many changes are noted in the Energy Fields and Chakras as the septenate forces unfold. A certain color may be associated with a functioning, ordinary chakra as normal, when in fact the chakra is still in its infant phase of development. The soul matures through stages of self-realization and the energy system reflects this transformation in the auric light. The Seven Rays expand, develop, advance, and establish the human into the HU-man, the Divine God Man, and prepares consciousness to enter the experience beyond earthly Karma—spiritual liberation.

The Seven Rays are carried by three major currents in the human body located in the spine which are the nexus of the Kundalini. The first is the *Golden Thread Axis*, also known in the Hindu tradition as the *Medullar Sushumna*. According to Ascended Master teaching, the Golden Thread Axis originates with our solar sun, and the vibrant life-giving current spiritually connects each individual to their I AM Presence throughout each individual lifetime. Light energy penetrates at the top of the head, moves through the spinal system, and then onward through the perineum—the Base Chakra. This ethereal cord travels onward through the earth where it roots to the core of the earth, also considered a latent sun. According to esoteric teachers the Golden Thread Axis connects Heaven and Earth. Its visual symbol is known as the *Rod of Power*, which depicts the two suns connected by a central beam. Ascended Master students and chelas frequently draw upon the energy of the sun and earth through the Golden Thread Axis for healing and renewal with meditation, visualization, and breath.

Light of Awakening

APPENDIX B

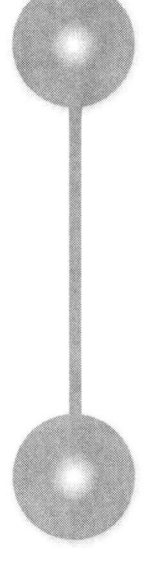

FIGURE 10-B
Rod of Power
The *Rod of Power* symbolizes the human energy system's connection to the sun and earth.

The vital energy of life—chi, or prana—pulsates through the Golden Thread, and its earthly presence is dissolved when the soul exits through death, or its energies are withdrawn by the individual to the spiritual planes through the Ascension Process.

Two vital currents intertwine around the Golden Thread Axis, and this foundation is distinguished in Yoga as the right and left eyes, representing the two petals of the Third Eye Chakra. Feminine energy travels up the spine by the inhalation (cooling) of breath through these six zodiacal signs: Aquarius, Pisces, Aries, Taurus, Gemini, and Cancer. Masculine energy descends into the spine by the exaltation (warming) of breath through the astrological signs of: Leo, Virgo, Libra, Scorpio, Sagittarius, and Capricorn. Yogic Astrology embraces the evolutionary fluidity of the Rays through the lunar energy (moon), known as the *Ida Current*, and the solar energy (sun), the *Pingala Current*. These currents intersect four times in their sacred journey around the axis, and each intersection creates a chakra ruled by specific planets and Ray Forces. The Seven Rays journey through these three important Nadis and chakras, and dispense Galactic energies according to the Karma and Dharma of the individual. This metaphysical human energy system is renown in ancient history and myth as the *Caduceus*.

The Caduceus is often confused with the *Rod of Asclepius*, the traditional symbol of medical practice; however, the two symbols share common ancestry in the Greek myths of Apollo. Today the Caduceus is a universal medical symbol and its two serpents and wings were popularized by the US Army medical corps in 1902.

The serpentine energy of the symbolic Caduceus winds down the rod and meets in four distinct areas; the Crown Chakra is represented as a set of heavenly wings. Ancient depictions of Mithra in the Roman Mithraeum of Ostia (190 A.D.) depict the Caduceus entwined six times by only one serpent, and four wings are said to represent the four seasons.

APPENDIX B

FIGURE 11-B
Caduceus
The ancient symbol for the Greek Messenger Hermes became the emblem of the U.S. Army Medical Corps. In the Human Energy System the *Caduceus'* center staff represents the Golden Thread Axis; its wings, the Crown Chakra; the two eyes of the serpents represent the Third Eye Chakra; and their entertwining bodies represent the kundalini. Chakras form at the four intersections.

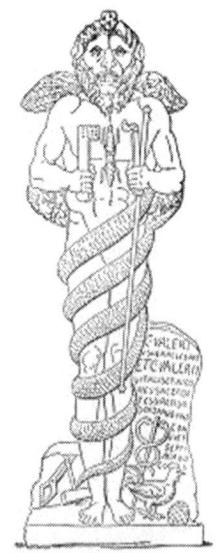

FIGURE 12-B
Mithra as Boundless Time
This is a reproduction of a statue found in the Mithraeum of Ostia (Italy), dedicated in the year 190 CE. The body is entwined six times by a singular serpent. The four wings are decorated with symbols of the Four Seasons. Symbols of the planets and ultimate authority, (sceptor, thunderbolt, wand of Mercury, the hammer and tongs of Vulcan), present Mithra as the embodiment of all of the powers of the Gods.

[Franz Cumot, *The Doctine of the Mithraic Mysteries*, http://www.sacred-texts.com/cla/mom/mom7.htm, (2010)]

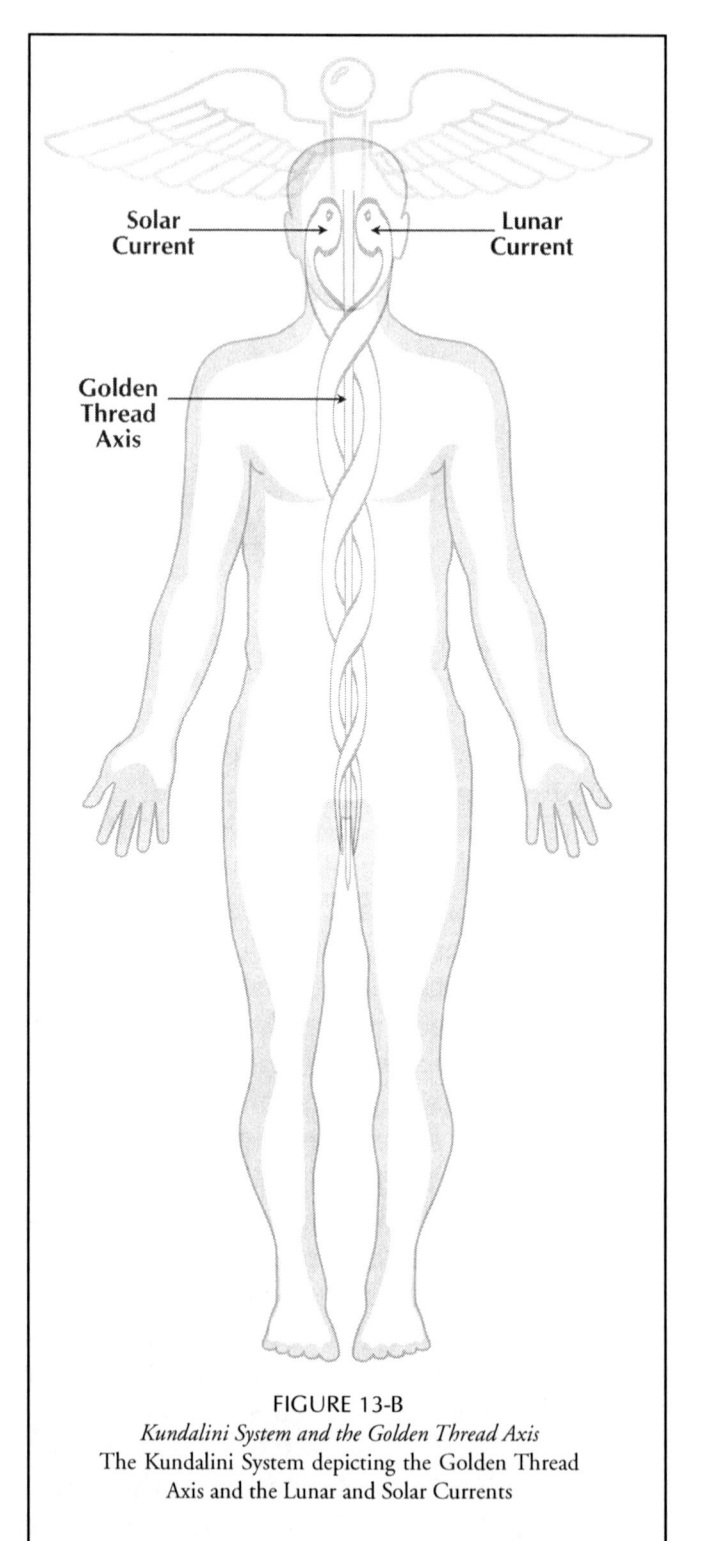

FIGURE 13-B
Kundalini System and the Golden Thread Axis
The Kundalini System depicting the Golden Thread Axis and the Lunar and Solar Currents

Light of Awakening

APPENDIX B

FIGURE 14-B
The Dharmic Bull of Truth
The Bull of Truth loses one leg as earth progresses through
each declining stage of the Cycle of the Yugas.

Kali-Yuga and the Rays

Vedic Rishis claim the evolutionary status of humanity is contingent upon the quality of Ray Forces streaming to earth as a non-visible quasar light from the Galactic Center—the Great Central Sun. While the Rays are invisible to the naked eye, their presence contains subtle electromagnetic energy and psychics may detect their luminous astral light. Ancient astrologers visually observed and experienced the Seven Rays of Light and Sound. Their astronomy, advanced beyond today's science, maintained that our solar sun was in reality a double star. Our sun rotates with a companion—a dwarf star which contains no luminosity of its own. This theory suggests that as our Solar System orbits the Great Central Sun, earth experiences long periods of time when the dwarf star impedes the flow of the Rays from the Galactic Center; likewise, there are times when this important stream of light is unhampered. Since the light energy from the Central Sun nourishes spiritual and intellectual knowledge on the earth, the Vedic Rishis expertly tracked earth's movement in and out of the flow and reception of this cosmic light. This cycle is known as the *Cycle of the Yugas,* or the *World Ages* whose constant change instigates the advances and deterioration of cultures and civilizations. There are four Yugas: the Golden Age (*Satya* or *Krita-Yuga*); the Silver Age, (*Treta-Yuga*); the Bronze Age, (*Dvapara-Yuga*); the Iron Age, (*Kali-Yuga*). The dharmic *Bull of Truth*—a Vedic symbol of morality—represents this cyclic calendar. According to Vedic tradition the bull loses a leg as a symbol of earth's loss of twenty-five percent of cosmic light with each cycle of time. During a Golden Age, the earth receives one-hundred percent cosmic light from the Great Central Sun. In a Silver Age, earth receives seventy-five percent light and in a Bronze Age, fifty percent light. We are now living in Kali-Yuga: the age of materialism when earth receives only twenty-five percent light.

Since the science of Vedic Astrology—Jyotish—was given to humanity in a time of greater light on earth, it is possible that many of the recognized planets ruling chakras

APPENDIX B

are functioning at abnormal levels. This is accounted for in the chakra tables that follow. [Editor's Note: Vedic and esoteric scholars speculate that the calculation for the timing of the Yugas may be faulty, and we are living in the infant stages of Dvapara-Yuga. This opinion is based on the calculations of *Sri Yuteswar*, guru of Paramahansa Yogananda. Some Vedic adherents of the *Puranas*—ancient, religious texts—allege we are currently experiencing a minor upswing of Galactic Light, the *Golden Age of Kali-Yuga*. It is important to understand the Golden Age of Kali-Yuga is not a full force one-hundred percent Krita-Yuga; however, the Master Teachers claim it is possible earth may receive up to fifty percent Galactic Light, equal to a Bronze Age Dvapara-Yuga at the height of this ten-thousand year period.

Chakras and the Endocrine System

Some esoteric scholars suggest certain chakras frequently represent the energies of the endocrine glands and their energies are responsible for the *rising of the kundalini*—a term for spiritual development. Specifically, two endocrine glands are linked to our psychic ability and regulate consciousness: the pineal gland and the pituitary gland. In recent studies at the Psi Research Centre in Glastonbury, England, researchers believe the pineal gland's production of *pinoline* is responsible for various psychic states of consciousness. "Pinoline is thought to act on serotonin to trigger dreaming. It also has hallucinogenic properties, and its chemical structure is similar to chemicals found in psychotropic plants in the Amazon. Studies suggest that the dream state is one in which we are most likely to have psychic experiences. Pinoline is believed to be the neurochemical that triggers this state of consciousness."[6] Animals and homing pigeons rely on the presence of *magnetite*—a magnetically sensitive compound of iron and oxygen—to sense the right direction during travel and seasonal migrations. Human sensitivity to magnetic fields may be explained by the presence of magnetite crystals located near the pituitary gland.

Color and Vibration

Human Energy Field researcher Dr. Shafica Karagulla (1914-1986) concluded chakras are affected and altered in color, luminosity, size, form, and texture during the disease process. An outgrowth of the detailed research discovered that medically diagnosed problems in the endocrine glands are also detected in the chakras. This research expanded knowledge regarding the traditional Seven Chakras, and added an additional chakra—the Spleen Chakra—located between the Creative and Solar Plexus Chakras. Her research also discovered the minor chakras that exist in the palms of hands, and soles of feet. Dr. Karagulla co-authored the book, *Through the Curtain*, with friend and theosophist Viola Petit Neal. The book was published in 1983 after Neal's death. A version of this table is published in the introduction of the book:

Chakra	Endocrine Gland
Base	Spine/Glandular System
Creative	Ovaries/Testes
Spleen*	Spleen/Liver

APPENDIX B

Solar Plexus........Adrenals/Pancreas
Heart...................Thymus
Throat.................Thyroid/Parathyroid
Third Eye............Pituitary
Crown.................Pineal

The table below is based on the research of Dr. Valerie Hunt, a professor of kinesiology at the University of California. Dr. Hunt has specialized in measuring human electromagnetic output to validate the existence of chakras. According to her research, the physical body emanates radiation in areas typically associated with the Seven Chakras. Her research data was mathematically measured by scientists in *hertz frequency* (Hz), the periodic speed of which something vibrates (movement) also known as *cycles per second*. Since the human eye can perceive only a small range of color, Dr. Hunt's research relied on information from auric readers and their use of clairvoyance. The results were remarkably consistent and these auric colors correlated with these frequency-wave patterns:

Color	Frequency
Blue	250-275 Hz plus 1200 Hz
Green	250-475 Hz
Yellow	500-700 Hz
Orange	950-1050 Hz
Red	1000-1200 Hz
Violet	1000-2000, plus 300-400; 600-800 Hz
White	1100-2000 Hz

[Editor's Note: The above table is derived from the book *Hands of Light*, by NASA research scientist and healer Barbara Brennan.]

Hunt's research expanded to include the frequencies of different types of individuals. She discovered the normal range for most people is around 250 Hz, which is the identical frequency range of the heart. However, when psychics were measured their frequency range was 400 to 800 Hz; mediums and channelers have a range of 800 to 900 Hz; and mystics—those continually connected to the I AM, or higher-self—were measured above 900 Hz. Cyndi Dale writes, "…the chakras can be stepping-stones to enlightenment, each inviting a different spiritual awareness and increasing the frequency of the subtle body."[7]

APPENDIX B

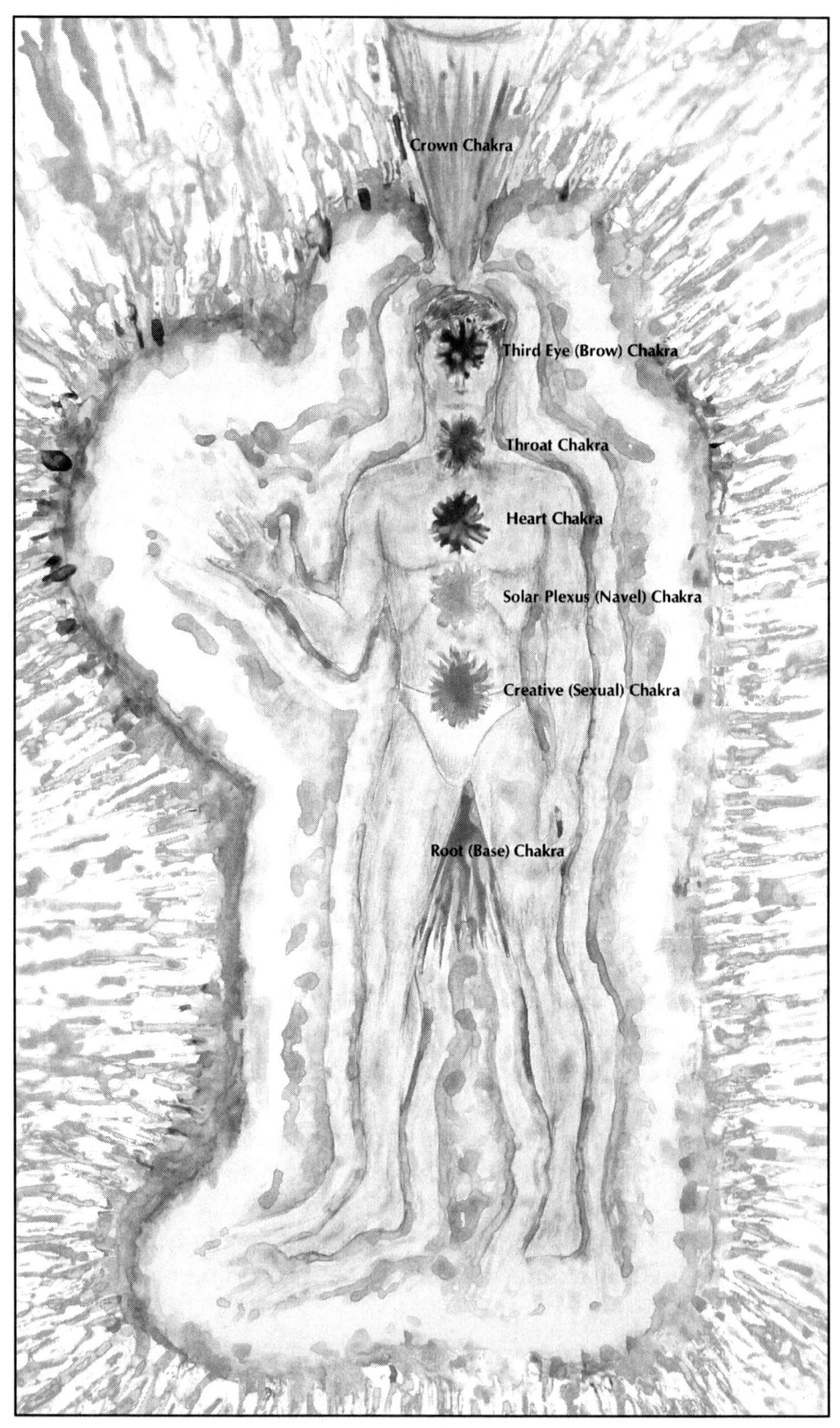

FIGURE 15-B
Layers of the Human Aura
The Hunan Energy System depicting the
Seven Major Chakras and Layers of the Energy Field

APPENDIX B

FIGURE 16-B
The Auric Blueprint
The *Auric Blueprint* depicting the
Seven Major Chakras and the
Energy Grids, Meridians, and Nadis

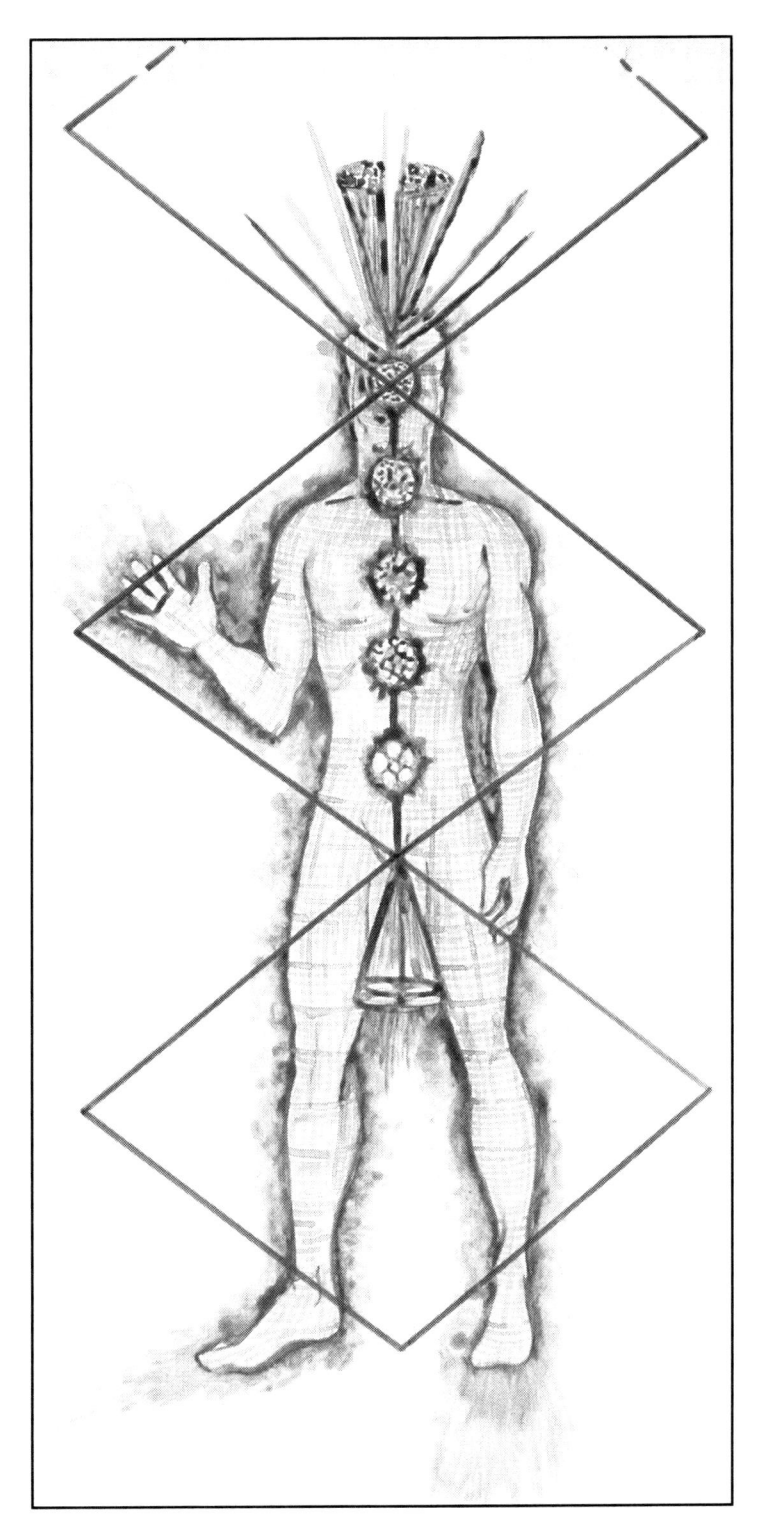

---

147   *The Golden City Series: Book Two*

APPENDIX B

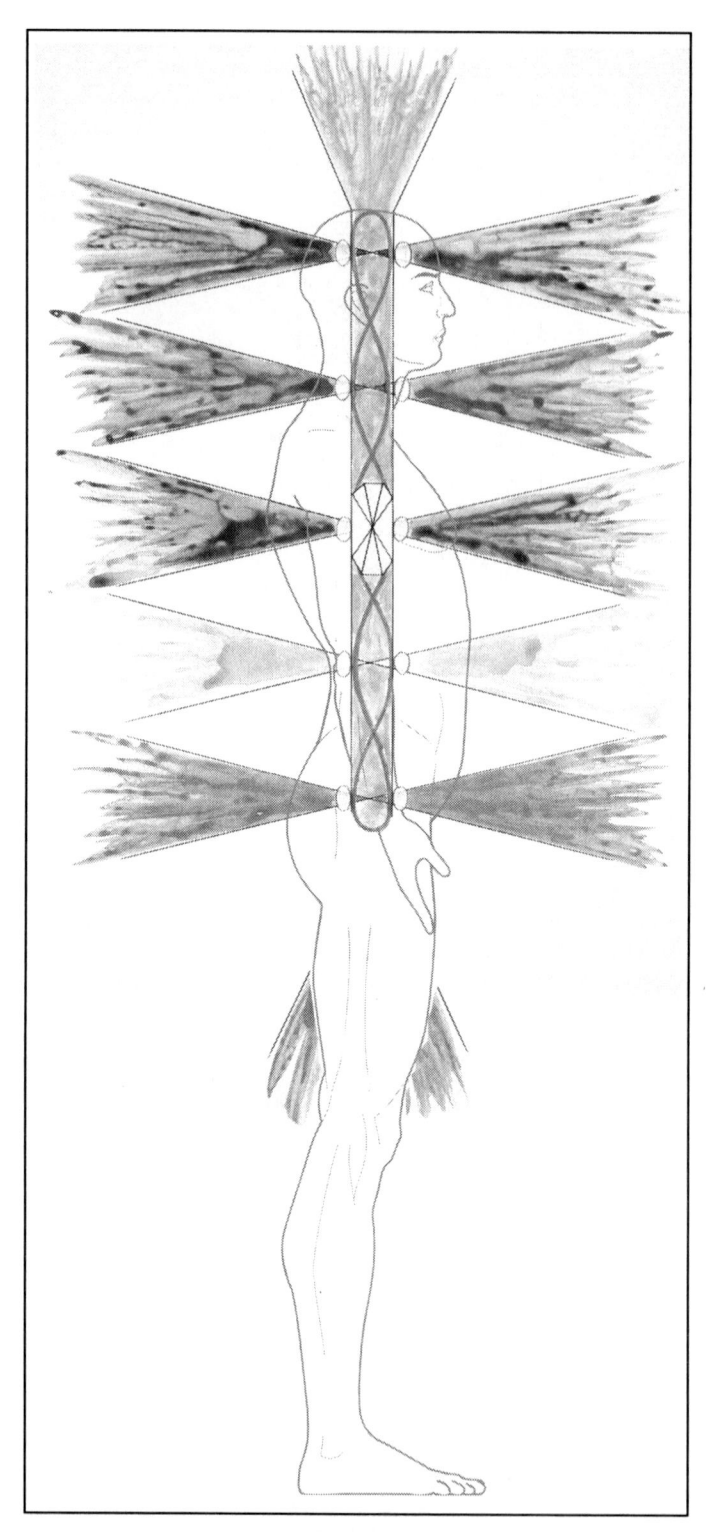

FIGURE 17-B
Golden Thread Axis
The *Golden Thread Axis* and
the Major Chakra System

APPENDIX B

First Chakra
Names: *Root Chakra, Base Chakra, Muladhara*

Ruling Planet:
    Average: Earth
    Evolved: Saturn
    HU-man: Mars

Colors:
    Average: Dark Red
    Evolved: Blue
    HU-man: Ruby

Rays:
    Average: Red
    Evolved: Blue
    HU-man: Ruby-Gold

Location: Base of spine—the perineum; the energy of this chakra flows between the legs downward and connects to Mother Earth.

Main Aspect: Security and the will to live; is grounded to our earth mother and lives in the present moment.

Astrological Signs:
    Lunar Current: Aquarius
    Solar Current: Capricorn
    Exaltation: Mars in Capricorn

Attributes: Due to the influence of Kali-Yuga on the human energy field, the average base or root chakras of most individuals are not in alignment with their environments. This may explain the lack of sustainability in many facets of current day affairs: economic, energy, climate, and government. This undeveloped chakra leads one to rashness and intensity without weighing the risks involved. However, this energy has good stamina and courage, which inevitably leads to development through the lunar current of Aquarius. Saturn rules elimination and support—the skeletal system, including the spine. Although it is a contracting planet and crude in nature, Saturn focuses and stabilizes the energies of the chakra towards structure, analysis, and science. Aquarius' sign of humanity civilizes the brash energies of the red Root Chakra, and Mars inevitably exalts in the solar current of Capricorn. This is the highest manifestation of Mars' qualities and the executive, hard-working efficiency of the *Divine Warrior* is present. The evolved base chakra resists disease and aging while focused on achieving goals through generous, protective acts.

APPENDIX B

Dark Side: Quick to anger and thinks it is okay to take from others; deceptive, reckless, and arrogant.

Second Chakra
Names: *Creative Chakra, Sexual Chakra, Sacral Chakra, Svadhisthana*

Ruling Planet:
- Average: Rahu (Moon's North Node)
- Evolved: Jupiter
- HU-man: Venus

Colors:
- Average: Orange
- Evolved: Yellow
- HU-man: White (In developmental states, pastel colors may be detected.)

Rays:
- Average: Will vary with each individual
- Evolved: Yellow
- HU-man: White

Location: Lower abdomen, between navel and genitals

Main Aspect: Procreation and creativity

Astrological Signs:
- Lunar Current: Pisces
- Solar Current: Sagittarius
- Exaltation: Venus in Pisces

Attributes: Rahu rules obsession and unpredictable behaviors, with a tendency towards materialism and worldliness. These lower energies influence the Creative Chakra in its developmental stages. Jupiter governs the reproductive system and the creative energy and the lunar current of this chakra in Pisces quickly evolves this chakra with wisdom, philosophy, spirituality, alongside a strong intuition and visionary ability. The lunar current of this chakra develops in Pisces and endows the individual with a nurturing and healing disposition, and a good family life with prosperous children. Jupiter's solar current in Sagittarius develops humanitarian social skills, and the capacity to inspire and lead others with progressive compassion. In the lunar half of Pisces, Venus exalts and is connected with the need to unite sex with love and harmony. The higher qualities of Venus and the White Ray are expressed through balanced artistic sensuality as the *Divine Feminine* is realized.

APPENDIX B

Dark Side: Overindulgent and too sacrificing; the individual may experience loss through misplaced sympathies, and is taken advantage of by marriage or partnership.

Third Chakra
Names: *Solar Plexus Chakra, Navel Chakra, Manipura*

Ruling Planet:
- Average: Jupiter
- Evolved: Mars
- HU-man: Sun

Colors:
- Average: Yellow
- Evolved: Dark Red (During development stages some orange may appear)
- HU-man: Ruby-Gold

Rays:
- Average: Yellow
- Evolved: Will vary throughout the development process, but will develop into the Ruby Ray.
- HU-man: Ruby-Gold

Location: Between the navel and base of the sternum

Main Aspect: An intense feeling (intuitive) chakra which is known as the Center of Power and Balance in relationship to everything in life

Astrological Signs:
- Lunar Current: Scorpio
- Solar Current: Aries
- Exaltation: Sun in Aries

Attributes: The Solar Plexus Chakra is our center of power, and distributes our ability to realize our goals and aspirations that inevitably lead to the fulfillment of our Dharma (purpose). Since this chakra manages digestion processes and digestive organs, it is also associated with our digestion of life's experiences as thoughts, feelings, and actions. Experience is the ultimate Guru, hence this chakra's affiliation with Jupiter in its seminal stages. Eastern systems relate digestion to the fire element, and as this chakra develops, it is associated with the planet Mars—considered by Vedic astrologers to be a good friend to Jupiter. The solar current of Mars in Scorpio manifests a strong warrior spirit with the ability to quickly resolve opposition with a sharp mind and intellect. However, as the Rays and chakra evolves, the lunar half of the energy current exalts the sun in Aries, and the quick, impatient temperament must integrate with the vital will.

APPENDIX B

The authority of the *Divine Father* is developed and realized through courage, leadership, innovation, and strength of character.

Dark Side: Too authoritative, dogmatic, impatient, active but incompetent, stubborn, and aggressive; these individuals are inept at sustaining or maintaining.

Fourth Chakra
Names: *Heart Chakra, Anahata*

Ruling Planet:
- Average: Mercury
- Evolved: Venus
- HU-man: Moon

Colors:
- Average: Green
- Evolved: Green to White (Pastel colors may be present during development)
- HU-man: White to Pink (Pastel colors of green and blue may be present during developmental stages.)

Rays:
- Average: Green
- Evolved: White
- HU-man: Pink

Location: The center of the chest; the heart

Main Aspect: Love and Relationships; our ability to feel compassion, forgiveness, and our own feeling of Divine Purpose—the Heart's Desire

Astrological Signs:
- Lunar Current: Taurus
- Solar Current: Libra
- Exaltation: Moon in Taurus; Saturn in Libra

Attributes: At the physical level the heart is the center of our body and emanates a thousand times more electricity and magnetism than our brain; and this is perhaps this chakra's foundational affiliation with the Green Ray.[8] As an individual evolves the spiritual heart must open beyond physical needs, and our attachments to new ideas, fads, fame, and money inevitably change. A mystical approach to life opens the heart and creates balance in thoughts, feelings, and actions. This is the movement of intelligence into Wisdom. This energetic movement is related to the Divine Feminine as art and beauty, with an overall humanitarian approach. As the heart evolves the lower solar energies, the frequencies of the solar current create the *Divine Will* through the

APPENDIX B

"higher principles of justice, order, and detachment, which are necessary in using our heart energy in the right way without bias or attachment."[9]

The lunar half of Venus evolves into the exalted Moon in Taurus. This is the birth of the *Divine Mother* within our heart and is the energy of openness, receptivity, generosity, and the fullness of life and love.

Dark Side: One may encounter over-indulgence, laziness, overly self-controlled, possessiveness, and jealousy; this makes one controlling in love, non-romantic, overworking, and fearful of change.

Fifth Chakra
Names: *Throat Chakra, Vishuddha*

Ruling Planet:
    Average: Saturn
    Evolved: Neptune, Mercury
    HU-man: Mercury

Colors:
    Average: Blue
    Evolved: Blue-Green (Aquamarine)
    HU-man: Green

Rays:
    Average: Blue
    Evolved: Aquamarine-Gold
    HU-man: Green

Location: Throat

Main Aspect: Expression of truth, emotion, creativity, knowledge, and the sciences; the Oral Tradition

Astrological Signs:
    Lunar Current: Gemini
    Solar Current: Virgo
    Exaltation: Mercury in Virgo

Attributes: Due to the influences of Kali-Yuga, Saturn's pressure on the Throat Chakra has decreased our command of languages, memory, and our ability to learn and absorb new information. Naturally, this limits human development and ambitions; but is good for focusing on details at a slower pace, especially in communication and self-expression. As the lunar current evolves this chakra in the sign of Gemini, an individual's thinking becomes developed, tactical, inventive, and quick-witted. The

APPENDIX B

mind readily absorbs music, literature, and technology. As the solar current evolves the Throat Chakra in the sign of Virgo, it reaches the point of exaltation and the sublime energies of the *Divine Messenger*. It is here that the intellect receives its highest levels of precision and advanced insight to readily absorb and express philosophically; initiate a quantum approach to the sciences; and receive advanced insight and intuition alongside a refined discrimination. This is the enlightened intellect of the Buddha.

Dark Side: Critical; lives in fantasy; demanding and argumentative; superficial, talks more than accomplishes; intellect interferes with common sense—*analysis paralysis*

Sixth Chakra
Names: *Third Eye Chakra, Ajna*

Ruling Planet:
    Average: Saturn
    Evolved: Moon and Sun
    HU-man: Jupiter

Colors:
    Average: Dark Blue, Indigo, Purple
    Evolved: Pink, Ruby, Gold
    HU-man: Yellow

Rays:
    Average: Blue, Violet
    Evolved: Pink, Ruby-Gold
    HU-man: Yellow

Location: Above and between the eyebrows

Main Aspect: The blending of thought and feeling as perception and projection for Co-creative activity

Astrological Signs:
    Lunar Current: Cancer
    Solar Current: Leo
    Exaltation: Jupiter in Cancer

Attributes: Solar and lunar currents meet and merge in the Third Eye Chakra, and due again to the lower energies of Kali-Yuga, humanity is yet to achieve the fulfillment of the Ajna Chakra. However, in the infant stages of the development of this chakra, the Third Eye is often subjugated by the other chakras, and is readily influenced by external factors; especially by social and cultural pressures via politics and religion. Disciplined use of visualization will open and develop the Third Eye and promotes the

APPENDIX B

expansion of engineering, science, and technology—areas humanity is currently developing as we enter the Golden Age of Kali Yuga. This promotes the evolution of the Third Eye Chakra through qualities of perception, sensitiveness, kindness, and wisdom through the lunar current of Cancer. The solar current of Leo further develops sensitivity through the royal sign of spiritual leadership. The developed chakra produces a blend of independent and intelligent insight that repels negativity with courage and stamina. At this stage, the chakra gains independence and initiates and directs the flow of consciousness. This gives rise to the exaltation status of the chakra, or the development of the Godman—the Divine HU-man, where the qualities of feeling and leadership expand into knowledge, devotion, merit, and a soft-yet-strong humane and spiritual ministration to humanity. This is the *Divine Guru.*

Dark Side: Over optimistic; indulgent; lazy; too sensitive and generous; susceptible to others troubles and becomes bossy, impatient, dominating and hot-tempered.

Seventh Chakra
Names: *Crown Chakra, Sahasrara*

Ruling Planet: All planets, including the Great Central Sun—the Galactic Center

Colors: White, Violet, Gold

Rays: All Seven Rays

Location: Top of or just atop of the head

Main Aspect: Connection to the spiritual planes

Attributes: The Seventh Chakra is perhaps the most unique of the seven chakras as this is where the Seven Rays enter the Chakra System. In the Hindu system the Crown Chakra is also known as the *Chakra of One-Thousand Petals* and "the petals represent the Sanskrit alphabet along with their twenty permutations."[10]

The Seven Rays, along with these subtle vibrations, govern and coordinate the other chakras according to the Divine Plan for the individual's spiritual growth and development for each lifetime. This chakra is easily located as it is the soft-spot at the top of the head in newborn babies. Some yogis claim as they liberate their Karmas from the earthly plane, Divine Rain falls from the petals of the lotus and dampens the head with the "dew of divinity."[11]

This chakra creates a sheath between the physical, astral, and causal bodies. As the HU-man fully develops and self-realizes through the Chakra System, the Ascension Process disintegrates the sheath and the soul is freed from the *Wheel of Karma.* According to certain Hindu traditions the freed soul enters into the three higher planes above the earthly body—Satyaloka, the *Abode of Truth.* Evolved yogis express this disintegra-

APPENDIX B

tion of the Anandamaya Sheath through the entrance into *Samadhi,* a state of bliss and transcendence of the Earth Plane.[12]

Satyaloka is the highest of the seven lokas in the Vedic Cosmology of created worlds, and is the alleged home of Brahma and the Gods.

Dark Side: Over optimistic; indulgent; lazy; too sensitive and generous; susceptible to others troubles and becomes bossy, impatient, dominating and hot-tempered.

[The information on the Seven Chakras was compiled from information contained in the I AM America Teachings from the School of the Four Pillars, Dr. David Frawley's, *The Astrology of the Seers, A Guide to Vedic (Hindu) Astrology,* William R. Levacy's, *Beneath a Vedic Sky, A Beginner's Guide to the Astrology of Ancient India,* and Cyndi Dale's, *The Subtle Body, An Encyclopedia of Your Energetic Anatomy.*]

APPENDIX B

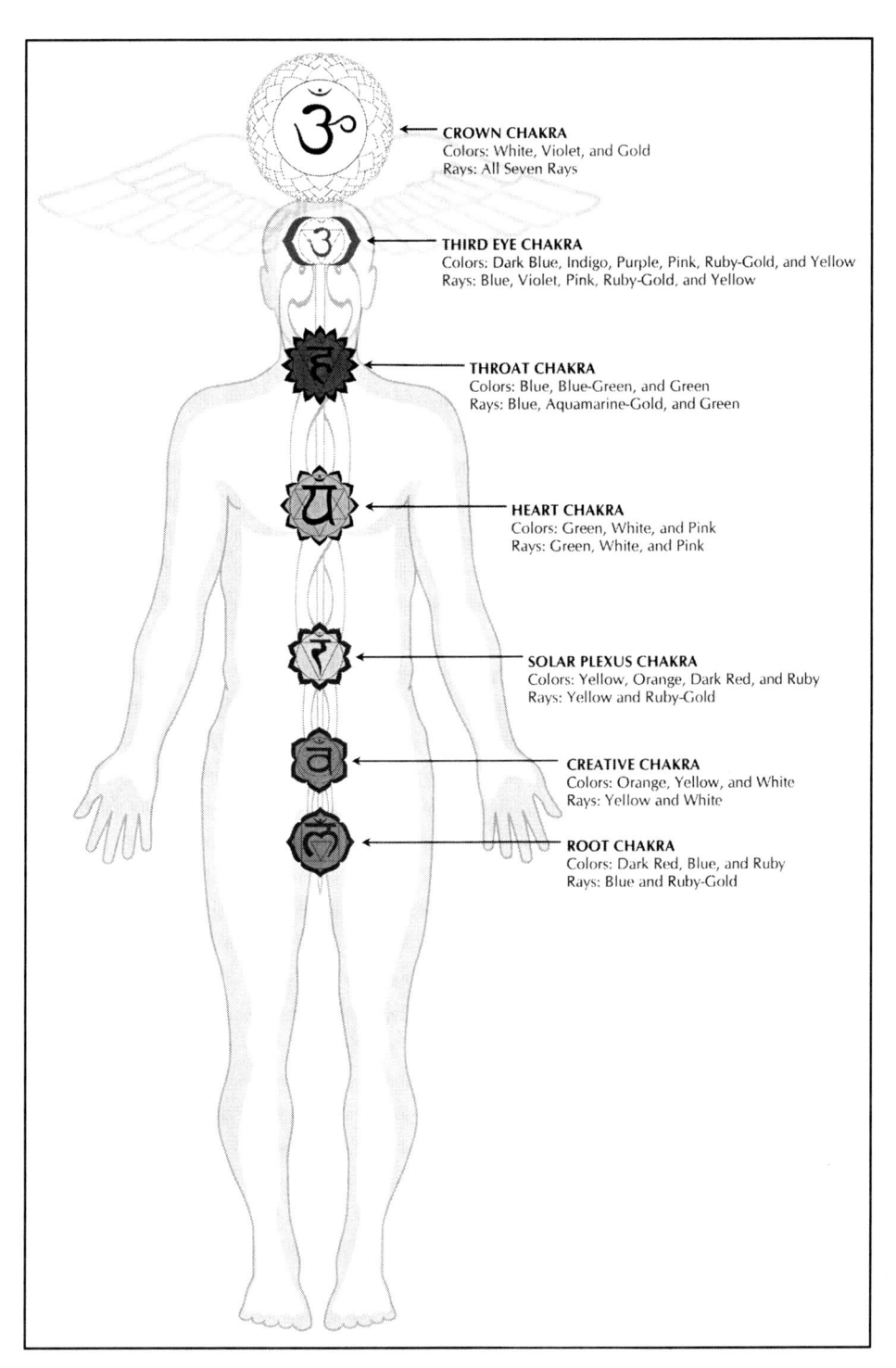

CROWN CHAKRA
Colors: White, Violet, and Gold
Rays: All Seven Rays

THIRD EYE CHAKRA
Colors: Dark Blue, Indigo, Purple, Pink, Ruby-Gold, and Yellow
Rays: Blue, Violet, Pink, Ruby-Gold, and Yellow

THROAT CHAKRA
Colors: Blue, Blue-Green, and Green
Rays: Blue, Aquamarine-Gold, and Green

HEART CHAKRA
Colors: Green, White, and Pink
Rays: Green, White, and Pink

SOLAR PLEXUS CHAKRA
Colors: Yellow, Orange, Dark Red, and Ruby
Rays: Yellow and Ruby-Gold

CREATIVE CHAKRA
Colors: Orange, Yellow, and White
Rays: Yellow and White

ROOT CHAKRA
Colors: Dark Red, Blue, and Ruby
Rays: Blue and Ruby-Gold

FIGURE 18-B
Kundalini System
The *Kundalini System* and the Seven Major
Chakras; the Ancient Caduceus

APPENDIX B

Will Chakras

Crown Chakra
Connects to the Galactic Center through our Solar Sun

Concentrative-Receptive Will

Expressive Will

Eight-Sided-Cell of Perfection
Houses the Unfed Flame, the Monad

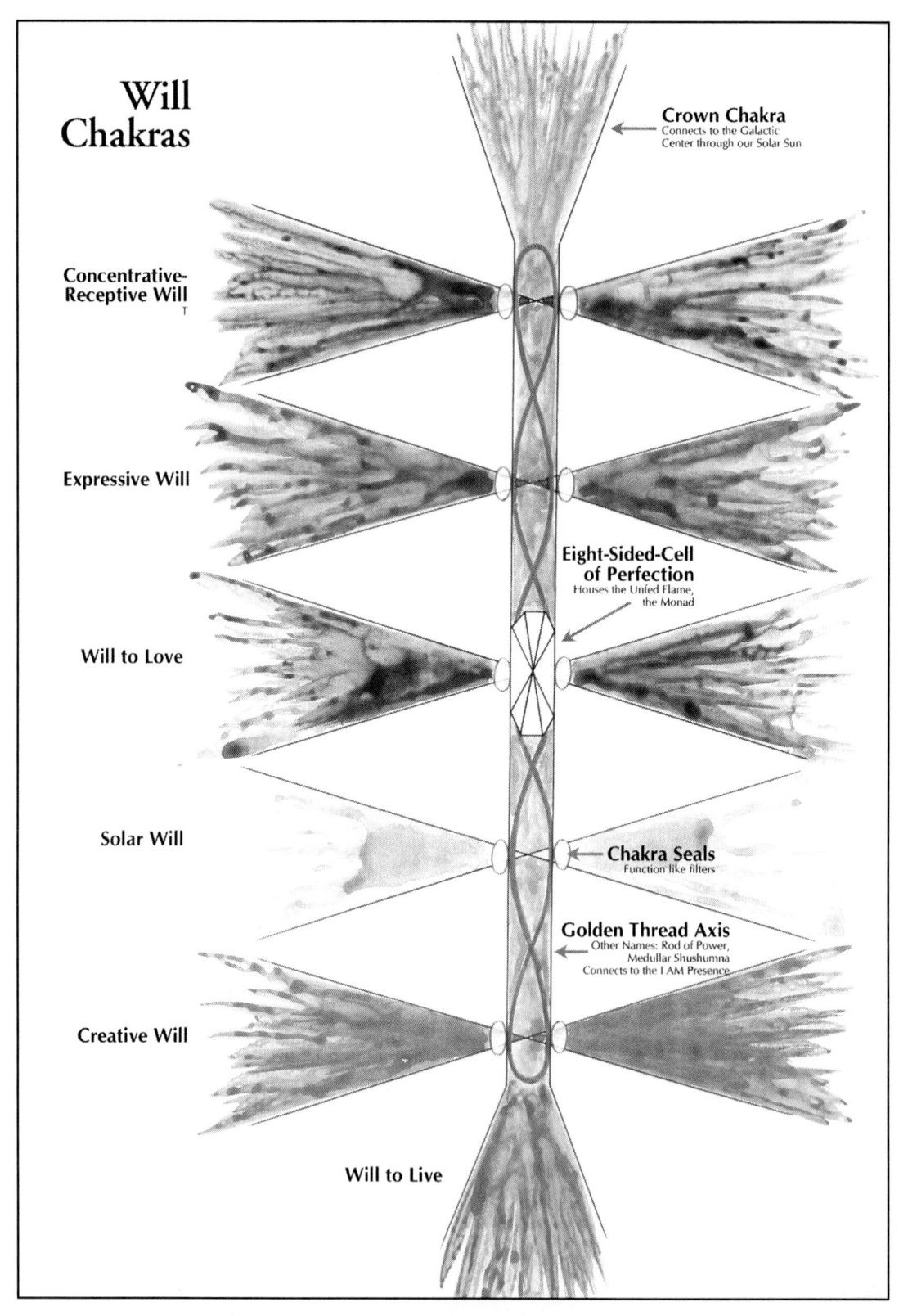

Will to Love

Solar Will

Chakra Seals
Function like filters

Golden Thread Axis
Other Names: Rod of Power, Medullar Shushumna
Connects to the I AM Presence

Creative Will

Will to Live

FIGURE 19-B
The Will Chakras
The Golden Thread Axis; Eight-Sided Cell of Perfection; and the *Will Chakras*.
(Side View: Left represents the back of the body; Right represents the front of the body.)

Light of Awakening

APPENDIX B

Will Chakras

The Will Chakras are a specific series of six chakras located on the back of the human spine and the Root Chakra (kundalini system), and enable the personal actions and choices of the individual. Like the Frontal Chakras, Will Chakras absorb and process light and sound energy from Ray Forces. The entire Human Chakra System affects the Human Aura. A chakra spins, in fact, in Sanskrit *chakra* literally means, "spinning wheel." The anatomy of a chakra contains both an outer portion and an inner portion. The inner portion of the chakra is comprised of sub-vortices; the number of sub-vortices varies according to the type of chakra. Chakra movement absorbs and releases the energy of the Rays. A healthy chakra absorbs Ray Forces through the clockwise movement of the outer chakra and releases the energies through the counter-clockwise movement of the sub-vortices. Will and Frontal Chakras both absorb and release energies; however, when energies enter a Frontal Chakra, the energy exits the Will Chakra; and vice-versa, when energies enter a Will Chakra, the energy exits through the Frontal Chakra. This flow maintains the health of the physical body through the balance of light and sound frequencies present in the Human Aura. Descriptions of the six Will Chakras follow:

1. Concentrative-Receptive Will: The ability to focus, while remaining open and receptive; centered and sensitive; Masculine and Feminine

2. Expressive Will: The will to express emotions and thoughts; the ability to communicate with clarity and personal truth; expansive and determined; Masculine

3. Will to Love: The Heart's Desire; Fulfills goals, aspirations, and desires conceived through the Creative Will. Nurturing and sustaining; Feminine

4. Solar Will: The ability to interact with others with personal power; receptive and protective; Masculine

5. Creative Will: The will to create through ideas, intentions, and goals; sensing; Feminine

6. Will to Live: Root Chakra connects to Mother Earth

APPENDIX B

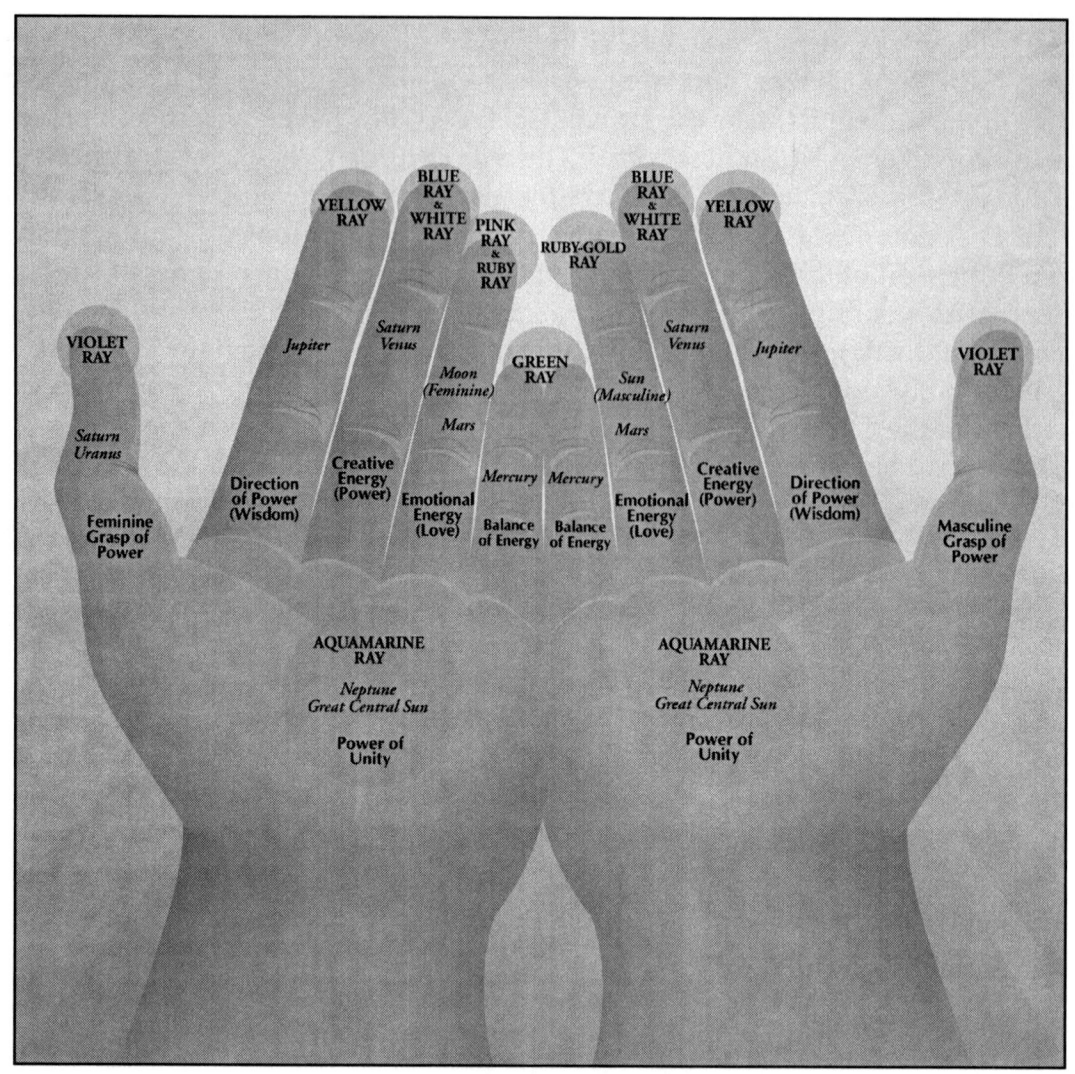

FIGURE 20-B
Flow of the Rays through the Human Hands
The Seven Rays and their corresponding locations and energy
emission from the human hands.

Flow of the Rays through the Human Hands

Certain Ray forces are said to flow through human hands. The preceding diagram illustrates each digit of the left and right hands, including their associated Ray Forces, assigned planets, and defining energies. Please note the difference between the feminine side (left) and the masculine side. Of the four terminal digits, the ring finger radiates perhaps the most powerful energy of the Rays—the left ring finger emits the feminine energies of the Pink Ray (moon) and the softer energies of the Ruby (Red) Ray (the healing, focused characteristics of Mars); while the masculine energies of the Gold Ray (sun) and the forceful, masculine energies of the Ruby (Red) Ray emanate from the right ring finger. The Ruby Ray of Mars evolves into developed physical energy and insight from violence and aggression. This Ray is also affiliated with the index

Light of Awakening

APPENDIX B

finger of both hands alongside Jupiter (Yellow Ray). The planets Saturn (Blue Ray) and Venus (White Ray) jointly govern the middle finger of the left and right hands. This energy represents converging sexual energy from the creative power of the developed will. Compassion, mercy, and forgiveness are characteristics of the Violet Ray. The thumb emits these qualities and represents an individual's developed grasp of power. As humanity evolves into the HU-man, according to the prophecies of the Ascended Masters, the Aquamarine Ray will emanate from the individual palms of both hands; it represents the power of unity and the consciousness of Unana.

A *mudra* is a symbolic ceremonial or spiritual gesture, mostly expressed by the hands and fingers. It is often used by evolved spiritual beings and Ascended Master to signify or emit spiritual energies. Mudras connect and link specific energy currents in the body, uniting Ray Forces symbolically and spiritually. Here are some classic Ascended Master mudras:

1. Index, middle, and ring fingers extended, thumb covers little finger: this is the mudra of love, wisdom, and power—a symbol of the Great White Brotherhood. In greetings the three fingers touch the heart (love), the third eye (wisdom), and the mudra is raised as a gesture to heaven (power).
2. Little and ring fingers touching palm; thumb and index and middle fingers extended. This is a common mudra often used by Sananda to transmit the energies of compassion, love, and mercy with force and direction.
3. Right hand held up, palm flat, all fingers extended pointing upward: greeting of unity and another symbol of the Great White Brotherhood.
4. Right hand held up, palm flat, all fingers extended pointing upward, left hand over heart. This mudra intentionally emits energies from the Heart Chakra of the individual and can be transmitted for Co-creative processes.

APPENDIX B

Flow of the Rays through the Human Feet

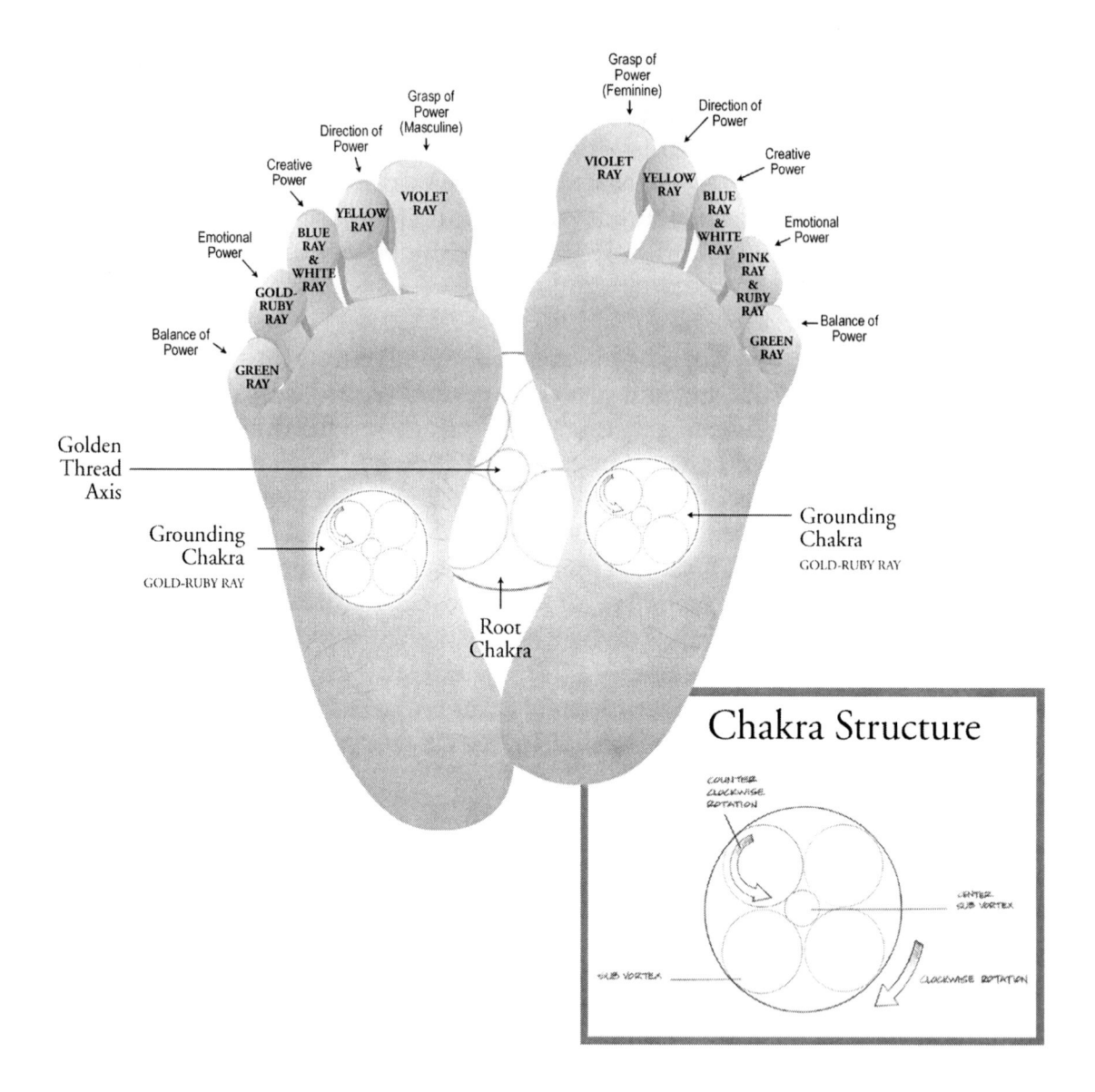

FIGURE 21-B
Movement of the Rays through the Human Feet

The Rays of Light and Sound move through the human feet in a similar manner like the flow of energy through the human hands. Two central grounding chakras anchor the human aura to the core of the earth, along with the Golden Thread Axis. This illustration also shows the structure of a chakra, and it contains four minor sub-vortices surrounding a smaller sub-vortex located in the center of the chakra. The Crown Chakra and Root Chakra are exemptions to this anatomy, and the Golden Thread Axis replaces the central sub-vortex in these chakras. The Crown Chakra connects the human aura to the I AM Presence; the Root Chakra connects the human aura to the core of the earth.

APPENDIX B

[1] *Hart de Fouw and Robert Svoboda, Light on Life, an Introduction to the Astrology of India,* (Penguin Books, 1996, New York, N.Y.), page 237.

[2] *Paramahansa Yogananda, Autobiography of a Yogi,* (Self-Realization Fellowship, 1946, Los Angeles, CA), page 400.

[3] *Right Brain vs. Left Brain,* http://www.funderstanding.com/content/right-brain-vs-left-brain, (2010)

[4] *Wikipedia, Sacred Geometry,* http://en.wikipedia.org/wiki/Sacred_geometry, (2010).

[5] *Wikipedia, Carolo Azeglio Ciampi,* http://en.wikipedia.org/wiki/Carlo_Azeglio_Ciampi, (2011)

[6] *Cyndi Dale, The Subtle Body, An Encyclopedia of Your Energetic Anatomy,* (Sounds True, Inc., Boulder, CO, 2009) Sounds True e-book.

[7] Ibid.

[8] Ibid.

[9] *David Frawley, The Astrology of the Seers: A Guide to Vedic (Hindu) Astrology,* (Passage Press, 1990, Salt Lake City, Utah), page 231.

[10] *Cyndi Dale, The Subtle Body, An Encyclopedia of Your Energetic Anatomy,* (Sounds True, Inc., Boulder, CO, 2009) Sounds True e-book.

[11] Ibid.

[12] Ibid.

APPENDIX C

Topics and Terms for Behind the Interplay

Planetary Life Forces
Writing Your Own Script
Service and Intention
The HU Sound Vibration
Teachings on Sound
Identifying Personal Sound Vibrations and Tones

Planetary Life Forces of Our Solar System

Vedic astrologers claim that our Solar System occupies the nine o'clock position in Sagittarius, in relationship to the Galactic Center. The Rishis of the prior ages of greater light traveled in their astral bodies to explore the planets, observe their qualities, and subsequently record the effect of the planets on humanity and life on earth. In fact, the bija-seed mantras attributed to the astrological planets are the alleged sounds of the planets heard by the Rishis as they journeyed to their faraway physical and supernal planes. Chanting each sound reproduces the life force and energy of the planet within our consciousness and spiritually activates the microcosmic Solar System within. Since the planetary force of the Rays structure and sustain life on earth, this supra-intelligence guides our thoughts, feelings, and actions. Dr. David Frawley writes, "The stars and planets are not just outer entities; they are alive within us as well. They exist within our own minds as our guiding lights. Or rather, one could say that our own inner lights take shape outwardly as the stars and planets to guide the world evolution. The outer comes from the inner and not vice versa, though the outer can affect the inner. The same Rays of creation function outwardly in the heavens and inwardly in the heaven of our own higher mind." [2]

Scientists theorize that our Solar System was formed 4.6 billion years ago after the collapse of a massive molecular cloud. The sun will burn itself into a white dwarf—about the size of earth—in about 5.4 billion years from now. The four smaller planets of Mercury, Venus, Earth, and Mars comprise the inner Solar System, and are dense and rocky, with minerals and metals with high melting points and no ring systems. The earth has one natural satellite—the moon—and Mars has two captured satellite asteroids: Deimos and Phobos. A system of yet again four more planets creates our outer Solar System, and they are known as the gas giants of Jupiter, Saturn, Uranus, and Neptune. These globes of hydrogen and helium with their gaseous rings and planet-sized moons circle our sun, along with the smaller planets, in the ecliptic plane inter-

APPENDIX C

spersed with comets, centaurs (dwarf planets that act like asteroids and comets), asteroid belts, and the Kuiper belt.[1]

The table below lists the spiritual life force of each planet in their highest potential as the representation of Cosmic Man:

Traditional Planets

Sun	Divine Self
Mercury	Divine Savior (Intelligence)
Venus	Divine Love
Earth	Divine Balance (Stability)
Moon	Divine Mind
Mars	Divine Energy
Jupiter	Divine Guru (Self-realization, Wisdom)
Saturn	Divine Will (Limitation and Impermanence)
Rahu (Moon's North Node)	Divine Expansion
Ketu (Moon's South Node)	Divine Liberation (Heaven)

Modern Planets

Uranus	Divine Awakening (Chaos, Change)
Neptune	Divine Inspiration (Imagination, Idealism)
Pluto	Divine Transformation (Renewal, Mastery)

Asteroids

Chiron	Divine Healer (Reconciliation)
Ceres	Divine Evolution (Cycles, Growth)
Juno	Divine Power (Relationship, Marriage)
Vesta	Divine Heart (Sacred Fire)

Harmony of the Spheres

Harmony of the Spheres is a philosophical concept associated with the notion of Sacred Geometry—that somehow everything in nature is organized according to a Divine Template. The Renaissance astronomer and mathematician, Johannes Kepler, was a proponent of *musica universalis,* music of the spheres. He viewed the movement of the cosmos in terms of a mathematical or providential harmony. Its foundation is rooted in Pythagorean tuning, a tuning technique that relies on a scale of intervals. These intervals are based on certain ratios, which can be applied to measure pitch—among something as small as notes on a page or as vast as the distances between planets. Pythagoras claimed an interval of one pitch exists between earth and moon; from moon to Mercury, an interval of one-half pitch; from Mercury to Venus, an interval of one-half pitch; from Venus to the sun, an interval of one and one-half pitches; from the sun to Mars, an interval of one pitch; from Mars to Jupiter, an interval of one-half pitch; from Jupiter to Saturn, an interval of one-half pitch; from Saturn to the *fixed stars*—stars which were believed to be one gigantic celestial sphere— an interval of one-half pitch. The chords of this ethereal music, however, can only be heard by those who have developed the *ears to hear*—clairaudience. The

APPENDIX C

mystic Manly Hall writes "The Pythagoreans believed that everything which existed had a voice and that all creatures were eternally singing the praise of the Creator. Man fails to hear these Divine Melodies because his soul is enmeshed in the illusion of material existence. When he liberates himself from the bondage of the lower world with its sense limitations, the music of the spheres will again be audible as it was in the Golden Age. Harmony recognizes harmony, and when the human soul regains its true estate it will not only hear the celestial choir but also join with it in an everlasting anthem of praise to that Eternal Good controlling the infinite number of parts and conditions of Being." [3]

Service

Service is described as a helpful act based on the Law of Love. According to the Twelve Jurisdictions, it is the fifth virtuous law for the New Times. This definition is expanded in *Behind the Interplay* and explains how service can balance and sometimes ameliorate difficult Karmas. Good Karma is often achieved through renunciation, detachment, discipline, and surrender to the Divine Will.

Intention

A deliberate, conscious thought that determines individual actions, the ensuing results, or both.

HU

HU is a sacred sound that represents the entire spectrum of the Seven Rays. That means when the sound is meditated on or chanted, HU can powerfully invoke the presence of the Violet Flame—the activity of the Violet Ray and its inherent ability to transform and transmit energies to the next octave. HU is also considered an ancient name for God, and it is sung for spiritual enlightenment. The spiritual leader, Harold Klemp, writes, "HU is woven into the language of life. It is the Sound of all sounds. It is the wind in the leaves, falling rain, thunder of jets, singing of birds, the awful rumble of a tornado ... Its sound is heard in laughter, weeping, (and) the din of city traffic, ocean waves, and the quiet rippling of a mountain stream. And yet, the word HU is not God. It is a word people anywhere can use to address the Originator of Life." [4]

Higher Self

Many Eastern religions and philosophies, such as Hinduism and Buddhism, refer to the immortal quality of mortality—the god within, the Higher Self. Referred to as Atma or Atman, this is the true identity of the soul that resides in the spiritual planes of consciousness. Though it is energetically connected to each individual in the physical plane, the Higher Self is free from the Karmas of the earth plane and identification with the material world. Ascended Masters refer to the Higher Self as the I AM Presence. Prayers and decrees to the Higher Self act with great efficacy, liberating the I AM presence from Third Dimensional restraints of time and space.

APPENDIX C

Sound

According to Ascended Master teachings, sound is the natural complement of light. In the physical world, sound is a wave of frequencies that travels through a solid, liquid or gas. Esoterically speaking, however, sound takes a different form: vibration. Master Teachers refer to sound as "vibrations per second." A musical note is akin to a musical atom; it is also a musical pitch with a certain frequency. Each Master Teacher is assigned a specific note.

El Morya	B
Mother Mary	F
Kuan Yin	F or C
Kuthumi	E or C
Saint Germain	G
Jesus Christ	E or C
Sananda	High F

Interplay

Reciprocal action and reaction

Teachings on Sound

1. Each Ray Force has a specific sound; Master Teachers claim that "light is complemented by sound."
2. Sound and light are best friends; these forces combine to form a *power*.
3. According to Saint Germain, sound seals and delivers *the essence of the lighted command*, which refers to the quality and force of sound. It allows light to carry forth a conscious intention in the Co-creative process.
4. Even though each Ray Force is assigned a sound vibration, chelas and students should meditate on a specific color instead. This process of discovery will lead the student to a personal experience of the sound. Sounds are individualized on a chela's various experiences, lifetimes on earth and working with certain Ray Forces.
5. Since sound will naturally seek its own level, the sound vibration heard during meditation is most harmonizing for that individual; it is a sound the student is best prepared to receive.
6. Some sounds carry high frequencies and may be difficult for a chela to absorb, harmonize, or apply at first. Revealing the individual sounds of the Rays within their light bodies through meditation assures a custom-fitted sound, designed to assist the interplay of light frequencies in the aura.
7. To find your unique sound for decree and mantra listen carefully for a recurring sound vibration during meditation.
    a. You will soon identify a particular sound beginning with a consonant (e.g., B, C, D, F, G, H …).
    b. This sound can be used to activate the Kundalini and open chakras and perception to higher spiritual arenas.

APPENDIX C

c. Often the intricate sounds heard during meditation are mathematical harmonies—an expression of the Interplay of the Rays—working to correct deficiencies of the Rays or harmonizing the Rays in the aura of the individual.
d. Continued use of the Violet Flame is always recommended while identifying and utilizing personal Ray tones and vibrations.
e. Saint Germain often reminds one "Only through your own practice can you experience the force of God working within you." This personal experience is vital to the evolutionary process; it incites clarity and understanding in the personal desire to serve the Light of God.

[1] Wikipedia, Solar System, http://en.wikipedia.org/wiki/Solar_System, (2009).

[2] David Frawley, The Astrology of the Seers, A Guide to Vedic (Hindu) Astrology, (Passage Press, 1990, Salt Lake City, UT), page 30.

[3] Manly Hall, The Secret Teachings of All Ages: An Encyclopedic Outline of Masonic, Hermetic, Qabbalistic and Rosicrucian Symbolical Philosophy, (The Philosophical Research Society, Inc., 1988, Los Angeles, CA), page 83.

[4] Harold Klemp, HU: A Love Song to God, http://www.eckandar.org/hu.html, (2010).

APPENDIX D

Topics and Terms for A New Day

The Internal Light—Ascension
New Wineskin—New Beliefs
Mother Earth, the Witness
Thoughts, Feelings, and Actions Model the Clay
A New Mind
Vertical Power Current
Birth of the Divine Will
Throw Away Old Beliefs and Fears
Sins against Self
Cast Time Aside
Live Life for Life!

Spiritual Prophecies
1. Humanity has been provided with the maps of the I AM America message of Earth Change. This information will help mankind embrace its Divine Destiny and prepare for a new evolutionary cycle.
2. Those who have opened their *eyes and ears* and are acquainted with the Fourth Dimension will develop *Clair Senses* and thus thrive in the Golden Age. Clair Senses include clairaudience (extrasensory sound); clairvoyance (extrasensory sight); clairsentience (extrasensory feeling); claircognizance (extrasensory knowing); clairgustance (extrasensory taste); clairalience or clairscent (extrasensory smell); clairtangency or psychometry (extrasensory touch); clairempathy or empath (extrasensory emotion); and the Channel (extrasensory mind and body).[1]
3. Humanity is prophesied to evolve and rise in vibration. This causes one to master and understand their internal light—a process also known as *Ascension*.
4. Many individuals have achieved Ascension throughout history. Still, this important time is *our* opportunity to accomplish this evolutionary goal. The following vibrational adjustments allow mankind to attain Ascension:
    a. Changes in the electromagnetic field of the human aura.
    b. The steady incidence of telepathy. This leads to Oneness, or Unity Consciousness—Unana.
5. Ascended Masters take on form *at will* to convey "Focused ideas, focused thoughts, and focused vibrations for the work at hand." Their stewardship of humanity guides individual and collective consciousness toward tremendous change.

APPENDIX D

Beliefs

A belief is a conviction or opinion of trust based on insufficient evidence or reality. This confidence may be based on alleged facts without positive knowledge, direct experience, or proof. According to the Master Teachers, beliefs may be negative, positive, or both. Often the unchallenged nature of beliefs form the nucleus of Co-creative activity. The spectrum of individual and collective beliefs can vary from innocent gullibility to unwavering religious faith and conviction.

Cellular Fear

According to the Ascended Masters, the emotion of fear accumulates in human light bodies and simultaneously affects DNA. An individual can carry some of this genetic toxicity to the astral plane after physical death. It can be passed on to the next lifetime until it is released by the soul.

Conscious Immortality

The consciousness of the soul is eternal and survives the physical death of the body; consciousness is immortal and does not cease to exist. This enduring light permeates all of our physical, emotional, mental, and spiritual bodies during, after, and between lifetimes. Recognition of this everlasting law naturally leads the individual to God Realization and the Ascension Process.

Divine Will

The notion of *Divine Will* has meant many things to many people, cultures, and belief systems. For instance, the Essenes—an ancient Jewish sect—believed that *Divine Will* was predetermined. Ascended Master teachings, however, accept Divine Will as the living presence of God—a presence that operates on individual free will.

Ever-present Now

Life in the consciousness of the ONE neither perceives the past nor anticipates the future: time loses all linear orientation. An individual in the ever-present now cognizes his or her experience in the continuous present with full recognition of inherent divinity.

Law of Cause and Effect

Every action causes an event, which is the consequence or result of the first. This law is often referred to as Karma—or the sixth Hermetic Law. "Every cause has its effect; every effect has its cause; everything happens according to law; chance is but a name for law not recognized; there are many planes of causation, but nothing escapes the law."[2]

Shroud of Darkness

Ascended Masters refer to the cloak of inhibiting beliefs that obscure the soul's direct contact with their innate Conscious Immortality as the *Shroud of Darkness*.

APPENDIX D

Vertical Power Current

The Vertical Power Current—also referred to as the Golden Thread Axis or the Rod of Power—is a cylindrical beam of light that centralizes its vertical energy along the spine. It enters through the Crown Chakra (top of head), exits through the Root Chakra (perineum), and generates the Kundalini (the untapped consciousness). This internal conduit channels the soul's vital current of energy; it simultaneously grounds the physical body to the earth and the I AM Presence. The Vertical Power Current activates several channels of energy within the body, including the Nadis (energy meridians); chi or prana (life force); and the seven chakras (energy centers). The vitality of the Vertical Power Current creates luminous human light bodies, also known as the layers of the human aura.

Structuring New Beliefs

One of humanity's greatest challenges today is restructuring personal beliefs to sync with those required during the New Times. Once that finally does happen, these new beliefs, attitudes, and ultimately social mores and cultural norms will begin to reflect the following ideas:

1. Consciousness is immortal; it cannot cease to exist or end. Often, Saint Germain affirms this new concept with the statement: "Down with Death! Conscious Immortality Arise!" Our consciousness survives death and our immortal thoughts travel with us from one lifetime to the next.

2. Conscious Immortality allows mankind to access comprehensive information surrounding certain circumstances or situations it may be encountering. The Ascended Masters explain that our inability to access our Conscious Immortality, described as *the Shroud of Darkness*, is the result of a personal inhibition of beliefs.

3. Humans unintentionally block information from other lifetimes through a belief in the Shroud of Darkness. As humanity enters the New Times, this soul-impeding energy is perceived and understood as nothing but an old-world credo. Humanity freely disregards this obstructive attitude, and in turn, embraces and maintains the New Consciousness.

4. As more thoughts grow toward our Conscious Immortality, individual feelings and actions obey the Co-creative pattern, and a new spiritual body is created. Known as the Ascension Body, this energy body is linked to the consciousness of Unana and to Mother Earth.

5. Since Mother Earth witnesses each and every life experience our souls encounter on earth, the Master Teachers often refer to her as the *Grand Teacher*. She assists the soul through life's continuous journey and tries to unify each individual from within. Her work readies the consciousness for physical birth and helps it identify levels of conscience. This process deepens the experience of Unity Consciousness. The Ascension and our Adeptship in Co-creation are achieved through this greater unification.

6. At this time in history, Mother Earth—as the cosmic being Babajeran—has offered to assist every individual effort to build the Ascension Body and to give aid to humanity's mass evolution and Ascension into the light.

APPENDIX D

Prophecies of Change

1. Ascended Masters perceive Golden City Vortices as sources of resplendent and revitalizing energy. Mother Earth has Co-created and Co-manifested the energies of Golden City Vortices to help humanity develop spiritually at this important time.

2. The anomalies of Time Compaction may make it difficult to identify and recognize our inner truth—our Conscious Immortality—our Divine Destiny. The deterioration of time confuses our reality. Meanwhile, constant illusions interfere with our ability to recognize important natural laws. Golden Cities are said to eliminate this distress; their energies help individuals begin to carefully, yet simply, recognize and understand the Law of Cause and Effect. The ever-present spiritual teachings of Mother Earth and the Elohim, along with the pervasive purity of Golden City Vortices, will help individuals navigate the illusiveness of Time Compaction.

3. The unwavering presence of Mother Earth and the Elohim in the Golden Cities initiates consciousness, which accelerates the ascension of body, mind, and soul. This important connection instigates a telepathic rapport with life (Unana), immortality, and the relationship to the ONE.

4. Saint Germain states "Life is for life, and death is an illusion." Comprehension of this spiritual subtlety removes Cellular Fear, which has been held for many lifetimes. Ascended Master teachers encourage the release of fear, especially the fear of physical death.

5. Indeed, it is our choice to start over and commence a New Day and a New Time. Saint Germain compares thoughts, feelings, and actions to clay on a potter's wheel—the medium is shaped by choices and the will. "The hands of God are your hands upon this piece of clay… through your choice and your will you begin anew."

6. Humanity is moving toward Unity Consciousness—Unana. This internal evolution within every individual creates the New Times, the Golden Age. According to Saint Germain, the prophesied changes of devastating Earth Changes can be thwarted if enough individuals embrace constructive change.

7. Mother Earth has offered herself to help humanity receive positive, constructive change. The acceleration of Ray Forces engenders the following results:
    a. A collective forgiveness among humanity. The release of past inequities and injustices—little hurts and little harms;
    b. The conscious light for the New Times and a New Age is planted within every heart;
    c. The individual will is realigned to realize the Divine Purpose;
    d. Humanity enters the realms of light—the spiritual liberation of Ascension.

8. Golden City Vortices are intentionally located around the planet, enticing people to seek out these spiritual locales and experience the healing energies within.

9. The Golden City Vortex of Wahanee radiates the energies of the Violet Flame.

10. The accelerated energies of Mother Earth—Babajeran—permeate the water, air, and plant life contained in Golden City Vortices. When ingested, these natural resources will help individuals increase their vibrations.

APPENDIX D

11. Certain Ascended Masters are assigned to specific Golden Cities. The presence of the Ascended Master provides additional vibration and consciousness-raising energy, which concentrates the spiritual focus of the Vortex. El Morya's presence, for example, disburses energies of the ONE throughout the Golden City of Gobean. This enables chelas, students, and vortex-seekers to co-opt the spiritual characteristics of Truth, Harmony, Cooperation, and Peace. Even brief exposure to the Gobean Vortex will compel light bodies to absorb these spiritual qualities. Thus, vortex-seekers are initiated into the consciousness of Unana.

12. Ascended Masters focus higher frequencies and spiritual energies on Golden City Vortices for the sake of mankind. The benefits for humans include a greater understanding of the ONE; a connection with the Earth Mother Babajeran; a unification with the I AM Presence; and a link with the Hierarchy of the Great White Brotherhood—both ascended and unascended members.

13. Until dysfunctional patterns of the past are identified and released, the New Times—or Golden Age—will be difficult to realize. Once emotional freedom is attained, however, one can fully accept a positive, hopeful future and grasp the *Ever-present Now*. According to the Ascended Masters, the Ever-present Now fluidly embraces the Oneship and gives our individual divine gifts and talents purposeful expression.

14. Traveling to Golden Cities to receive spiritual blessings and vibrational quickening is not necessary. In fact, other means and methods to accelerate thoughts, feelings, and actions do exist. Even so, experiencing Golden City energies firsthand gives students an advantage: prophesied perceptions of time are altered and the body's sleep requirements are decreased.

El Morya's Spiritual Teachings on Starting Anew—Restructuring Beliefs, Old Patterns, and Creating a New Mind

1. First, identify your intention. The word intention derives its meaning from the Latin word *intentio*, or *purpose*. Further Latin derivations of *proponere*—purpose—means I declare or I propose. It is based on the Latin root word *pono*: *to put* or *to place*. The intentions, purposes, and thoughts we plant in our consciousness, according to El Morya, will define certain outcomes and subsequent actions.

2. Our intention should properly reflect our purpose and plan: it should closely align or be in harmony with our will. Since our will is simply defined as *the individual actions chosen*, El Morya asks that we carefully consider our choices as a reflection of our will. The Ascended Masters often refer to the will as the *Vertical Power Current*.

3. The inspiration to change is always found inside our hearts—this decision usually has no outer influence. Therefore, change often comes from internal thoughts and feelings. According to El Morya growth is "sparked from within" and travels energetically through its own current. Consider again the Vertical Power Current. Kundalini energy flows upward along its midline channel, influencing the Seven Chakras and an individual's light bodies.

APPENDIX D

4. The creation of a new mindset often involves aligning the individual will to the Divine Will; however, El Morya's teachings state that this is not necessary. To restructure old patterns, beginners may choose instead to focus on an unattained desire or a simple wish. As time moves forward and the chela gains experience with this practice, intention becomes infused with conscience. This is the birth of the purposeful Divine Will.

5. Equality is the underlying theme of any fresh start. Realizing the God-force within empowers "the body, the mind, and inevitably the consciousness to start fresh." Recognizing our equal divinity with the God-source induces new levels of harmony and cooperation—necessary components to achieving Ascension. El Morya suggests meditation to identify self-inhibiting beliefs, patterns, and fears. Discovery and identification of these limitations prepare our consciousness to release old ways and embrace new beginnings. "When one releases these fears, one becomes ready to begin anew! Make the choice from within."

6. Take the time to evaluate your life; identify situations and circumstances that are not working. This may be difficult so have courage. Then write an outline of a personal plan you see for your life. Meditate upon this plan. "Have the courage to feel it, live it, and act it out," suggests El Morya. As a result of this process you'll gain experience and knowledge of what works for you and what doesn't.

Write and Burn Technique

The Write and Burn Technique helps students and chelas transmute any and all unwanted situations and circumstances, primarily undesirable dysfunctional life patterns. A venerated practice of the Ascended Masters, this type of journaling involves a handwritten letter—a petition—to the I AM Presence for Healing and Divine Intervention. The process encompasses two objectives: identifying and releasing unwanted and outdated energy or attracting and manifesting new and evolving energies. After the letter is written, it is then burned, either by fire or by light. Most students prefer to burn by fire. If, however, you choose to burn by light, place the document under a light source for twenty-four continuous hours. Insidious problems and complex-manifestation petitions may require up to one week of light exposure. The success of the light method and the subsequent acceptance of a petition depend on the reliability of the light source; the concentration of light must be continuous and without problems, e.g. blackouts, burnouts, and so on. If the issues are profound, you may need to probe deeper by identifying and addressing personal problem or life patterns. You may also want to consider rephrasing your approach to the problem, rewriting the letter, or both. Write and burn templates are provided below.

A. **Transmute and Release Energy Patterns:** Make one handwritten copy of this letter. *In the name of I AM THAT I AM, I release this to the Universe to be transmuted. (List the energy or behavior patterns you have identified. Some students also insert various alchemic decrees to the Violet Flame to dissolve, consume, and transform the energy.)* Sign and date the letter. Burn the letter by fire or by light.

APPENDIX D

B. Attract and Manifest New Energy Patterns: Make two handwritten copies of this letter. *In the name of I AM THAT I AM, I release this to the Universe to be fulfilled, maintained, and sustained in perfect alignment to the Divine Will. (List the new energy or behavior pattern you would like to Co-create.)* Sign and date the letter. Burn one copy by fire or by light. Keep the other copy in a sacred place (e.g. personal altar, family bible, favorite spiritual book) until you have achieved your goal or desired behavior change, and then burn that copy by fire.

Ascension Teachings of El Morya

1. Release the concept of drudgery! Seize life and all of its amazing experiences and gifts. "Live life for life!" Embrace the interconnectedness that exists in all circumstances and situations.
2. Use of the Violet Flame evokes the Blue Ray into action through light bodies. The Blue Ray clarifies intentions and assists the aligning of the will.
3. Time spent alone allows the unessential to fall away. Embrace spiritual simplicity when it comes to healing, solace, and important inner reflection. These principles engender introspection and inspired answers.
4. Don't expect to receive answers right away! El Morya encourages spiritual students to cast aside time. Some students may only need one day to identify their greater plan and connection to the ONE; for others, this may take many years. El Morya reminds us to remain patient with ourselves and not measure our results by earthly, illusive time. Personally integrating our experiences and feeling Unity from within are essential.

Saint Germain's Teachings on Starting Anew

The Violet Flame is known for its comprehensive healing properties, especially in matters of self-transformation and Karmic balancing. Saint Germain suggests the use of the Violet Flame to mitigate the following:

1. Harmful Cycles: release outdated, broken, and dysfunctional patterns. Lack of perfection: self-doubt, worry, and guilt. Saint Germain suggests the following decree to diminish fears of all kind:

Violet Flame I AM, God I AM.
Violet Flame, come forward in this instant.
Manifest perfection in, through, and around me!
Violet Flame I AM, God I AM Perfection, Violet Flame.

This decree is powerful enough to crack the voltage of the Blue Flame within the will. Its power is on a par with the electricity-producing force of lightning. Uttering this decree will create the *Lightning Crack of Divine Intervention*. The simple decree, "Violet Flame I AM, God I AM Violet Flame," from Saint Germain is meant for everyone. It instantly infuses the Violet Flame in our hearts. This decree lifts human-

APPENDIX D

ity out of suffering, limitation, death, and destruction, and into the hopeful vista of a New Day.

2. Forgiveness of Self: The Violet Flame assists the forgiveness of self. Use of its transforming fires transmutes any type of guilt. The Violet Flame is particularly helpful in transmuting the cause and effect surrounding memories that harness our consciousness with negativity and suppress our spiritual growth and evolution.

3. Sins of Self: Our own perceptions keep us trapped in a paradigm of death, decay, destruction, and catastrophe. Saint Germain sees this as a *sin against self* and encourages the dismantling of these destructive forces by applying the restorative energy of the Violet Flame and its Ray of transmuting light.

4. Know Thyself: Self-knowledge, along with the acknowledgement of our own doubts, limitations, strengths, and talents, is a key component of personal freedom.

---

[1]*Barbara Murphy, The Clairs,* http://www.quantumpossibilities.biz/clairs.htm, (2010).
[2]*The Kybalion,* http://www.kybalion.org, (2010).

APPENDIX E

Topics and Terms for A Quickening

The Fires of Purification
Living in New Dimensions and the New Times
Teachings on the E-motion
Human Gravity
The Violet Plume
The Gobean Star and Adjutant (Strategic) Points
The Light is without Judgment or Shame
The Reality of Oneness
Gobean Star and Doorways

Focus
   A central point of attraction, attention, or activity; often Ascended Master teachings refer to a *focus* as an intention, prayer, or meditation for spiritual growth.

Harmony
   Harmony finds its root in the Greek word *harmonia*, which means joining, concord, or music. However, when referred to in Ascended Master teachings, Harmony likely means *agreement*. Harmony is the first virtue of the Twelve Jurisdictions; it is based on the principle of agreement.

Prophecies of Change
   1. We are entering a time when we will be tested at many levels, including personally and spiritually.
   2. The effects of Time Compaction permit an individual to experience a constant arena of choice, which in turn, allows the fulfillment of a greater multitude of desires.
   3. Encountering and fulfilling many desires creates stress and tremendous tension. Though this satiation actually aids the liberation process, individuals encounter the closure of many different circumstances and situations as well. The Ascended Masters call this constant cycle of gratification and termination the *Fires of Purification*.
   4. The fires of self-purification move many individuals toward refined experiences of the Co-creative process. This is also known as *Instant-Thought-Manifestation*.
   5. Time Compaction helps many individuals to suddenly understand their personal thoughts, feelings, and actions.

APPENDIX E

6. Instant-Thought-Manifestation prepares consciousness to enter into the ONE—Unana.
7. Unity Consciousness encourages humanity's collective movement as "One Body of Light."
8. Humanity will experience an entirely New Dimension upon the birth of Unity Consciousness in the New Times.
9. Time Compaction opens the akashic records of prior lifetimes and purposely exposes many thoughts, feelings, and desires of the past. Our ability to define, understand, and positively heal and create with this morass of energy will usher our entrance into the New Times.

APPENDIX E

The Co-creative Thought Process as taught by Saint Germain

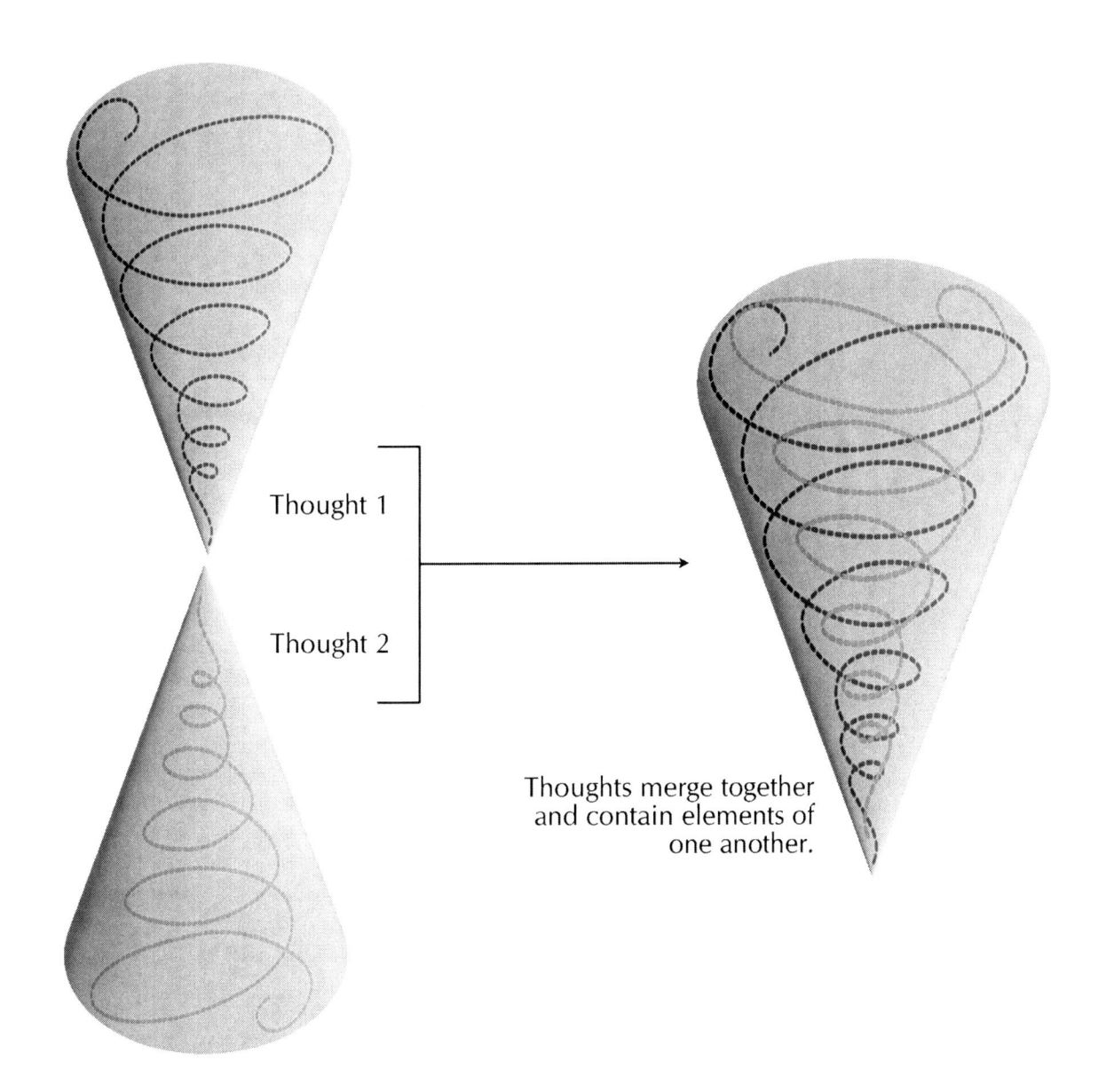

Thought 1

Thought 2

Thoughts merge together and contain elements of one another.

FIGURE 1-E
The Co-creative Thought Process
A diagram of the Co-creative thought process as diagrammed by Saint Germain in *The Quickening*.

APPENDIX E

The Co-creative Thought Process Under Time Compaction

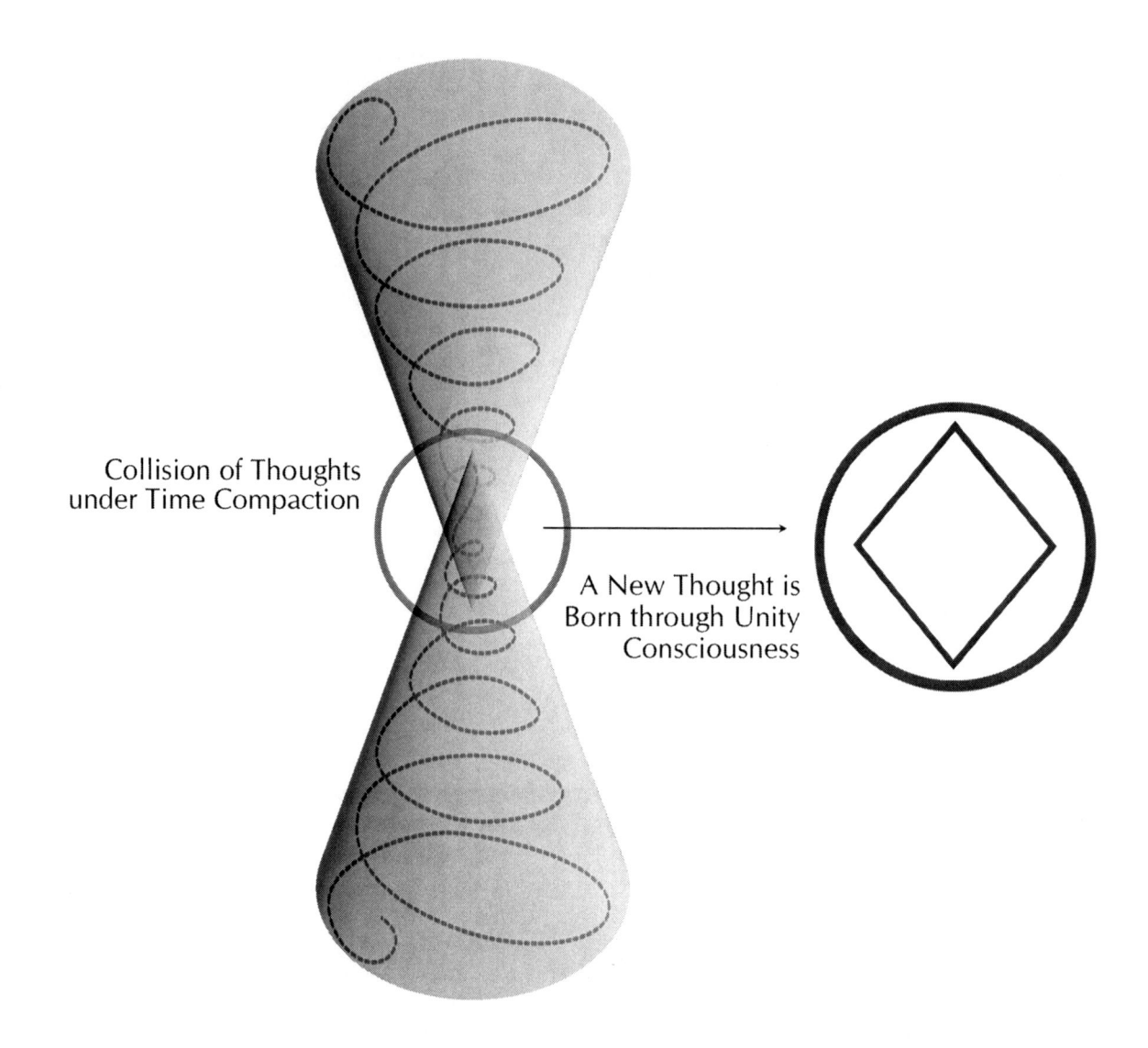

Collision of Thoughts under Time Compaction

A New Thought is Born through Unity Consciousness

FIGURE 2-E
Thoughts and Time Compaction
Time Compaction changes our thought patterns through the Co-creative process, and introduces a new thought that functions beyond dualistic identity. This ushers our entrance into Unity Consciousness, the ONE, and the New Times.

Light of Awakening

APPENDIX E

FIGURE 3-E
Native American Butterfly Symbol

The diamond symbol is perhaps one of the most sacred geometrical designs, and its esoteric meaning is linked to immortality, harmony, time and space, and the Ascension Process. It's enclosure in a circle represents the consciousness of ONE, Unana, and humanity's spiritual transformation process and entrance into the New Times.

Native Americans utilize the imagery of the diamond in the familiar design known as the butterfly. The butterfly lives a migratory existence, and in one lifetime may travel thousands of miles. Indigenous tribes welcome the annual return of the butterfly as the spiritual *Homecoming*. Most symbologists identify the butterfly as an icon of metamorphosis, transformation, and rebirth; however, the yearly return of the colorful Monarch also implies a profound metaphor of the soul's long journey to its true home. *Avia Venefia* writes about this insightful connection, "This encapsulates the divine journey in which man is born, moves through his world ever-gleaning more insight into his true identity and finally returns to the site of his first breath to realize he is immortal in his existence because of the path he chooses. In other words, man leaves a legacy, which is his key to immortality."

FIGURE 4-E
The Dagaz Symbol

The Runic Alphabet, based on Germanic languages before the Latin alphabet was embraced, features a butterfly shaped symbol—*Dagaz*. It is possible the twenty-fourth symbol is derived from Lepontic inscriptions from ancient northern Italy; however, Dagaz is associated with this Anglo-Saxon poem, "Day, the glorious light of the Creator, is sent by the Lord; it is beloved of men, a source of hope and happiness to rich and poor, and of service to all."[1] Esoteric symbologists associate the Dagaz with the spiritual concepts

APPENDIX E

of awakening, insight, clarification, epiphany, and new beginnings. Venefia writes, "It is also emblematic of time and space as complimentary elements. This rune speaks of the partnership between night and day with the center-point represented as the dawn."[2] The ancient Dagaz possesses similarity to Saint Germain's illustration of thoughts under Time Compaction; a metaphor to the dawn of the New Times and humanity's prophetic embrace of non-dualistic spiritual consciousness.

Ancient European groups often used the diamond as a symbol of life and depict the birth canal through the diamond motif. This association with the feminine and the birth of the New Energies through the cultivation of the intuition and the opening of Humanity's Heart is included in Saint Germain's new emblem for humanity's spiritual evolution.

E-motion

E-motion plays a critical role in the Co-creative process by melding and balancing thoughts and emotions. E-motion is also considered a type of "charge," which ignites and propels a kernel of thought-feeling into action. This charge represents the all-important impetus that compels and characterizes Co-creation. Enthusiasm, joy, and passion are essential components of a harmonious E-motion and Co-creative process. Anger, frustration, and revenge are the essential activators of the disharmonious E-motion. The harmonizing vibration of sound is sometimes defined as feeling.

Time of Tribulation

According to prophecies, humanity and planet earth may experience an era of conflict, struggle and cataclysmic Earth Changes—known as the Time of Tribulation. This devastating period can be thwarted, however, depending on the quality and quantity of mankind's collective spiritual growth and evolution. Darkness and negativity may be recalibrated if humanity can raise its spiritual conscience.

Discharging Negative or Disharmonious Situations

Holding on to negativity perpetuates individual and collective darkness. Moving toward spiritual growth, however, is about releasing adversity and replacing it with light. Saint Germain recommends the following steps to alleviate personal discord:

1. Using the Violet Flame on a daily basis provides assistance during self-purification.
2. Time spent alone, in the solace of mediation and silence, can quell disharmonious E-motion. This practice calms the mind and eases thoughts.
3. *Resting the E-motion*, that is, quieting the triggers of disharmonious thoughts and feelings can help achieve serenity.
4. According to Saint Germain, serenity ignites the true fires of freedom, which assists our return to wholeness, grace, and harmony while living in difficult times.
5. Saint Germain offers the following decree to discharge negativity and disharmony:
    Mighty Violet Flame, come forth through the I AM that I AM.
    Mighty Violet Flame, from the Grace of the Divine Heart, I AM!
    Violet Flame, come forth.
    Blaze in, through and around, all that keeps me from my Divine Path!

APPENDIX E

Violet Flame I AM, God I AM Violet Flame!
So be it.

(Sing the Bija-seed mantra of *HU*—a sound vibration prayer to the Creator/Creative Force; call upon the assistance of Master Teachers and spirit guides before uttering this decree.)

The Violet Plume

According to the Master Teachers, in ancient times of greater light on earth, the masses frequently used the Violet Flame to achieve spiritual growth. As a result, it increased to such strength and power it became a visible, ubiquitous violet-purple light in the human aura—the atmosphere was suffused with it. Meanwhile, the Rays of our sun and the luminous moon continuously reflected its vibrant lavender tone day and night. As humanity entered Kali-Yuga, the final stage of the dark age, and consciousness denigrated on the earth, the Violet Plume retreated to the subtle tones often observed at sunrise and sunset. Darker shades and vibrations of the Violet Plume can also be detected during certain phases of the full moon.

Teachings on the Golden Cities by Saint Germain and El Morya in the Quickening

1. Inside Golden Cities, the Ascended Masters and Babajeran—Mother Earth—will interact to create peace, stillness, harmony, and an understanding of the ONE during the Time of Tribulation on earth.
2. The Stars of Golden Cities consolidate the energy of that city's qualifying Ray, focusing its energy on a central location. The Master Teachers say that energy is concentrated in its most "direct force" in these specific areas.
3. The Star of the Golden City of Gobean is activated along with other Stars of Golden Cities during the Time of Change. Golden City activations create magnetism and psychic gravity inside the vortex. This type of radiation pulls students, chelas, aspirants, and initiates toward these geophysical locations for ceremony, prayer, and meditation. As humanity enters the New Times, many students will move to Golden City Stars to cultivate the spiritual attribute inherent in each Golden City Vortex. *See following activation table.* [Editor's Note: See *Points of Perception, Appendix B, Activations and Subtle Energies.*]
4. Each Golden City Star is a template of perfect thought, perfect feeling, and perfect action. These energies can be accessed and integrated for spiritual growth and evolution.
5. Certain Strategic Points inside Golden Cities are prophesied to physically manifest the energies necessary to move earth and humanity toward the New Times. [Editor's Note: See *Points of Perception, Adjutant Points.*]
6. Geophysical points inside the Gobean Golden City Vortex and the Star of the Gobean Vortex increase psychic awareness. Individuals who travel to, meditate in, and live near these geophysical points will develop spiritual insight and knowledge that will assist the manifestation of their choices and transformation and harmony processes while working within groups.

APPENDIX E

7. The infusion of Golden City energies present in the Stars and Adjutant Points of Gobean create an inner harmony with the Divine Will.
8. Stars and Adjutant Points of Golden Cities are interconnected. This connectivity first travels through the Stars of Golden Cities, then onward toward the Adjutant Points. Energies are subsequently disbursed throughout the Vortex. This is known as the Golden City Network, which El Morya refers to as *Template of Consciousness*.
9. El Morya, Michael the Archangel, and Hercules the Elohim hold the Blue Ray in the Gobean Vortex. The Blue Ray blesses humanity with harmony in all of its creations for the New Times.
10. To sharpen your understanding of the Divine Intervention of Harmony, El Morya suggests traveling to the Adjutant Points of the Gobean Vortex and spending a day there to reflect "upon the intention" of your soul "to create Unity and Harmony within." The following cities and towns are near Adjutant Points in the Golden City Vortex of Gobean. [Editor's Note: According to estimates, a Golden City Adjutant Point can have up to a ten to twenty mile radial electromagnetic energy flux. For more information see the I AM America United States Golden City Map.]

Socorro, New Mexico
Magdalena, New Mexico
Belen, New Mexico
Portal, Arizona (Chiricahua Mountains)
Safford, Arizona (Mount Graham, Pinaleno Mountains)
Benson, Arizona (Dragoon Mountains)
Globe, Arizona (Salt River Peak, near Lake Roosevelt)
Phoenix, Arizona (South Mountain Park, South Mountains)
Punkin Center, Arizona (Haystack Butte)
Sunflower, Arizona (Sycamore Creek and Diamond Mountain)
Cordes Junction, Arizona (Aqua Fria National Monument) [Editor's Note: This is near Arcosanti, an experimental town founded on the principle of *arcology*—ecological architecture—by the architect Paolo Soleri.]
Holbrook, Arizona (Painted Desert)
Payson-Heber, Arizona (Colcord Mountain)

APPENDIX E

Golden City Vortex Activation Dates

GOLDEN CITY	VORTEX ACTIVATION (Year)	STAR ACTIVATION (Year)	MASTER TEACHER	COUNTRY
GOBEAN	1981	1998	El Morya	United States
MALTON	1994	2011	Kuthumi	United States
WAHANEE	1996	2013	Saint Germain	United States
SHALAHAH	1998	2015	Sananda	United States
KLEHMA	2000	2017	Serapis Bey	United States
PASHACINO	2002	2019	Soltec	Canada
EABRA	2004	2021	Portia	Unites States, Canada
JEAFRAY	2006	2023	Archangel Zadkiel, Amethyst	Canada
UVERNO	2008	2025	Paul the Venetian	Canada
YUTHOR	2010	2027	Hilarion	Greenland
STIENTA	2012	2027	Archangel Michael	Iceland
DENASHA	2014	2031	Nada	Scotland
AMERIGO	2016	2033	Godfre	Spain
GRUECHA	2018	2035	Hercules	Norway, Sweden
BRAUN	2020	2037	Victory	Germany, Poland Czechoslovakia
AFROM	2022	2039	Claire and SeRay	Hungary, Romania
GANAKRA	2024	2041	Vista	Turkey
MESOTAMP	2026	2043	Mohammed	Turkey, Iran, Iraq
SHEHEZ	2028	2045	Tranquility	Iran, Afghanistan
ADJATAL	2030	2047	Lord Himalaya	Afghanistan, Pakistan, India
PURENSK	2032	2049	Faith, Hope, and Charity	Russia, China
PRANA	2034	2051	Archangel Chamuel	India
GANDAWAN	2036	2053	Kuthumi	Algeria
KRESHE	2038	2055	Lord of Nature, Amaryllis	Botswana, Namibia
PEARLANU	2040	2057	Lotus	Madagascar
UNTE	2042	2059	Donna Grace	Tanzania, Kenya
LARAITO	2044	2061	Lanto and Laura	Ethiopia
MARNERO	2046	2063	Mary	Mexico
ASONEA	2048	2065	Peter the Everlasting	Cuba
ANDEO	2050	2067	First Sister, Constance, Goddess Meru	Peru, Brazil

APPENDIX E

Golden City Vortex Activation Dates

GOLDEN CITY	VORTEX ACTIVATION (Year)	STAR ACTIVATION (Year)	MASTER TEACHER	COUNTRY
BRAHAM	2052	2069	Second Sister	Brazil
TEHEKOA	2054	2071	Third Sister	Argentina
CROTESE	2056	2073	Paul the Devoted	Costa Rica, Panama
JEHOA	2058	2075	Kuan Yin	New Atlantis
ZASKAR	2060	2079	Reya	China
GOBI	2062	2079	Lord Meru	China
ARCTURA	2064	2081	Arcturus	China
NOMAKING	2066	2083	Cassiopea and Minerva	China
PRESCHING	2068	2085	Archangel Jophiel	China, North Korea
KANTAN	2070	2087	Great Divine Mother and Archangel Raphael	China, Russia
HUE	2072	2089	Lord Guatama	Russia
SIRCALWE	2074	2091	Group of Twelve	Russia
ARKANA	2076	2093	Archangel Gabriel	Russia
MOUSSE	2078	2095	Kona	New Lemuria
DONJAKEY	2080	2097	Pacifica	New Lemuria
GREIN	2082	2099	Viseria	New Zealand
CLAYJE	2084	2101	Orion	Australia
ANGELICA	2086	2103	Angelica	Australia
SHEAHAH	2088	2105	Astrea	Australia
FRON	2090	2107	Desiree	Australia
CRESTA	2092	2109	Archangel Crystiel	Antarctica

Light of Awakening

APPENDIX E

Golden City Energies

The Mineral and Vegetable Kingdoms that flourish amid the Stars and Adjutant Points of Golden City Vortices are imbued with the energies of that particular Golden City. As a result, water and produce are beneficially charged with Vortex-infused minerals. According to El Morya, each doorway of the Golden City of Gobean releases the following benefic Vortex energies into the air, water, and locally grown foods:

>Gobean Northern Door: ... The Inner Growth of Harmony
>Gobean Southern Door: .... Healing of Disease and Disharmony
>Gobean Western Door:........ Higher knowledge and understanding of Harmony, Peace, and Cooperation
>Gobean Eastern Door:........ Harmony among family, friends, and groups
>Gobean Star: .... Acquisition of a new understanding of Harmony; Transformation

[Editor's Note: See I AM America United States Golden City Map for more information.]

---

[1] *Wikipedia, Dagaz,* http://en.wikipedia.org/wiki/Dagaz, (2010).
[2] *Avia Venefia,* http://www.whats-your-sign.com/diamond-symbol-meaning.html, (2009).

APPENDIX F

Topics and Terms for Golden City Rays

Ray Forces
Integration of Ray Forces
Living in a Golden City
Gobean and the Blue Ray
Malton and the Ruby-Gold Ray
Changes Within the Elemental Kingdoms
Star Seeds and Ray Forces
The Dominant Ray
Wahanee and the Violet Ray of Brotherhood
Shalahah and the Healing Green Ray
Energy Anomalies of Ascension Valley and the Transportation Vortex
Klehma and the White Ray of Purity
Mantras of the Golden Cities

Integrate

To bring together, as a part into a unified whole, especially when incorporating the Rays for spiritual growth and evolution

Chakra Breathing

Chakra Breathing is a form of meditation and visualization that focuses primarily on unblocking one chakra at a time. A practitioner accomplishes this by intentionally calibrating his or her breathing with a mental image. This relaxation technique is most commonly used to heal the body, mind, and spirit. Chakra Breathing has more specific applications as well. It can help the integration process when it comes to assimilating new energies currently present on earth. Chakra Breathing can be augmented with other types of breathwork, such as yogic breathing. Based on the creation of *Pranayama*—the practice of filling breath with life, vital force, or control—this Hindu-based practice regulates respiration, thereby carrying more oxygen to the brain. According to many practitioners, this technique activates the subtle energy system and gives an individual control over the life energy in the body, which awakens innate and dormant powers.[1]

Spiritual Migration

An individual can transmute personal Karmas and initiate the Ascension Process by living near a Golden City Vortex, thereby deliberately and physically accessing its energies. Known as *Spiritual Migration*, this process involves embracing and understanding the metaphysical knowledge of the four doorways—or four directions—of a Golden City. A chela's passage through the energies of each doorway is literal and metaphoric on all levels: physical, emotional, mental, and spiritual. The journey begins in the Northerly area of the Vortex, also known as the Black Door. The spiritual course progresses to the Blue Door (East), onward to the Red Door (South), and to the final door, the Yellow Door, found in the West. It concludes at the Star, the center or apex of a Golden City. This gradual evolutionary expedition is designed to introduce a student to the higher frequencies of a Golden City, but it is not a voyage taken alone. Presiding Ascended Masters, archetypes of evolution who steward Golden City Vortices alongside the physical presence of specific Golden City Power Points—namely Golden City lei lines—and Golden City Adjutant Points provide the necessary Fourth- and Fifth-Dimensional mentoring. Golden City energies must be carefully integrated before entering the intense energies of Golden City Adjutant Points and Golden City Stars.

First, it is suggested that chelas visit or live near the outer perimeters of the Vortex to acclimate to the energy—one to forty miles within a Golden City Vortex should be sufficient. Once that step is completed, a chela can then carefully migrate inside, to the inner perimeters and power points of the Vortex. Students should have developed the ability to contact the appropriate Golden City Master Teacher and the capacity to maintain this contact during the critical moments of this arduous passage. Advanced students may take as few as twenty-one days to complete their spiritual migration—one day for each of the twenty-one major power points present in a Golden City Vortex—whereas others may journey for years.

The number twenty-one is sacred, not only in the realm of theosophy but in matters of creation. It represents many things—the meeting of spirit and matter, the beginning of *HU-man* individuality, the transition from youth to adulthood, and the sacrosanct vessel of God and the Holy Temple. The number twenty-one also contains elements of destruction and renewal; it prepares our consciousness to receive the master number twenty-two, a powerful integer associated with initiates and the Master Builder.

The ability to integrate Golden City energies depends on the spiritual depth and development of a student. His or her capacity to adapt, to transmute self-inhibiting Karmas and desires, to rely on the innate *HU-man* divinity, and to remediate problems and obstacles are key indicators of spiritual maturity. A chela should rely on the physical and spiritual presence of Golden City energies during his or her spiritual migration. The experiences and disciplines learned throughout this metaphysical pilgrimage will help guide the chela toward spiritual transformation and unfolding and inevitable self-realization and mastery. According to the Ascended Masters, as more individuals become aware of the spiritual power inherent in the Golden Cities, the process of spiritual migration will shepherd humanity's collective entrance into the New Times and onward to the Golden Age.

Saint Germain's Teachings on Golden City Rays
1. Ray Forces enter each Golden City through the apex under the direction of the Great Central Sun. These energies move in a circular motion and are disbursed by a process of emanation and radiation.

APPENDIX F

2. Individuals who seek to strengthen, integrate, or purify a Ray Force can achieve this goal by living near the apex or star of a Golden City Vortex. This produces the following results:
    a. As one begins to work with Ray Forces, his or her energies function homeopathically, meaning a little of a Ray's healing energy goes a long way. Therefore, Saint Germain suggests practicing patience with the integration process. Deliberately living in a Golden City to absorb a specific Ray Force will take time.
    b. When new energy is first absorbed, the opposite results are often experienced. For instance, in Gobean, which focuses the energies of the Blue Ray, disharmony takes the place of harmony. According to Saint Germain, this is akin to personal spiritual purification—cleansing the astral field of unwanted thoughts, feelings, and past experiences.
    c. Do not become alarmed—things may worsen before they improve. As the Ray Force integrates with light bodies, energies align light frequencies and vibrations with the Ray's inherent power and force-field. Accordingly, seekers may also experience the need for more sleep as the body adjusts. Disharmonious relationships and other physical anomalies are also common.
    d. The integration process is basically the same in all Golden Cities. The difference, however, is the Ray. Students may have different experiences, depending on the specific action and Divine Purpose of the Ray of a particular Golden City Vortex.
3. Ray activity affects the surrounding environment, including the Animal, Vegetable, Mineral, and Elemental Kingdoms contained in Golden City Vortices.
4. Breathwork is a great tool. Use it to integrate the Ray Force from the light bodies with the physical body. Chakra Breathing is a simple yet effective form of breathwork.
5. Energy work—or Energy Balancing—can also produce positive Ray Force integration. [Editor's Note: Types of Energy Balancing include the Four Pillars Technique, based on Ascended Master teachings; the Brennan Healing Science Technique, developed by NASA physicist, Barbara Brennan; Core Energetics, developed by John Pierrakos, M.D.; Reiki, developed by Buddhist, Mikao Usui; and Healing Touch, developed by holistic nurse Janet Mentgen.]
6. According to Saint Germain, various DNA, mixed genetics, and Karmas from past lifetimes may create challenges when identifying and assessing a student's dominant Ray Force. In these cases it may be necessary to utilize the energies of more than one Golden City Vortex to identify the Ascension process of an initiate. Most often, personal choices, preferences, and inclinations will reveal an individual's dominant Ray Force, disclosing its harmonizing yet balancing service.
7. Humanity has been subject to many embodiments on earth. As a result, each individual has experienced different combinations of Ray Forces and a variety of genetic and racial types over time. This incarnated wisdom enhances the self-knowledge of the soul and the ability to work with light and sound.

APPENDIX F

8. In Saint Germain's Golden City of Wahanee, the Violet Ray creates a Divine Intervention, one that that releases cellular fear from the physical and light bodies via the following process:
    a. The Violet Ray first works on the Solar Plexus Chakra, transmuting energies associated with death consciousness and cellular fear.
    b. This process can drastically affect the physical body, causing flu-like symptoms and intestinal upset.
    c. In its beginning stages, the Violet Ray galvanizes the Heart Chakra, moving energies along the Kundalini to the Crown Chakra—this is where the Ray's higher purpose begins.
    d. Saint Germain's decree to transmute death consciousness with the Violet Ray is "Down with death! Conscious immortality, arise!"
9. Saint Germain reminds students that healing is about repairing the body, the mind, the spirit, and the soul. Initiates can find this type of rejuvenation in Shalahah (Idaho and Montana, United States). This is where the Green Ray of Healing is located.
10. The Green Ray fosters revivification on many levels, including spiritual consciousness. It also repairs humanity's separation from God—or the Creator. As this level of healing progresses and is accepted from within, an individual will experience the Oneship. After this initiatory process, the chela is ready to move toward New Dimensions.
11. As the body, mind, and spirit are brought into balance and harmony, the result is natural abundance. Saint Germain encourages students who wish to manifest abundance and prosperity in their lives to travel to the Golden City of Shalahah. "Align yourself to the Green Ray," he says. Saint Germain also claims that this process deeply affects Heart and Solar Plexus energies. Growth and development culminate in true abundance and prosperity.
12. Safety. Overidentification with physical materialness makes one feel unsafe. "Safety is truly a matter of the heart."
13. Abundance streams forth into our lives by cultivating clarity and living in beauty (balance). "Abundance streams forth with clarity and beauty."
14. Ascension Energies of the Golden City of Klehma are similar to Shalahah; however, the White Ray assists the individual during the final release of the death urge. The White Ray completes the initiatory process that was instigated by the Violet Ray and Green Ray.

APPENDIX F

Initiation and the Golden Cities

Spiritual migration is not a static process and virtuosity is never fully achieved. The journey can take a lifetime. Once a student or chela masters the spiritual migration of one Golden City, he or she may advance to other Golden Cities to experience the Ray Forces, Master Teachers, qualities, and characteristics within. Every Vortex embodies explicit spiritual teachings that are designed to reveal the presence of each Ray Force, its promise of personal integration, and the mastery of its distinct spiritual process.

In all, fifty-one Golden Cities are located around the planet. Three individual sequences, or Ascension methods, consist of seventeen cities each, which are listed below.

Seventeen Initiations of the I AM America Map: *Realization of and integration with the I AM Presence and establishment of the I AM Race.*

	Golden City	Location	Presiding Ray	Master Teacher
1.	GOBEAN	United States	Blue Ray	El Morya
2.	MALTON	United States	Gold-Ruby Ray	Kuthumi
3.	WAHANEE	United States	Violet Ray	Saint Germain
4.	SHALAHAH	United States	Green Ray	Sananda
5.	KLEHMA	United States	White Ray	Serapis Bey
6.	PASHACINO	Canada	Green Ray	Soltec
7.	EABRA	Canada, United States	Violet Ray	Portia
8.	JEAFRAY	Canada	Violet Ray	Archangel Zadkiel and Amethyst
9.	UVERNO	Canada	Pink Ray	Paul the Venetian
10.	YUTHOR	Greenland	Green Ray	Hilarion
11.	MARNERO	Mexico	Green Ray	Mary
12.	ASONEA	Cuba	Yellow Ray	Peter the Everlasting
13.	ANDEO	Peru, Brazil	Pink and Gold Rays	The First Sister, Goddess Meru, Beloved Constance
14.	BRAHAM	Brazil	Pink Ray	The Second Sister
15.	TEHEKOA	Argentina	Pink and Violet Rays	The Third Sister
16.	CROTESE	Costa Rica, Panama	Pink Ray	Paul the Devoted
17.	JEHOA	New Atlantis [The Eastern side of this Vortex is present-day Saint Lucia Island in the Caribbean.]	Violet Ray	Kuan Yin

The Golden City Series: Book Two

APPENDIX F

Seventeen Initiations of the Greening Map: *Personal and transpersonal healing of the feminine to balance Mother Earth and awaken her ecological alchemy.*

	Golden City	Location	Presiding Ray	Master Teacher
1.	Adjatal	Pakistan, Afghanistan, India	Blue and Gold Rays	Lord Himalaya
2.	Purensk	Russia, China	Blue, Yellow and Pink Rays	Faith, Hope, Charity
3.	Prana	India	Pink Ray	Archangel Chamuel
4.	Zaskar	China	White Ray	Reya
5.	Gobi	China	Ruby-Gold Ray	Lord Meru / Archangel Uriel
6.	Arctura	China	Violet Ray	Arcturus / Diana
7.	Nomaking	China	Yellow Ray	Cassiopea and Minerva
8.	Presching	China	Yellow Ray	Archangel Jophiel
9.	Kantan	China, Russia	Green Ray	Great Divine Mother and Archangel Raphael
10.	Hue	Russia	Violet Ray	Lord Guatama
11.	Sircalwe	Russia	White Ray	Group of Twelve
12.	Arkana	Russia	White Ray	Archangel Gabriel
13.	Grein	New Zealand	Green Ray	Viseria
14.	Arkana	Russia	White Ray	Archangel Gabriel
15.	Clayje	Australia	Pink Ray	Orion
16.	Angelica	Australia	Pink Ray	Angelica
17.	Sheahah	Australia	White Ray	Astrea

APPENDIX F

18. Fron	Australia	Blue Ray	Desiree

Seventeen Initiations of the Map of Exchanges: *Self-realization of the HU-man through the exchange of heavenly energies on earth that usher in the Golden Age.*

Golden City	Location	Presiding Ray	Master Teacher
1. Shenta	Iceland	Blue Ray	Archangel Michael
2. Denasha	Scotland	Yellow Ray	Nada
3. Amerigo	Spain	Gold Ray	Godfre
4. Gruecha	Norway, Sweden	Blue Ray	Hercules
5. Braun	Germany, Poland, Czechoslovakia	Yellow Ray	Victory
6. Afrom	Hungary, Romania	White Ray	SeRay and Claire
7. Ganakra	Turkey	Green Ray	Vista
8. Mesotamp	Turkey, Iran, Iraq	Yellow Ray	Mohammed
9. Shehez	Iran, Afghanistan	Ruby-Gold Ray	Tranquility
10. Gandawan	Algeria	Ruby-Gold Ray	Kuthumi
11. Kreshe	Botswana, Namibia	Ruby-Gold Ray	Lord of Nature and Amaryllis
12. Pearlanu	Madagascar	Violet Ray	Lotus
13. Unte	Tanzania, Kenya	Ruby-Gold	Donna Grace
14. Laraito	Ethiopia	Yellow Ray	Lanto and Laura
15. Mousee	New Lemuria [Present-day Pacific Ocean, Northwest of Hawaii]	Aquamarine-Gold Ray	Kona
16. Donjakey	New Lemuria [Present-day Pacific Ocean, Northwestern Hawaiian Islands, Midway Islands]	Aquamarine-Gold Ray	Pacifica
17. Cresta	Antarctica [Antarctic Peninsula]	Aquamarine-Gold Ray	Archangel Crystiel

Most numbers that show up in Ascended Master teachings have special metaphysical significance, and the number seventeen is no different. To humanity, it represents the Star of the Magi and the birth of Christ Consciousness. Ancient Chaldean numerology refers to the seventeen as the eight-pointed Star of Venus. Meanwhile, the seventeenth card of the Tarot—the Stars—signify the Divine Powers of Nature.

Ascended Masters claim the nascent energies of the Christ Consciousness physically appear through three sets of seventeen Golden Cities; individuals who aptly apply esoteric principles begin this important development. The three sets of seventeen Golden Cities represent three separate spiritual techniques to rouse the internal sacred fire and actualize the Divine God Man—the *HU-man*.

While many Ascended Master students may choose to perfect the twenty-one movements of Spiritual Migration contained in a singular Golden City Vortex, the Master Teachers claim that any of the three sequential Ascension practices will quickly ad-

APPENDIX F

vance the chela. Perhaps the first initiatory sequence is considered the most straightforward; and most of the Golden Cities in this series are accessible.

Seventeen Initiations of I AM America

The Seventeen Initiations of I AM America is a spiritual process that helps students awaken and realize the power of the I AM Presence. As personal mastery and command of the I AM Presence is achieved, individuals will join together to reestablish North America, Central America, and South America as ONE expression of the I AM Race. An anagram derived from the word *America*, the I AM race is the prophesied new breed of man destined to serve as the nucleus of the New Times. The Violet Ray, the Pink Ray, and the Green Ray are the principal Rays of I AM America Golden Cities. The Archangel Zadkiel and various Master Teachers and Elohim serve as stewards of these Vortex cities.

Seventeen Initiations of the Greening Map

Mother Earth plays a central role in the Greening Map of Asia and Australia. The migratory path of these Golden Cities is intended to restore the Earth Mother physically, emotionally, and mentally by balancing prevailing oppressive male energies with the influence of the feminine. White and Pink Rays dominate this sequence, which means spiritual initiation focuses on the balance and integration of personal and collective feminine energies. The journey of healing through the seventeen Golden Cities of the Greening Map awakens Fourth- and Fifth-Dimensional attributes of Mother Earth to the magical and sensual expression of Ecological Alchemy. This spiritual practice opens initiates to the ONE and forges an indelible connection to the Earth Mother. This Ascension method is crucial in calibrating earth's consciousness to the incarnating New Children. Meanwhile, many new and different species of flora and fauna are prophesied to inhabit earth throughout the New Times. The Golden Cities of the Greening Map may instigate the healing of the tyrannical male energies—in governments, religions, cultures, and economies—that have dominated earth's timely passage in Kali-Yuga. As individuals integrate and apply the energies of these feminine Golden Cities, the global culture will heal the pain of harsh, exploitive power and open the Divine Heart of Humanity. Five Archangels serve in the seventeen Golden Cities of the Greening Map and assist the awakening of earth's light grids and lei lines. Archangel Chamuel, Archangel Jophiel, Archangel Raphael, Archangel Gabriel, and Archangel Uriel comprise this cadre of spiritual stewards.

Seventeen Initiations of the Map of Exchanges

The initiatory progression of the Map of Exchanges, which includes Europe, Africa, and the Middle East, is perhaps the most difficult spiritual sequence of all. It requires the guiding wisdom and focus of the Yellow Ray —the Divine Guru. The interplay of the Gold Ray in cosmic partnership with the Ruby-Gold and Aquamarine-Gold Rays helps the student realize the Yellow Ray's hidden power, or *Shatki* and the Divine HU-man. The progression of Golden Cities in this particular map

APPENDIX F

is prophesied to anchor heaven on earth and usher in God-actualized humanity. It is the birth of Unana. Throughout the seventeen Golden Cities of the Map of Exchanges, a student's Fourth- and Fifth-Dimensional light bodies are trained to step down heavenly energies that transmute and exchange with energies of the Third Dimension. It is an extensive Ascension process: doubt is exchanged for knowledge; fear is exchanged for courage; hate is exchanged for trust; and darkness is exchanged for light. Energies from the Galactic Center permeate the seventeen Golden Cities contained in the Map of Exchanges, lifting humanity and the planet toward the prophesied New Times and Golden Age. As earth progresses toward the final exchange of enlightened energy, the heavenly filaments of the Galactic Web will illuminate the entire globe. This web of enlightened awareness is prophesied to link and expand individual consciousness beyond this planet and onward, toward a Galactic Consciousness that embraces the lokas—or the levels of spiritual development on all planets. Archangel Michael and Archangel Crystiel oversee the spiritual Ascension of humanity and earth:

When encountering inaccessible Golden Cities, such as the submerged New Atlantis and New Lemuria, travel as close as possible to the Golden City's location to absorb spiritual energies. Students can also use the Star Meditation technique, which is as follows: Enter the Star of one Golden City Vortex and access the energies of any Golden City via the Fourth- and Fifth-Dimensional Golden City Network. This technique, however, is not for the novice. It requires patience and practice. [For more information see *Points of Perception: Golden City Activations and Subtle Energies, Golden City Activation.*]

Prophecies of Change

1. The Golden City of Malton (Illinois and Indiana, United States) plays a vital role in assisting the purification of the Elemental Kingdoms, which includes nature beings—Devas, fairies, gnomes, sylphs, and undines. The activity of this Golden City will help restore balance by cleansing the earth of environmental pollutants and toxins. [For more information see *Points of Perception, Devas and Elementals, Appendix F.*]
2. The spiritual guidance of the Ruby-Gold Ray currently influences earthquakes, tidal waves, and volcanic eruptions. These so-called natural disasters are destined to create balance among all systems of the earth. A modicum of despair, death, and destruction must be endured during this time, but it is merely part of the process. These seemingly disharmonious events will adjust and harmonize earth and its Nature Kingdoms, creating consonance at yet another level and ushering in the Oneship and the higher consciousness of Unana.
3. During the Golden Age, certain souls will choose to incarnate or live in Golden Cities that align with their dominant Ray Force. A soul is attracted to its *Soul Family*, a term Master Teachers often refer to as *Star Seed*. Since all Star Seeds contain some elder members who have evolved to the Fifth Dimension, certain

APPENDIX F

Golden Cities and the appropriate Ray Forces can more efficiently support and address individualized Ascension processes.

4. As the energies of the New Times grow, and more individuals embrace the Ascension process, those living near the Star of Wahanee (Augusta, Ga., United States) may experience regeneration, a phenomenon that occurs when a tremendous amount of life-giving energy—chi or prana—is concentrated in a Star location. This energy also assists chelas in transmuting and eliminating death consciousness.
5. The Golden City of Wahanee (Georgia, South Carolina, United States) with the help of the Violet Ray build a higher consciousness on earth, allowing humanity to drop the energies of cellular fear and create a united Brotherhood and Sisterhood on earth.
6. The Green Ray in the Golden City Vortex of Shalahah initiates healing at optimum levels, which will help human consciousness experience the ONE and the New Dimensions. Two energy anomalies are prophesied to usher in humanity's entrance into the New Dimensions of the Golden Age:
    a. Ascension Valley: Located in Idaho (United States) near Moscow, Idaho, SouthEast of Spokane, Wash., this energy Vortex prepares students to integrate their light bodies and spiritual consciousness into the ONESHIP, the divinity within. It further readies the body, mind, and spirit to experience and travel to the New Dimensions.
    b. Transportation Vortex: Prophesied to develop as humanity enters the New Time. A model of this energy anomaly will exist in the Golden City of Shalahah near Coeur d'Alene, Idaho (United States). This interdimensional portal works with the developed projection of the mind. As humanity's understanding of Ray Forces evolves, physical bodies will assume a finer quality in light and substance. Humans will be able to bi-locate—or be in two places at once—with the help of these energy Vortices. In the New Times, bi-location will become an accepted form of travel.
7. The Golden City of Klehma (Colorado, United States) will become the new capital of the United States. Many rulers of the historical past, including Native American leaders, will reincarnate and come forward to govern the United States in the New Times. Their spiritual guidance will usher the United States toward a higher intention and purity of mind and service.

Determining the Dominant Ray Force

The presence of a Ray is usually obvious; an individual's dominant Ray can be expressed several ways. Physical appearance, personality traits, habits, and characteristics often provide many clues. A tall, thin, austere man shows the influence of the Saturnine Blue Ray; a beautiful, feminine woman embodies the White Ray of Venus, while a talkative, information-oriented personality reveals the Mercurial Green Ray. Sometimes, however, determining the dominance of a Ray Force is difficult. That's because several Rays may be vying for predominance in a person's life patterns. In this case

APPENDIX F

Vedic Astrologers turn to Jyotish techniques to glean additional information, specifically *Shadbala* and *Atmakaraka*.

Shadbala measures the ascendency of a planet in an individual's horoscope. The power of a Ray is calculated by determining the strength of six planetary factors.
1. Positional strength (or the sign a planet resides in a chart);
2. Directional strength (or cardinal direction: North, East, South, West);
3. Temporal strength (based on time and date of birth);
4. The strength of motion (forward, direct, stationary, or retrograde);
5. The visual radiance of a planet (in this sequence: Sun, Moon, Venus, Jupiter, Mercury, Mars, and Saturn);
6. Aspectual strength (the strength a planet gains from being in proximity to other planets or Ray Forces).

By applying Shadbala, a particular planet and its Ray Force always gain prominence. The Ray that is discovered is considered the dominant Ray of that individual's current lifetime.

The Atmakaraka, or soul indicator, is the most important planet and Ray Force in a person's chart. The influence of the *significator of self* often reveals the disposition of an individual who embodies the natural aptitude, qualities, and characteristics of a particular Ray or planet. Some esoteric astrologers say the Atmakaraka indicates the soul group (or Star Seed) or Ray Family of origin, which defines the soul's purpose. The planet positioned most powerfully in Shadbala is often seen as the Ray carrying the individual's obvious aspirations in a particular lifetime, whereas the Atmakaraka, also referred to as the Atma, indicates the essence of the soul and its core identity. For instance, an individual with the Sun (Ruby-Gold Ray) in the highest position in Shadbala may be driven toward leadership roles; however, the position of the Atmakaraka will indicate the area of leadership. For instance, an individual with a Mercury (Green Ray) Atma may prevail in commerce, business, science, or teaching; matriarchs or patriarchs may have a Moon (Pink Ray) Atma; and those who lead by their counsel or spiritual wisdom may possess a Jupiter (Yellow Ray) Atma. The power of a Ray relies on strengths and weaknesses to direct the course of lives and sculpt individual experiences. Low-strength Ray forces denote areas that may need improvement or refinement in this lifetime, known by Vedic Astrologers as *Gnati Karaka*—an astrological benchmark that defines a person's greatest obstacles and challenges in this lifetime.

The strongest Ray Force and Atma placement will also determine a person's preference for spiritual development and the most effective techniques for spiritual liberation. A strong Sun can provide great devotion; a powerful Moon, the ability for unconditional love; a well-placed Venus, a proclivity for forgiveness; Saturn fosters discipline, detachment, and self-negation; Jupiter provides the gifts of listening, direction, and advice (good teachers—gurus); and a solid Mercury offers the intelligence to grasp spiritual subtlety, nuance, and the ability to quickly integrate.

Abundance

APPENDIX F

Based on the Law of Choice, the second of the Twelve Jurisdictions is the principle of overflowing fullness in all situations and circumstances. Abundance, from the perspective of Ascended Master teaching, is the natural result of Harmony, the First Jurisdiction. [For more information on the Twelve Jurisdictions, see *New World Atlas, Volume One*.]

Mantra

Certain sounds, syllables, and sets of words are deemed sacred and often carry the power to transmute Karma, purify the spirit, and transform an individual. These are known as a *mantras*. The mantra is a foundation of Vedic tradition and often treated as a devotional *upaye*—a remedial measure of difficult obstacles. Mantras, however, are not limited to Hinduism. Buddhists, Sikhs, and Jains also utilize mantras. The Ascended Masters occasionally provide mantras to chelas to improve resonation with certain Golden Cities.

My teacher of Vedic tradition gave this explanation regarding the anatomy of the mantra:

MAM + TRA = MANTRA

Chants + Protects = MANTRA

He was particularly avid about adding the sound HREEM before chanting the mantra to transmute difficult Karmas. His explanation:

H = Sins

REEM = Removes

HREEM = Removal of Sins

Mantras for the Five Golden Cities of the United States

According to Saint Germain, individual mantras infuse Golden City Ray Forces into light bodies (auras), a practice that evolves the conscious life experience toward Ascension Consciousness. He suggests that the efficiency of a Ray is best understood when used in a Golden City Vortex, where the energy of a mantra works concurrently with the centrifugal force of the Golden City Star. Uttering mantras is most effective in the Star of a Golden City, but don't let that prevent you from the practice. If you can't make it to the Star, saying mantras in any part of a Golden City is beneficial. The following mantras should be used simultaneously with the initiatory Ray work in each Golden City.

GOBEAN	*Om Shanti*	Produces peace and harmony
MALTON	*Om Eandra*	Produces harmony and balance for the Nature Kingdoms. It is also associated with instant thought

Light of Awakening

APPENDIX F

manifestation.

WAHANEE	*Om Hue*	Aligns the chakras with the Vertical Power Current, or Golden Thread Axis, and evokes the Sacred fire—the Violet Flame. Since this mantra is a Vibration of Violet Flame Angels, it invokes their Healing presence, which helps purify and heal the body.
SHALAHAH	*Om Sheahah*	Evokes the consciousness of the ONESHIP—Unana. This mantra means, "I AM as ONE."
KLEHMA	*Om Eandra*	Used as a decree for Instant-Thought-Manifestation of Ascension, glory, and conclusion.

Angels of the Violet Flame

The Angels of the Violet Flame protect the purity of the Flame, dispense its transforming vibration, and carry the transmuting energies of the Flame whenever called upon. These angels can be summoned to assist with decrees and meditation regarding spiritual growth, governmental freedoms and rights, wealth and supply, and to hasten the Ascension Process. Perhaps Angels of the Violet Flame are best known for their ability to expedite healing. Edna Ballard of the I AM Activity writes:

> "When you want to call forth the Healing Flame to assist someone, hold the picture of the Violet Flame Angel, and watch from the Sun Presence of its heart the projection of a Flame, the center part pink, the outer violet and the outer radiance blue, reaching out and going forth to enfold your Loved Ones, or any one to whom you wish to give assistance.
>
> This can also reach out and into the mental and feeling world of an individual, quiet disturbance, purify and raise the vibratory action of the Inner Bodies into the same Great Purity and Love which the Healing Angels project!" [2]

The following is a decree from the I AM Activity teachings to the Violet Flame Angels for healing:

> *"Beloved Mighty I AM Presence and Blessed Nada!*
> *I DEMAND the Healing Flame of Love from the Angels of the Violet Consuming Flame COME FORTH in and around me and all under This Radiation, to purify and perfect our bodies! I DEMAND the Violet Flame Angels of Healing Love come and abide with me and heal all I contact!"* [3]

APPENDIX F

Golden City Names

The names of the Golden Cities are unusual, and each City's meaning is secret knowledge closely held by the Master Teachers. Through the years of our work with the Ascended Masters, several definitions of the names of Golden Cities have emerged, but never in great detail. Yet, each curious name is important, and reveals hidden qualities and spiritual characteristics of each Golden City. Some occultists refer to the veiled language of the mystics as *Owaspee*—the native tongue of Angels. The Divine Language, or the language of the Gods, is referred to in religious traditions including the Adamic language—the language spoken by Adam and Eve; Hebrew—the Jewish language of God; Greek, the mathematical language of harmony; and Sanskrit, the Divine Language of the Gods through Vedic spiritual traditions.

Divine Languages are often known as *form languages*. My Vedic teacher once explained the etymology of Sanskrit as "a Mother tongue," similar to the syntax and semantics of computer languages. According to Vedic legend our entire earth was programmed, or created, through the spoken words of Sanskrit. Speaking a form language is powerful and commanding, and each spoken syllable has the ability to exactly create in form and substance its subject. Perhaps the creation story of Genesis says it best, "Then God said, 'Let there be light,' and there was light." (Genesis 1:3 New American Standard Bible)

The names and meanings of the Golden Cities, which originate in the causal plane of the Fifth Dimension, carry their emotive light and sound through the feeling worlds of the Fourth Dimension and integrate their activity to evolve the HU-man of earth's Third Dimension. Golden City names are founded on the multiple languages of earth. Their individual syllables are based on archetypal words from many cultures of the world, including ancient Sanskrit, Greek, Persian, Phoenician, and the lost tongue of Moriori. Their sounds also include Native American languages: Algonquian, Navajo, Shoshoni, and Cahto. Surprisingly, modern languages appear in the syllables of the names of Golden Cities: the universal language of peace, Esperanto; Tolkein's fictional language of Middle Earth, Elfish; and the contemporary, linguistic Minimalist Language.

The sounds and meanings of the Golden Cities's names are the evocations and myths for the New Times. Their resonance is the hope and the aspiration for progressive, positive change on behalf of humanity and the earth. The theosophist George William Russell wrote, "The mind of man is made in the image of Deity, and the elements of speech are related to the powers in his mind and through it to the being of the Oversoul. These true roots of language are few, alphabet and roots being identical."[4]

APPENDIX F

Meanings of the Fifty-One Golden City Vortices

ADJATAL: *The Big Rainbow* derives its meaning from the Suabo-Indonesian word *adja* ("big") and the Pashto-Pakistanian word *tal* ("rainbow"). The Golden City of Adjatal is located in Pakistan, Afghanistan, and India; the historical Khyber Pass (the ancient Silk Road) is located on the Western side of this Vortex city.

AFROM: This Golden City name means, "A Devotion." This meaning originates with the word *from*, which in German, Norwegian, and Swedish means "pious" or "devoted." The Ascended Masters claim this Golden City also means "to affirm."

AMERIGO: This European Golden City is Spanish for "I AM Race."

ANDEO: The Golden City of the South American Andes is likely named for this mountain range; however, the source of this Golden City of the Feminine is rooted in the Albanian word *anda*, which means "strong desire" and the Huli (New Guinea) word *andia*, which means "mother." Andeo's meaning translates into this phrase: "the Mother of Desire."

ANGELICA: The Native American Algonquian word *ca* means "at present" or "present"; therefore, Angelica's full meaning is "Angel Present," or "Angels at Present."

ARKANA: The nineteenth century created language of peace—Esperanto; and the Polish language both state that the word *arkana* means "Mystery."

ASONEA: The Golden City of Cuba and ancient Atlantis derives its meaning from the pristine Ason River of the Cantabria province in Spain and its mythological race of supernatural undines—the *Xanas*.

BRAHAM: *Braham* is also known as the Second of Three Sisters who preserves a maternal radiance over South America. Braham is the feminine version of *Brahma*, and this Golden City meaning is the "Mother of the New Manu."

BRAUN: The Golden City of Germany, Poland, and Czechoslovakia means "the Shining Strong One."

CLAYJE: Dialects from the Netherlands create this Golden City's name through the word *kla*—"clear." The word *je* in Bosnian, Croatian, Serbian, and Slovak languages means "is." The combination of these words constructs this Australian Golden City's meaning: "Is Clear."

CRESTA: In Spanish, Italian, and Brazilian Portuguese the word *cresta* means "the ridge or peak."

APPENDIX F

CROTESE: Located in the Cradleland of Central America, this Golden City means "the Attentive Cradle." Its meaning is derived from the French *cro*—"cradle," and the Etruscan *tes*—"to care for or pay attention."

DENASHA: This Golden City derives its meaning from the modern English name Denesa, which means the "Mountain of Zeus." This mythological Greek father of both Gods and men is also known in Roman myths as Jupiter, an ideal symbol for this European Golden City of the Yellow Ray.

DONJAKEY: Located on new lands prophesied to rise from the Pacific Ocean in the New Times, this Golden City's name comes from the Italian word *don*—"gift," and the Indonesian word *key*—"tree." Donjakey means "Gift of Trees," and is associated with new species of flora prophesied to appear on earth.

EABRA: "The Feminine in Eternal Balance." This name is a derivative of several words, namely *bra* or *bodice*, which means "the pair" or the "wearing of pairs." *Ea* has several meanings: in Frisian (German) *ea* means "ever," in Romanian *ea* means "she." The word *pair* numerically indicates two, a number associated with femininity and balance.

FRON: The meaning of this Australian Golden City is "throne" in Albanian. In the Creole language, *fron* means "pious" and "devoted." The combination of these definitions creates Fron's meaning: "the Devoted Throne."

GANAKRA: The ancient Turkish City of Ankara means "anchor" in Greek; in Portuguese *gana* means "desire"; and *kra* is a Creole word for "mind." Ganakra's combined meaning is "Desires Anchored by the Mind," or "Desires of the Mind."

GANDAWAN: From the Sanskrit word *Gondwanaland* means "Forest of the Gonds." Located over the Sahara Desert, this Golden City represents this ancient culture that claimed to survive in present-day India. Contemporary Gond legends mirror the emergence stories of Southwest Native American tribes, and the Gond Gods surfaced from a cave and were adopted by the Hindu Goddess Parvati (Divine Mother) and were assisted by their tribal Goddess Jangu Bai. According to myth, the Gonds emerged from their cave in four distinct groups.[5]

GOBEAN: The Ascended Masters claim the earth's first Golden City for the New Times means to "go beyond." However, Gobean's etymology suggests the meaning: "Go Pray." This phrase is derived from the word *bea* or *be*, which in Frisian (German) and Norwegian means "prayer."

APPENDIX F

Gobi: Named for the Great Desert of China, Gobi in Mongolian means "the waterless place." Ascended Masters claim the Golden City of Gobi is a step-down transformer for the energies of the earth's first Golden City—Shamballa. Gobi's esoteric definition comes from the Chinese translation of "go—across," and *bi* in Indonesian (Abun, A Nden, and Yimbun dialects) means "star." The Golden City of Gobi means "Across the Star," or "Across the Freedom Star." "Freedom Star" is a reference to earth in her enlightened state.) Gobi aligns energies to the first Golden City of the New Times: Gobean.

Grein: *Grein* is an Icelandic, Norwegian, and Swedish word which means "branch." The Ascended Masters maintain that the New Zealand Golden City of Grein means "the Green Branch"—a symbol of the peaceful olive branch.

Gruecha: The Golden City name of Norway and Sweden is a Norwegian word and means "Hearth."

Hue: According to the Ascended Masters, the word *hue* invokes the Sacred Fire, the Violet Flame. In Tibetan dialects, however, the word *hue* or *hu* means "breath."

Jeafray: The Golden City of the Ever-present Violet Flame meaning translates to "Yesterday's Brother." This is based on the Gaelic word *jea*, which means "yesterday"; the word *fra* is English for "Brother" (friar). Since Archangel Zadkiel and the Archeia Amethyst serve in this Vortex retreat, "Yesterday's Brother" is a reference to the work of Saint Germain—as Sanctus Germanus (the Holy Brother)—and the many other archetypes of consciousness who tirelessly work for humanity's freedom and Ascension through the use of the transmuting fire.

Jehoa: It may be that this Golden City's name is based upon the Tetragrammaton YHWH; however, the etymology of this sacred haven of the Caribbean is based on the Russian word *YA*—meaning "I AM"—and *hoa*, which means "friend," from the Tahitian, Hawaiian, Maori, and Rapa Nui (Easter Island) languages. This translation elevates the various interpretations of Jehovah, the jealous God into the uplifting phrase, "I AM Friend."

Kantan: This Golden City of China and Russia derives its name from the English (Cornish) word *kan*—which means "song," and the Korean word *tan*, meaning "sweet." The full meaning of this spiritual Vortex is the "Sweet Song."

Klehma: The meaning of the fifth Golden City of the United States is based on several Native American words. The first syllable *kle* (pronounced clay) comes from the Navajo word *klê-kai*—which means "white." The second syllable *ma*, is a derivative of the Shoshoni word *mahoi*—around, or encircling. Klehma's esoteric definition is the "Circle of White."

APPENDIX F

KRESHE: This African Golden City is known to the Ascended Masters as the "Silent Star," an esoteric reference to Venus. *Kres* is also a Celtic word for "peace."

LARAITO: This Ethiopian Golden City's meaning is "Our Home." Laraito's definition comes from the Brazilian, Portuguese, and Spanish word for home—*lar. Ito* is a Tanzanian word for "ours."

MALTON: The Ascended Master Kuthumi's Golden City meaning is derived from the Phoenician word *maleth*—which means "a haven."

MARNERO: Mexico's Golden City's steward is Mother Mary and the first syllable of Marnero—*mar*—is a Spanish, Italian, and Portuguese word which means "sea" or "ocean." The remainder of the name—*nero* translates into *ner*, a Hebrew word for "candle." The Golden City of Marnero's meaning is the "Ocean of Candles."

MESOTAMP: The Golden City of Turkey, Iran, and Iraq is likely linked to the ancient word *Mesopotamia*, which means the "land between rivers." The higher meaning of *Mesotamp*, however, is linked to the New Guinea word *meso*—"moon," and the Turkmen word, *tam*—"house." Mesotamp's meaning translates into the "House of the Moon."

MOUSEE: This Golden City for the New Times means the "Ocean of Fish." This spiritual haven, prophesied to appear near Hawaii, combines the New Guinea word *mou*—"fish," and the Afrikaan word *see*—"sea" or "ocean." New flora and fauna is prophesied to appear as earth enters the New Times.

NOMAKING: This Chinese Golden City means "Name of the King." Its meaning is based on the word *noma* (or *nama*) and in many languages ranging from Italian to Sanskrit simply means "name."

PASHACINO: "The Passionate Spirit." This Canadian Golden City's meaning is derived from the English word for "passion"—*pash*, and the Kurdish and Turkish word for "spirit"—*cin*.

PEARLANU: Madagascar's Golden City's meaning is based on the Malagasy (the national language of Madagascar) word *lanosina*, which means "to be swum in." Pearlanu's meaning translates to "Swimming in Pearls."

PRANA: Located in the heart of India, this Golden City of the Pink Ray meaning is "Life-giving Energy."

PRESCHING: This Chinese Golden City's meaning is linked to its topography. *Pres* is an English word which means "meadow," and *ching* is a Native American (Cahto) word for "timber and forest." Presching means the "City of Meadows, Grasslands, and Forests."

APPENDIX F

PURENSK: This Golden City means "Pure Intelligence" or the "Pure Message." This Russian and Chinese Golden City derives its esoteric meaning from the Danish, English, German, and French name *pur*—"pure," and the Turkish word, *esk*, for "intelligence" or "message."

SHALAHAH: Sananda is the steward of this United States Golden City which in Sanskrit means a "Sacred Place Indeed!" The syllables break down with these meanings: *shala*—"sacred place", "sanctuary"; *hah*—"indeed."

SHEHEZ: This Golden City located in Iran and Afghanistan is a Persian word that means "large," or "grand."

SHEAHAH: The Ascended Masters claim that the meaning of this Australian Golden City is, "I AM as ONE." The etymology of this Vortex meaning is undoubtedly related to the Feminine Energies prophesied to dominate and direct the New Times. The syllable *aha* in Tanzanian and Uganda means "here"; in Czechoslovakian *aha* stands for "I see." Therefore Sheahah's hidden meaning is actually prophetic: "She is here," or "She, I see."

SIRCALWE: The Russian Golden City of the White Ray derives its sacred name from the Turkish and Chinese languages—*sir*, which means "secret"; and the Elfish language of Middle Earth—*cal*, meaning "light." The word *we* in the English, Korean, and Italian language is defined as "ours." These languages combine to give this Golden City Vortex name its meaning: "Our Secret Light."

STIENTA: This Golden City's name means "the path" in Norwegian.

TEHEKOA: Since this Golden City represents one of the Three Sister Golden Cities of South America, its meaning springs from the lost Moriori language and the Hebrew word *Teku'a*: "the City of Tents," "secures the tents." These meanings merge and Tehekoa means the "Wise Woman who Secures the City."

UNTE: This Golden City—located in Tanzania and Kenya—means in Brazilian, Spanish, and Portuguese "to anoint."

UVERNO: The Canadian Golden City of the Pink Ray translates in Slovak to "trust well."

WAHANEE: The third Golden City of the United States derives its name from *Wahabu*, the Nigerian name for the "God of Love." The etymological meaning of the final syllable *nee* in English, Italian, and French is "born." Wahanee's esoteric meaning is the "God of Love is born."

APPENDIX F

Yuthor: In minimalist language, *Yu* means "union." *Thor* is the Scandinavian God of Thunder—"Power." The Golden City of Greenland's hidden meaning is the "Power of Union."

Zaskar: This Golden City of the White Ray derives its meaning from the Czech and Slovak word *zas*—"again," "over again"; and the Basque word *kar*, which means "flame." This Chinese Golden City means the "Repeating Flame."

[Editor's Note: The *Webster's Online Dictionary with Multilingual Thesaurus Translation* was used extensively in creating this translation.]

---

[1] Cyndi Dale, The Mayan Energy System, An Encyclopedia of Your Energetic Anatomy, (Sounds True, Inc., Boulder, Colo., 2009) Sounds True e-book.

[2] Saint Germain Press, I AM Angel Decrees Part Two, (Saint Germain Press, Inc., 1974, Chicago, Ill.), page 36.

[3] Ibid., page 35.

[4] Wikipedia, Divine Language, http://en.wikipedia.org/wiki/Divine_language , (2011).

[5] Countries and Their Cultures, Gonds, http://www.everyculture.com/wc/Germany-to-Jamaica/Gonds.html , (2010).

APPENDIX G

Topics and Terms for Blue Illumination

Gobean and the Ancient City of Shamballa
The Blue Race and Shamballa
The Immortal Leader: Sanat Kumara
Retreat of Shamballa to the Ethereal Planes
Kali-Yuga
Shamballa and the Golden City of Gobi
Time of the Golden Perfections
Instant-Thought-Manifestation
Quetzalcoatl and Akhenaten
Serapis Bey, Guru to El Morya

El Morya's Historical Teachings on Shamballa and the Golden Cities:
1. The Golden City of Gobean aligns to, or is associated with the Golden City of Gobi—located in China. This Vortex covers the geophysical area which was once the earthly location of the fabled ancient Golden City of Shamballa.
2. All of the Golden Cities of the earth are interconnected.
3. The Blue Ray Force is said to have brought earth's first Golden City into physical manifestation. While many of Shamballa's first inhabitants came from the planet Venus, Mercury also played a significant role in populating the opulent city. Other planets from different solar systems were also involved in the population of Shamballa. The Ascended Masters refer to this galaxy-migrating populace as the *Blue Race*.
4. Members of the Blue Race were immortal; death did not exist.
5. The deterioration of Shamballa came about as the populace was invaded by other planets (Star Seeds). Through this influence, the physical genetics and spiritual teachings of immortality were weakened and the Death Consciousness grew in strength. This brought the first disharmony, and thereafter strife and conflict spread through the once harmonious city. As the emanation of Shamballa deteriorated, the Masters of Wisdom decided to move the Golden City. However, this time the City of Perfection was physically built in such a manner that Shamballa was hidden; and entrance was given only to those who purposely sought its radiance and perfected vibration. Once again the city flourished as an abode for the immortals.
6. According to El Morya, perfection is an emanation: "Seek your own perfection. (First) idealize it as a perfect crystalline thought in your mind."

APPENDIX G

7. The second Golden City of Shamballa grew in energy and, through the principle of conductivity, once again influenced the earth with perfection and harmony.
8. Shamballa's second incarnation was again maligned by its citizens. This time the city's enlightened populace, who had risen in consciousness along with the venerated immortals, engaged in material excesses. The leaders of Shamballa made the decision to again destroy and rebuild the Golden City of Shamballa. However, the entrance to the new Golden City of Shamballa would not be built on the physical plane.
9. The immortal leader Sanat Kumara set forth the edict for Shamballa's restructuring on the ethereal immortal plane, assuring that only those who had properly developed their light bodies (Astral Body) could enter the sacred city.
10. Ashrams were established throughout Eastern Asia to train future members of the Shamballa community in the essential fundamentals of higher consciousness, which are the essential keys to open its Golden Gates.
11. As the ethereal Crystal City of Shamballa flourished, directly underneath its radiating fifth-dimensional aura a new civilization of the Gobi Desert thrived. According to El Morya, this is the spiritual Law of "As above, so below," and this ancient culture advanced spiritual knowledge and healing techniques.
12. The physical civilization that was once embraced by the golden ethers of the City of Shamballa disappeared upon earth's entrance into the age of lesser galactic light: Kali-Yuga.
13. By the order of leader Sanat Kumara, the city limits of the Golden City of Shamballa were restricted to the ethereal Fifth Dimension; however, remnants of this once physically opulent metropolis can still be detected by archaeologists. The energies of Shamballa intertwined with the ancient light fields of the once physical civilization of Gobi. The process of ethereal consciousness, emanation, and conductivity produced the Golden City Vortex of Gobi.
14. The Golden City of Gobi aligns to the First Golden City for the New Times: Gobean. Golden Cities represent a co-creation of Heaven and Earth. [Editor's Note: The Golden City of Gobi is located over the Qilian Shan Mountains, with the Gobi Desert to the North. The word *Qilian* is pronounced *Chee-layn*, and closely resembles the word *chela*, a term commonly used by the Master Teachers which means *disciple*. Qilian is a Xiongnu word, and in this language means *sky*. Qilian Shan Peak is 5,547 meters, or approximately 18,199 feet high—the center, or apex of the Gobi Vortex and one of the highest mountain peaks in the Chinese Gansu Province.[5]]
15. The Golden City of Gobean and the Golden City of Gobi are connected, not only through the grid of worldwide Golden Cities, but through a spiritual, etheric connection. According to El Morya, meditation performed in the Golden City of Gobean can instantly transport your body. This is due to the level of perfection present in Shamballa. The process of bi-location is achieved through the Mastery of Perfection as perfect consciousness streams into body, mind, and heart.
16. Through accessing the Blue Ray of Truth in the Golden City of Gobean, El Morya teaches that through meditation students and chelas can access Akashic Records of

APPENDIX G

ancient times and civilizations. This allows information to be relayed seamlessly to fit each individual's educational spiritual developmental level. This technique circumvents recorded history slanted by another's perspective or beliefs that may dilute the effect of the information for the student. As each student or chela receives direct information, they also obtain ever-important experience.

17. The Golden City of Gobean is permeated with the historical Akashic records of the earth.
18. According to El Morya, the lands that now comprise the physical proximity of the Gobean Vortex were once visited by the spiritual teacher and King of Egypt, Akhenaten (1351–1334 BC). Since he was able to project his consciousness to the higher planes, it is claimed that Akhenaten traveled in his light bodies to the ancient American Southwest and shared his teachings with the Native Peoples. This was one of the first initiatory preparations of Gobean, and from these earliest spiritual sparks, the Vortex grew in energy and power. Today, the Golden City of Gobean aligns in historical provenance to the Ancient Giza Plateau.
19. According to El Morya, Shamballa is seen by the Master Teachers as the "Hall of Wisdom," and through its venerated teachings of the eons, it has guided humanity's spiritual growth and evolution.

Star Seed

The Ascended Masters assign two associated definitions to this term. The first defines the Star Seed as a family or soul group whose members have evolved to Fifth-Dimensional awareness. Star Seeds can also contain members who have not yet evolved to this level and are still incarnating on earth. The second definition of Star Seed is somewhat literal and refers to populating groups, or soul groups, originating from other solar systems and galaxies. Some Star Seeds intentionally leave their homeland planets to inhabit earth and adapt their DNA through reproduction with humans. Other Star Seed souls and soul families enter the earthly evolutionary Wheel of Karma, and spiritually incarnate in human form. Occult historians claim that earth is now riddled with Star Seeds through genetics and spiritual connection.

Gobi Desert

Theosophists claim this desert region of China was once a fertile plain which bordered an inland sea and contained the "Sacred Island." This esoteric geology is said to date back to the times of Atlantis, Rama, and the Ancient Uiger civilization—an evolved culture that asserts the prehistoric use of aircraft (Vimanas). The *Sons of Will and Yoga* took shelter on the mythological Sacred Island as humanity fell into states of lower consciousness. Theosophical texts define this time in humanity's history as one when, "Daityas prevailed over the Devas and humanity became black with sin." In Hinduism, Daityas were a race of evil giants, who resisted the Gods, or immortals; the Devas are the immortals who maintained the sanctity of Divine Creation. Cataclysm drained the inland sea, leaving the once bountiful land a wild and arid desert of mountains and sand.[1]

Prior to this catastrophe, the spiritual elders reestablished their school and library of teachings, known as the Thirteenth School in present-day Tibet. Occultists claim the Great

APPENDIX G

White Brotherhood evolved from this early Mystery School and the famed philosopher Lao Tzu (born 604 BC) journeyed to its western headquarters—the mythological land of Hsi Wang Mu.[2]

Psychic Edgar Cayce referenced the Gobi Desert in many of his life readings and identified this area as the "Sun Land." Cayce also referred to a city buried under the desert sands as the *City of Gold* and prophesied its future discovery. His readings claimed that the Gobi civilization mirrored the prehistoric mound-builders of North America, and their architecture included terraced buildings and temples. Today the A.R.E.—the Association for Research and Enlightenment founded in 1931 by Cayce—alleges that a small ethnic group from the Gobi contains X Haplotype DNA, theorized to be related to the *Atlantean Genetic Type*, and a genetic link to the North American Iroquois tribe, ancient Iberia, and the Basques.[3,4]

The Gobi Desert traverses Northern and Northwestern China and Southern Mongolia; it is the fifth largest desert in the world. The Himalaya mountain range creates the rain shadow that blocks rain from falling in the Gobi.

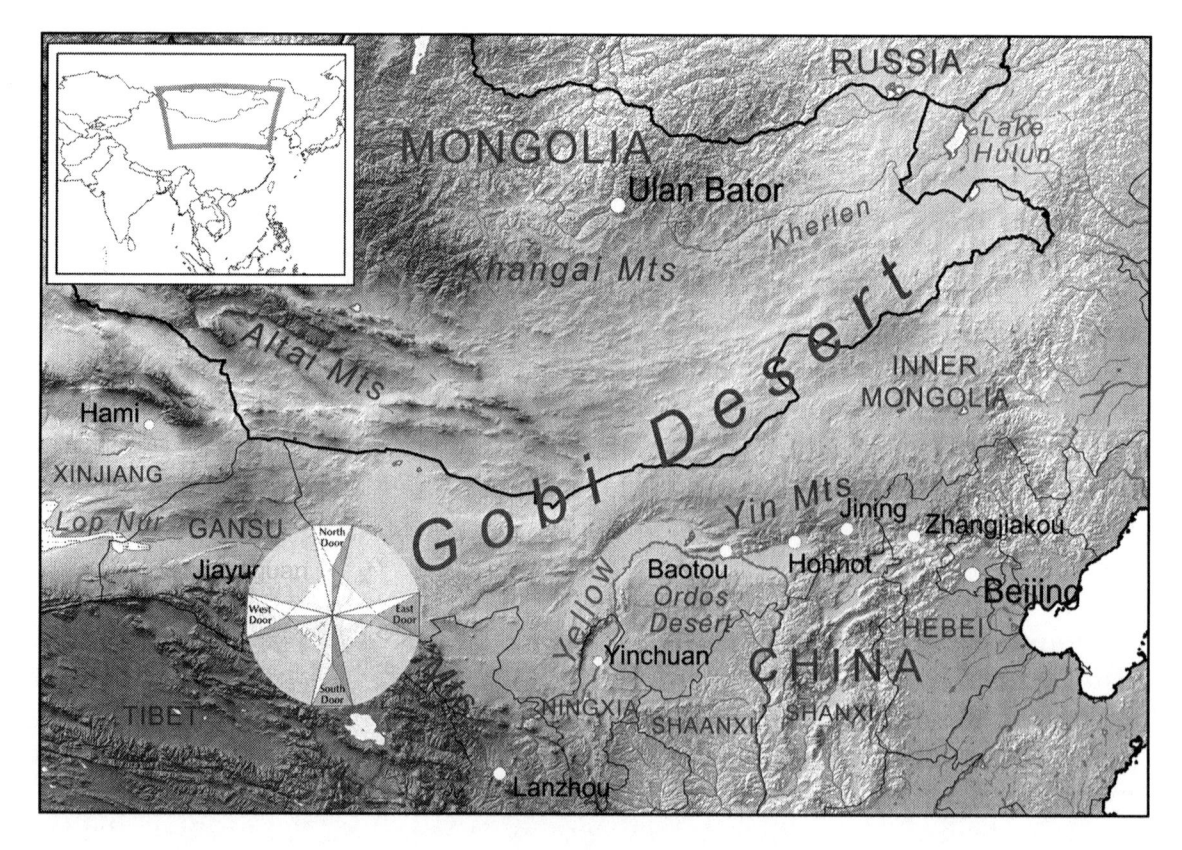

FIGURE 1-G
Golden City of Gobi
The *Golden City of Gobi* is located in China and Mongolia: Tibet is to the Southwest and the Gobi Desert to the North and Northeast. These areas are the People's Republic of China (PRC) Provinces and Administrative Divisions of: Gansu; Qinghai; Inner Mongolia. (Golden City Figure not to scale.)

[Map Base Art: *Wikimedia Commons*, Kmusser, Map showing the Gobi Desert and surround area. Elevation data from SRTM, all other features from Vector Map (2011).]

APPENDIX G

The Lineage of Shamballa to the Golden Cities

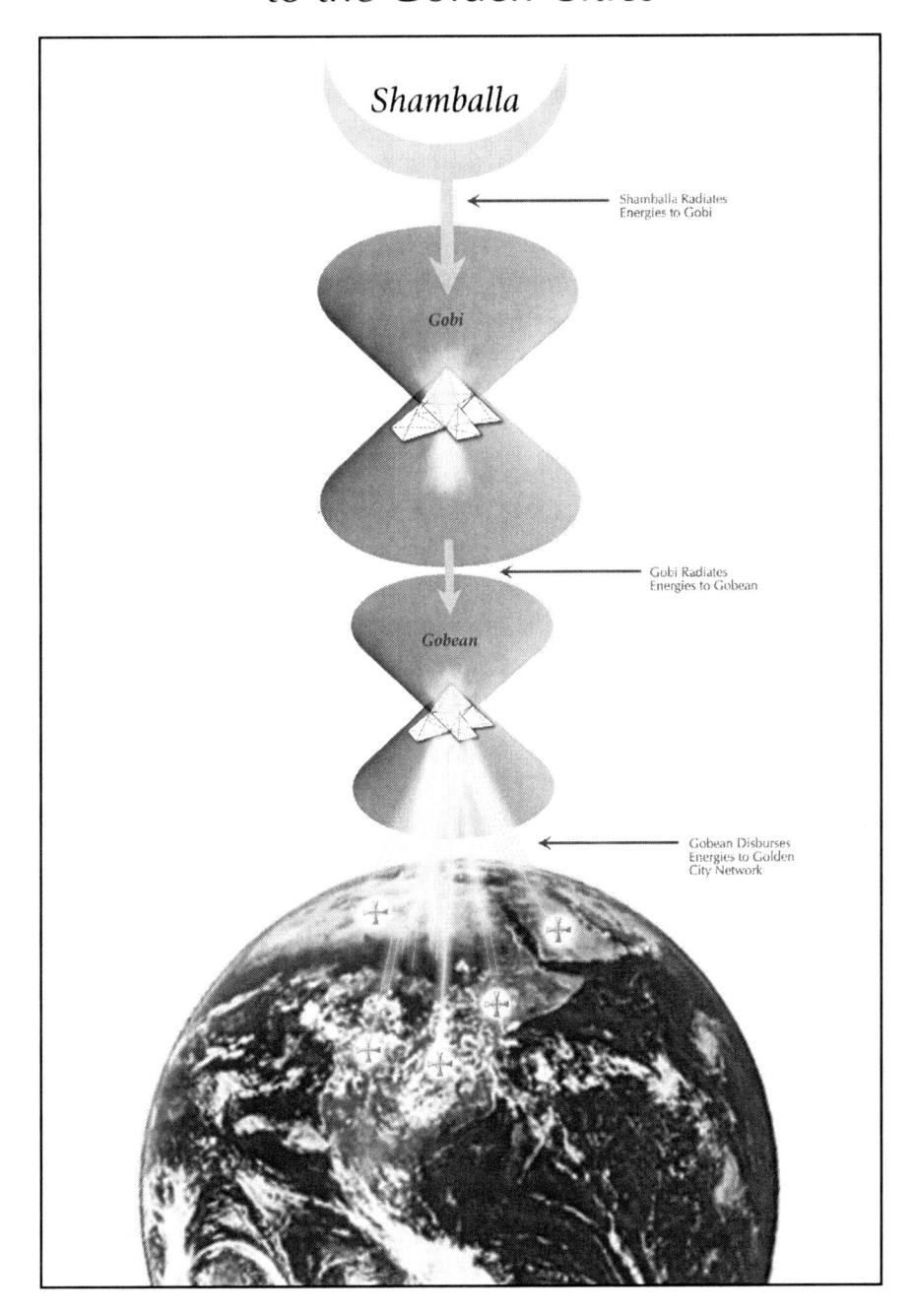

FIGURE 2-G
Lineage of Shamballa to the Golden Cities
This illustration depicts the flow of spiritual energies from Shamballa to the Golden City of Gobi (China); the energies step-down from the Golden City of Gobi to the Golden City of Gobean (Southwest, US); the Golden City of Gobean disburses the energies of Shamballa to all other Golden Cities through the Golden City Network. Fifth dimensional energies flow through a spiritual grid on the earth and enter through the apex (center) of each Golden City Vortex.

APPENDIX G

Sanat Kumara

Sanat Kumara, the venerated leader of the Ascended Masters, is best known as the founder of Shamballa, the first Golden City on earth. He is also known in the teachings of the Great White Brotherhood as the *Lord of the World* and is regarded as a savior and eminent spiritual teacher. Sanat Kumara is revered in many of the world religions as the familiar *Ancient of Days* in Judeo-Christianity, *Kartikkeya* in Hinduism, the Persian deity *Ahura Mazda* in Zoroastrianism, and as Moses' challenging teacher and the Sufi initiator of Divine Mysteries *Al Khdir*. C. W. Leadbeater and Alice Bailey referred to Sanat Kumara as the *Youth of Sixteen Summers*—a paradox to his Ancient of Days identity—and the *One Initiator*, as the Master of spiritual ceremonies of initiation. According to esoteric historians, Sanat Kumara was one of the few Ascended Masters who revealed his four-fold identity as the Cosmic Christ: first as *Kartikkeya*, the Hindu commander of God's Army; second, as *Kumar* (Kumara), the holy youth; third, as *Skanda*, son of Shiva; and fourth, as *Guha*—a Sanskrit term for the secret place in the heart, as he lives in the cave of all hearts.[5]

Sanat Kumara's Vedic and Buddhist Connection

The leader of the Spiritual Masters of the World appears historically in Vedic religious texts as a rishi who was one of the four sons of Brahma, the Creator. The four sons are born as liberated souls, and in early life take vows of celibacy. Since they are young, unmarried males, this becomes their eternal appearance, and the four sons are naturally attracted to devotional service to humanity. The four sons, or Kumaras, are known as: Sanaka Kumara; Sanandana Kumara (Sananda); Sanatana Kumara; and Sanat Kumara. In Sanskrit the name Sanat Kumara means *eternal youth*. Vedic scholars claim that the four sons are actually one incarnation manifesting on different planes of spiritual and physical reality.[6]

Santana Kumara	Supra Cosmic Plane
Sanaka Kumara	Solar Plane
Sanandana Kumara	Earth Plane
Sanat Kumara	Earth Planet

Sanat Kumara's affiliation with the earth is often referred to by esoteric researchers as the station or office of Planetary Logos—a soul whose evolutionary journey leads them to oversee entire planets. Dr. Joshua Stone describes this cosmic position: "The job of the Planetary Logos is to set up a framework on the physical level for all evolving life forms which allows them all to evolve and grow. The Planetary Logos could be symbolically likened to a mountain and the paths on the mountain which the life forms travel to evolve. The Planetary Logos is also at the top of the mountain so he can guide all life forms toward the top."[7] Perhaps this understanding alone gives explanation for Sanat Kumara's abiding presence in Shamballa, known in ancient India as the true spiritual center of earth, akin to earth's Sahasrara—Crown Chakra.

The Vedic epic of ancient India, the Mahabharata, states that Sanat Kumara is reborn as the son of Lord Krishna, Pradyumna. Pradyumna was an incarnation of the God of Love—Kama—and met a Karmic death at Dwaraka, one of the seven sacred cities of ancient

APPENDIX G

India. With this final earthly Karma completed, Pradyumna resumes his cosmic identity as Sanat Kumara and secures his rightful seat as the Planetary Lord of Shamballa.

Buddhist lore defines Shambhala (Shamballa) as the place of happiness, tranquility, and peace; and where the records of the Kalachakra Tantra—advanced spiritual practices, spiritual philosophies, and meditation techniques—are claimed to be safeguarded. The teachings of Vajrayana Buddhism declare the King of Shambhala as King of the World, and this royal lineage descends from the Kalki Kings who maintain the integrity of the Kalachakra teachings. Early Tibetans claim Shambhala's location to be North of Lake Manasarovar, the highest fresh-water lake in the world, and nearby Mount Kailash, which derives its name from the phrase *the precious one* and is considered a sacred mountain of religious significance to the Bon, Buddhism, Hinduism, and Jainism. This area is considered the hydrographic center of the Himalaya, and its melted snows are the source for the Brahmaputra River, the Indus River, and Karnali River—an important tributary of the Ganges River. It is thought that all of the earth's dragon currents—energy lei-lines—intersect at Mount Kailash.[8]

Evolution and Training of a Planetary Logos

Sanat Kumara's evolution is said to have occurred primarily on an earth-like planet located in the Milky Way Galaxy. It is claimed that after sixty-nine lifetimes, he achieved the Ascension. After a brief study of the Music of the Spheres, he elected the path of Planetary Logos. This training was arduous and spiritually challenging and the Master divided his consciousness into 900,000 fragments with each portion strewn to a different planet of the galaxy. From there he wove each individual piece back into the ONE through unconditional love and equanimity. After this great test of Mastery, Sanat Kumara was required to take on a physical body to continue his training on the Planet Venus, where he encountered the cosmic being Adonis who became his guru. It is claimed that Sanat Kumara was educated in the beautiful Fourth Dimensional temples of Venus for 2,000 years. During his epoch tenure on Venus, Sanat Kumara was assigned to work with the Venusian Planetary Logos. As the Master grew in experience and knowledge of planetary infrastructure and patterns, he evolved his spiritual Mastery to embrace Unity Consciousness, integration, balance, and the power of choice. These important spiritual precepts ultimately groomed the young Lord for his chief assignment: earth.[9]

Some esoteric texts claim Shamballa existed more than 60,000 years ago, while others claim Sanat Kumara was sent to earth to build the restorative Golden City more than 18,000,000 years ago. This complex timeline may be explained by the cosmic susceptibility to the progression of the Yugas (periods of Vedic timekeeping) and their correlation with cataclysmic Earth Changes. The provenance of Shamballa states that the wondrous City of Light was destroyed and rebuilt three times. The first Golden City on earth, however, was in all of its various stages of planning, construction, destruction, modification, and transformation, under the stewardship of Sanat Kumara. His assignment was simple but relatively complex: raise the consciousness of humanity. Should he fail in his mission, earth would likely be destroyed. The compassionate Venusian Lord offered his light to balance the planet's metaphysical darkness and disharmony.[10] [Editor's Note: For more information, read *Points of Perception, Appendix M, Shamballa*.]

APPENDIX G

Prior to Sanat Kumara's descent to earth, he was given a well-deserved vacation of fifty years. Upon his return, he was given a party where it was announced that Sanat Kumara would be accompanied by the Venusian volunteers Lord Gautama and Lord Maitreya. Along with the angelic Serapis Bey, these two Lords would play invaluable roles in humanity's spiritual history and development.[11,12]

As Sanat Kumara entered earth, his three Brothers—the immortal Kumaras—held their focused energies to assist the heavenly incarnation. Today this is known as the Astrological Spiritual Trinity transmitted to the earth through Jupiter, the Sun, and Mars. And to this day, energies of the Galactic Center triangulate to the earth through these planets. While Sanat Kumara's incarnation took effect immediately, another 1,000 years was needed to properly seat the celestial powers and link the supreme consciousness to earth. During this 1,000-year period, occult historians claim the earth's atmosphere was filled with electrical storms. Sanat Kumara and his stalwart volunteers patiently calibrated the earth's energy fields and established their spiritual headquarters located near the Himalayan Mountains, near the present-day Gobi Desert.[13]

Sanat Kumara: Shamballa and the Great White Brotherhood

H. P. Blavatsky first coined the phrase "Lords of the Flame," to describe Sanat Kumara's association with humanity's Divine Evolution. Yet it was the theosophists Leadbeater and Annie Besant who claimed Sanat Kumara deployed thirty *Lords of the Flame* to accompany him on his spiritual mission to earth. Classic Ascended Master teachings concur with this legendary story, however Sanat Kumara's group numbered 144,000 Venusian volunteers—pledged to enlighten earth at a time of collective spiritual darkness.

One hundred of Sanat Kumara's volunteers arrived on earth 900 years beforehand to proliferate light, propagate the Flame of Consciousness, and prepare for the coming of the Golden City of Shamballa. Esoteric teachings say fellow Venusian Serapis Bey served as Sanat Kumara's first volunteer. With an affinity for architecture, this Master Teacher—along with the Seraphic Hosts he served with on the planets of Mercury, Aquaria, and Uranus—offered to oversee the creation of Shamballa. Serapis Bey, the exalted being of light, performed one of the greatest sacrifices in Ascended Master legend by descending into a physical body. On earth, with his legions of seraphim, Serapis Bey oversaw the building of Shamballa—the City of White—for nine centuries. His sacrifice awarded him the honor of the Divine Architect of Shamballa.[14]

The builders of Shamballa modeled it after the opulent Venusian City of the Kumaras. On a white island in the sapphire-colored Gobi Sea (present-day Gobi Desert), workers erected the Elysian metropolis of light and consciousness. An ornate bridge of marble and gold connected the White Island to the mainland. They adorned the city with hundreds of white, dome-and-spire-capped temples—that's where Shamballa earned its moniker, the City of White. Against this whitewashed backdrop, the luminous Temples of the Seven Rays and their corresponding hues—blue, pink, yellow, pearl-white, green, ruby, and violet—stood prominently along a landscaped avenue. At its terminus rose the Temple of the Lord of the World, Sanat Kumara's annular, golden-domed sanctuary. Here, the Ascended Master; three other Venusian Kumaras (lords); and thirty high priests, also known as Lords of the Flame, held conscious light for earth to sustain her place in the solar system. Dur-

APPENDIX G

ing his time in Shamballa, Sanat Kumara provided more than a spiritual safe harbor for earth's denizens. He also formed the Great White Brotherhood—the fellowship of the Ascended Masters.[15]

Sanat Kumara's Return to Venus

Before Sanat Kumara's appointment as Lord of the World, Sri Magra held the office in earth's spiritual-political hierarchy. After millions of years of service to earth, Sanat Kumara was granted his freedom on January 1, 1956 and the noble Lord returned to his beloved Venus and his Divine Consort, Lady Master Venus. His three beloved Venusian volunteers—Lord Gautama, Lord Maitreya, and Serapis Bey—had successfully developed and advanced their sacred mission.

Serapis Bey became renowned as the *World Architect* and was also revered as the Hindu deity VishvaKarma.

Lord Maitreya became the leader of the Great White Brotherhood as a representation of the *Cosmic Christ*. He is the magnificent guru of Jesus, Kuthumi, El Morya, Saint Germain, and many other Masters, saints, and spiritual teachers. Through the process of overshadowing, this avatar "enfolded Jesus in His Cosmic Consciousness through Jesus' form."[16] The overshadowing process is described by Joshua Stone, PhD, in *The Complete Ascension Manual*:

> "Overshadowing was a process of melding his consciousness from the spiritual world into the physical body and consciousness of Jesus. In a sense, they shared the same physical body during the last three years of Jesus' life. Most people do not realize this. Many of the miracles and sayings attributed to Jesus were really those of Lord Maitreya who holds the position in the Spiritual Government as the Christ. Jesus so perfectly embodied the Christ Consciousness that it enabled the Lord Maitreya, who is the Planetary Christ, to meld his consciousness with that of Jesus."[17]

Using the same technique initiated by Lord Maitreya as *the World Teacher*, Sanat Kumara overshadowed and accelerated the earth's spiritual development through Venusian Lord Gautama's earthly embodiment as Prince Siddhartha Gautama, an Indian prince (563–483 BC). Through Sanat Kumara's careful guidance, their consciousness melded as ONE, and Lord Gautama became the *Enlightened One* and qualified as earth's first Buddha. According to A, D. K. Luk in the *Law of Life*, the activity and service of a Buddha is, "to step-down the high spiritual vibrations and radiate them to nourish, expand, and sustain the light in all beings during their development on the planet. He is to radiate God's love to a planet and its evolutions; to draw and hold the spiritual nourishment around a planet for all evolving lifestreams on that planet both while in and out of embodiment, sustaining them spiritually and developing their inner God natures especially the emotional bodies. He guards and sustains the flame of the least developed soul, so that it will not go out. A Buddha's work is through radiation, by radiating."[18]

Buddha's radiation of the indwelling spiritual consciousness of humanity paved the pathway for the development of humanity's conscious mind and the Christ activity, or *Christ Consciousness* in self-realization. Lord Buddha also assumed Sanat Kumara's vacant

APPENDIX G

position at Shamballa as present-day Lord of the World, an honor bestowed from the now seasoned Planetary Logos: Sanat Kumara—mentor, guru, and friend.

Sanat Kumara Today

Presently the ethereal City of Shamballa is open to all who have acquired *the eyes to see, and the ears to hear* from December 17th to January 17th on an annual basis. During this time, Sanat Kumara returns to Shamballa and gives guidance to the Brotherhoods and Sisterhoods of Light for their yearly plan for humanity's spiritual growth and progress. Sanat Kumara's visit is accompanied by the Celebration of the Four Elements: a twenty-eight day festivity centered on devotional sacraments dedicated to the elements of earth, air, water, and fire in conjunction with thanksgiving, gratitude, love, friendship, intention, and unity. [Editor's Note: For more information see *Points of Perception, Appendix M*, and *The Celebration of the Four Elements*.]

Sanat Kumara is the guru of four of the *Twelve Jurisdictions*—spiritual precepts on Co-creation designed to guide human consciousness into the New Times. As he gave this important wisdom, his ethereal presence was often accompanied by the Golden Radiance of the Solar Logos: Apollo. Here is a synthesis of Sanat Kumara's four teachings.

> **The Masculine Principle of Cooperation**: The spiritual teachings of Cooperation, the seventh of the *Twelve Jurisdictions*, are taught by both Lady Master Venus and Sanat Kumara. Cooperation is the spiritual knowledge that teaches every individual to *honor their divinity*. Both Lady Master Venus and Sanat Kumara share their philosophies on this topic. Lady Master Venus gives the feminine point of view. Sanat Kumara elaborates from a male perspective. In his teachings Sanat Kumara states, "Your enlightenment has always been and will always be. That is unchangeable. Bring your conscious awareness, your focus, to the sustaining, and cooperate with yourself in this great magnificence that you are. Cooperate with all others in the great magnificence that they are."[19]

> **The Principle of Charity**: The eighth of the *Twelve Jurisdictions* is the spiritual guidance to *live with love and equity*. Sanat Kumara advises, "Charity is a distribution, and it is the equalizer when there is un-justice and inequity."[20]

> **The Principle of Desire**: The ninth of the *Twelve Jurisdictions* is based on a new perception of desire based on the true etymology of the word. *De* is a French word that means *of*, and the English word *sire* means *forefather, ancestry,* or *source*. From this context, Sanat Kumara teaches the *Heart's Desire is the source of creation*. He states, "Desire springs not only from the heart, it comes from the soul, the spark of creativity."[21]

> **The Principle of Stillness**: Stillness is the eleventh of the *Twelve Jurisdiction* and Sanat Kumara explains this important spiritual knowledge as the *Law of Alignment*. The practice of this immutable law was likely perfected during the creation of Shamballa, and the Lord of the World states, "Stillness is the space where energy is gathered and

APPENDIX G

aligned to come forth in a manifestation."[22] [Editor's Note: For more information on the *Twelve Jurisdictions* see *New World Atlas, Volume One*.]

The Spiritual Contributions of Sanat Kumara

The spiritual role played by Sanat Kumara in earth's history and humanity's spiritual enrichment is truly invaluable and, without question, almost impossible to measure. There are, however, several significant and remarkable accomplishments worth noting.

Sanat Kumara spearheaded the mission to graft the sublime *Unfed Flame*—a Flame of Divinity and spiritual consciousness—to the carnal human heart. The Unfed Flame urges humanity to evolve beyond its present state of spiritual consciousness through Co-creative thought, feeling, and action and the Divine Tenets of Love, Wisdom, and Power. This empowers humans to achieve a higher sense of consciousness, thereby assuring humanity a type of spiritual immortality. With an etheric silver cord, Sanat Kumara connected the Unfed Flame to every life stream incarnation on earth. This ensured the development and growth of spiritual consciousness among individuals.[23]

During the 1,000-year period while earth energies were purified to receive the spiritual presence and teachings of Sanat Kumara, the esteemed Lord performed yearly sacred fire ceremonies to clear earth's etheric atmosphere of darkness. These ceremonies assisted the spiritually awakened to maintain contact with their I AM Presence. It is claimed that many attended these rites, and each attendee would take home a piece of the sacred wood used for the fire—likely sandalwood—to keep throughout the year. These ceremonies forged an indelible bond between Sanat Kumara and those he once served. A. D. K. Luk writes, "Sanat Kumara came ages ago to give assistance to the earth when it would have been dissolved otherwise. He offered of his own free will to supply the light required to sustain her and keep her place in the system until enough of mankind could be raised to a point where they could carry the responsibility of emitting sufficient light . . . Now when people first come in contact with his name they usually feel a sense of happiness come over them. This is because of his connection with their lifestreams through radiation during the past."[24]

The sacred City of Shamballa is said to be both "a location and a state of consciousness."[25] Sanat Kumara's service to advancing spiritual students is never static and always unfolding; and along with various counsel meetings among the Spiritual Hierarchy, Sanat Kumara's purpose at Shamballa is to continue the initiatory process of students and chelas and to provide a haven for those who have successfully passed the fifth initiation. The seven levels of human evolution and their initiatory processes are:

1. The spiritually un-awakened, yet conscious human
2. The *Aspirant*—a newly awakened, ambitious student
3. The *Chela*—the disciple who has entered a formal student relationship with a guru or teacher
4. The *Initiate*—personal experience by degree, test, and trial that is encountered morally, mentally, and physically
5. The *Arhat*—one who has overcome antagonistic craving, including the entire range of passions and desires—mental, emotional, and physical

APPENDIX G

6. The *Adept*—one who has attained Mastery in the art and science of living; a Mahatma
7. The *Master*—"human beings further progressed on the evolutionary pathway than the general run of humanity from which are drawn the saviors of humanity and the founders of the world-religions. These great human beings (also known by the Sanskrit term Mahatma 'great self') are the representatives in our day of a Brotherhood of immemorial antiquity running back into the very dawn of historic time, and for ages beyond it. It is a self perpetuating Brotherhood formed of individuals who, however much they may differ among themselves in evolution, have all attained mahatma-ship, and whose lofty purposes comprise among other things the constant aiding in the regeneration of humanity, its spiritual and intellectual as well as psychic guidance, and in general the working of the best spiritual, intellectual, psychic, and moral good to mankind. From time to time members from their ranks, or their disciples, enter the outside world publicly in order to inspire mankind with their teachings."[26]

In metaphysical terms, Sanat Kumara may be seen as a *mastermind* of earth's spiritual evolutionary process. A *mastermind* contains *organized effort*—a true measure of everlasting power. Sanat Kumara had the ability to hold the focus of the Elemental and Fourth Dimensional energies to create Shamballa on earth and then actively engage the help of literally thousands of Lords, Masters, sages, saints, angels, Elohim, and adepts throughout our galaxy. Esoteric scholars claim that the entire spectrum of the Seven Rays are indeed embodied in Sanat Kumara and distributed through the synthesizing radiance of the Lord of the World.

FIGURE 3-G
The Four Kumaras
The four youthful, immortal Brothers are depicted in this Indian print.

[Samkadi Muni Bhagaven, source is from Editor in Chief: Sri Vasudeva Srana Upadhayaya of Sarvesvara Press, Sri Nimbarkacar, Wikimedia Commons (2011).]

APPENDIX G

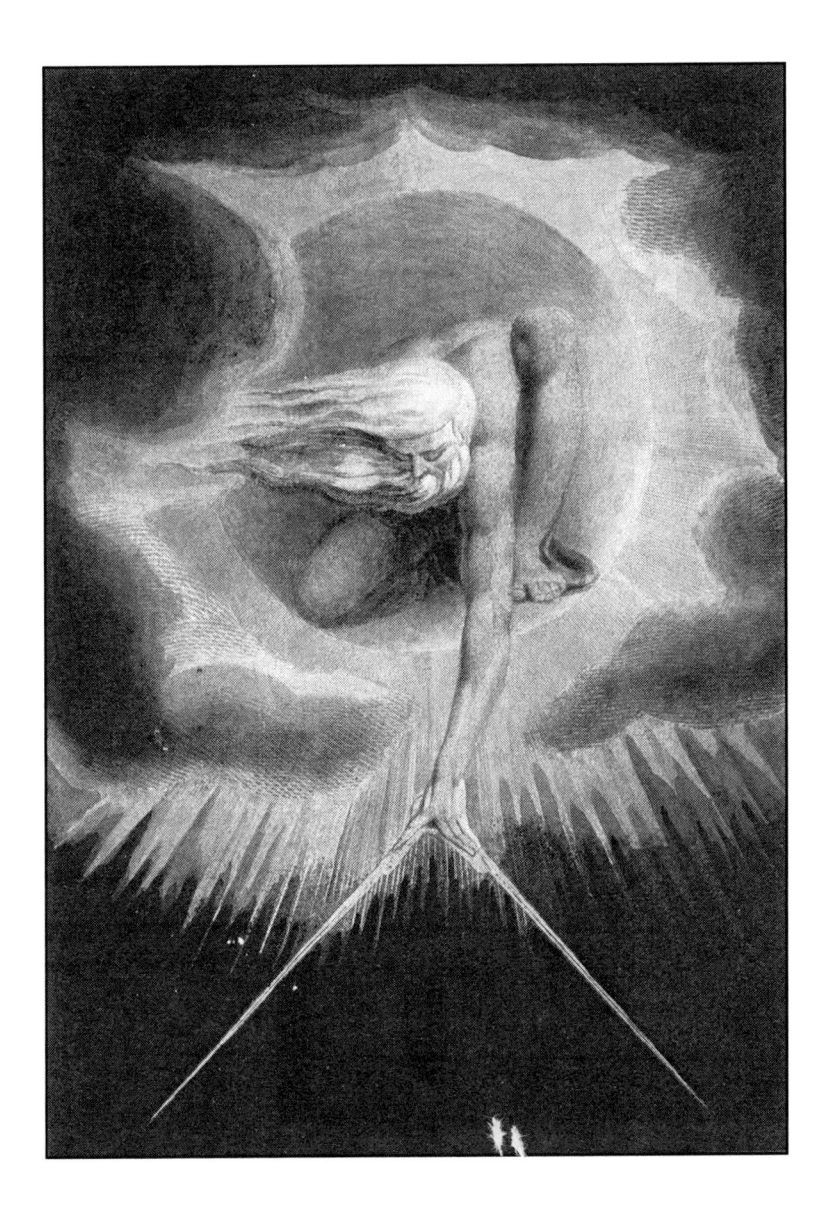

FIGURE 4-G
The Ancient of Days
by William Blake (1757—1827)
Sanat Kumara, portrayed by the visionary artist William Blake as *The Ancient of Days*, holds his spiritual compass as if to engineer the spiritual city Shamballa. This portrait is housed in the British Museum, London, and is claimed to be Blake's final painting, commissioned by Frederick Tatham.

[William Blake, The Ancient of Days, Wikimedia Commons, Public Domain, (2011).]

APPENDIX G

FIGURE 5-G
Kartikkeya
First Century coin with the deity Kartikeya from the Yaudeya Gana, an ancient state of India once located between the Indus and Ganges Rivers. This coin resides in the British Museum Collection.

[WikiMedia Commons, (2011).]

FIGURE 6-G
Ahura Mazda Investiture
Ahura Mazda (right) with Ardeshir I (left) in this archaeological relief at Naqh-e-Rustan (Iran). This rock carving is from the birth of the Sassanian Empire (224—651).

[Ginolerhino, Naqshi Rustam Investiture d'Ardashir, Wikimedia Commons (2002).]

Prophecies of Change

1. El Morya prophesies the end of Kali-Yuga and humanity enters a new period that is designed to move everyone forward into a new evolution.
2. Many individuals will be accelerated in their physical bodies, minds, and light-bodies in the New Times. This acceleration, referred to by El Morya as the *Times of the Golden Perfections*, gives the ability to bi-locate, which is the capability to be present in more than one place at a time in the physical dimension.
3. *Time Compaction* aids humanity in acquiring the Golden Perfection of the body, and it is prophesied that as the New Times progress, the deathless body and the idea of physical immortality will be better understood.
4. The *Cellular Awakening* assists this acceleration and is essential to access the advanced energies of the Golden Cities. Since the Golden Cities contain an abundant, condensed form of *prana* (chi, orgone), this higher, revolving energy source restores the physical body and produces miraculous healing, especially in Southern Door

APPENDIX G

locations of Golden City Vortices. [Editor's Note: see *Points of Perception*, Appendices E and G.]

5. In the New Times, Northern Doors of Golden Cities assist students and chelas to practice and obtain *instant-thought-manifestation*.
6. The Golden Cities serve as a *Divine Intervention* during the Time of Change, providing humanity with the necessary support and spiritual guidance to enter the ever-important Golden Age.

The Candle Meditation as Taught by El Morya

The Candle Meditation by El Morya is one of the first steps to experience the Divine Light within and calm the mind. Use a long tapered candle, not a jarred glass candle. For this exercise I prefer a white candle, but any color should work. Light the candle and establish a constant, stable flame.

First, sit comfortably; you may use a chair for back support if needed. Look and concentrate on the candle and give attention to the different layers of the light of the flame. You will notice these layers: the outer glow; the yellow-white layer of fire; the center of the wick; and the central inner glow, which sometimes contains a blue or violet hue at the base of the flame. Focus on the overall glow of the candle until you identify the layers of light. Breathe evenly and gently as you concentrate on the light.

As you observe the Flame of Light, continue your rhythmic breath as the light begins to expand and absorb the space between you and the flame. Continue this breathing until you have established a large ovoid of light, including the candle and yourself.

Remain focused in the circle of light and you will begin to notice you are in the flame; the light is even, and it flows with your breath. You may notice a pulse in the energy field you share with the flame. At this state you are ONE with the light.

Individuals who practice the Candle Meditation have reported feeling calm and peace, even in extremely stressful conditions. Sometimes this is accompanied by a high-pitch ring. El Morya asserts the application of the Candle Meditation imparts experience with the consciousness of the ONE and develops human consciousness into the HU-man. The Candle Meditation can be performed individually or in groups.

Instant-Thought-Manifestation

As you become more perfectly aligned and in harmony with your thoughts, feelings, and actions, your individual focused, directed desires may quickly manifest. This Co-creative activity is known by the Master Teachers as *Instant-Thought-Manifestation* and moves the *Initiate* to the beginning stages of *Arhat*. As initiates perfect this process, they may notice that the period of time between thoughts and manifestations diminishes; this is a common quality of HU-man development.

Akashic Records

From the Sanskrit word *akasa*, which means *to be visible, appear, shine*, or *be brilliant*, the *Akashic Records* are built from ether, the fifth cosmic element. Occultists claim the Akashic Records contain the history of all created things from time immemorial, including recorded details of past lifetimes and personal factors related to the

APPENDIX G

soul's spiritual growth and development. Akasa encompasses all of space and records all events, from the seemingly insignificant to the critical and decisive moments that change us forever. Akashic Records permeate our dimension; however, we may not have the ability to access or sense their content. For this reason, interested individuals may seek out mediums that are sensitized to the psychic undulations of akasa. The Ascended Masters, however, encourage our personal development through meditation to develop this ability.

According to esoteric teachers, the Akashic Records are purer than Astral Light, and exist in the Fifth Dimension. Since the Astral Body composes our Karmic pattern of emotion, it is influenced by our state of consciousness and does not extend beyond the Fourth Dimension. Mystics explain that the Astral Light is "the tablet of earth and of its child, the animal-man," and Akashic Light contains the memory of the Spiritual Hierarchy that manages and organizes our Planetary Logos and the souls that inhabit it. Akasa is known as the crucial agent in religion, occult electricity, an aspect in the HU-man energy system and Kundalini, and it "enters into all the magical operations of nature, producing mesmeric, magnetic, and spiritual phenomena." The book of Genesis describes akasa as the *waters of the deep*; and Gautama Buddha considered only two aspects of creation as eternal: akasa and nirvana.[27]

Akhenaten

Born in 1388 BC, the only surviving son of Amenhotep III, the King of Upper and Lower Egypt, Akhenaten strove to reform the Egyptian priesthood and unite the peoples of Egypt through a monotheist God, Aten. United in marriage at the age of twelve to the Egyptian Queen Nefertiti, Akhenaten was known to have fragile health, was a gentle and loving regent with an inclination to visions and dreams.

At the age of nineteen, Akhenaten broke with the corrupt priesthood of Amen. Historians record this fracture within the ancient Egyptian socio-political scene for several reasons. First, Amenhotep IV, known as Akhenaten, spiritually identified with the principles of Aten—symbolized by the Solar Disc—as a deity of one truth, and one light, who could unite the many secular deities of Egypt. Akhenaten—who had discovered the universal spiritual substance of light, good, and truth while meditating on the cosmic sun—realized that, "the sun did not shine upon Egypt alone, nor did its light and heat protect only the cities where it was honored. Its Rays shone beyond the mountains and beyond the deserts. Its light cheered the barbarians and sustained even the enemies of Egypt."[28]

Akhenaten's unfolding consciousness of the ONE and the unity of all life led him to issue orders that the name of Amen, and its implication of hierarchical adversity, be expunged from every inscription in Egypt. His break with the polytheistic religion of the kingdom created problems throughout the cultural state of Egypt, especially in ancient Thebes, the venerated City of his ancestors. To further implement his faith of Aten and his break from the traditional ancient faiths, Akhenaten relocated his capital City of Egypt on the East bank of the Nile River, approximately 160 miles South of present-day Cairo, where he constructed the intentional community of *Khut-en-Aten*

APPENDIX G

(the Horizon of Aten) at the present-day site of Amarna. This is where Akhenaten oversaw the building of several of the most massive temples of ancient Egypt, including the *Temple to the Formless One*.[29]

A pioneer of monotheistic religion, Akhenaten embraced the Christ Consciousness, and some esoteric historians view him as a spiritual forerunner who led the way for the incarnation of Jesus, the Christ. Charles Potter in the *History of Religion* writes, "He was also the first pacifist, the first realist, the first monotheist, the first democrat, the first heretic, the first humanitarian, the first internationalist, and the first person known to attempt to found a religion. He was born out of due time, several thousand years too soon."[30]

According to the Master Teachers, Akhenaten is one of the prior lifetimes attributed to Ascended Master Serapis Bey, and in his lifetime as Akhenaten was able to split his consciousness to physically appear in the Southwest United States. Due to their discovery of an ancient rock-cut cave, esoteric archaeologists theorize that Ancient Egyptians may have left clues to their presence in the Grand Canyon. An April 5, 1909, *Phoenix Gazette* article alleged that the Smithsonian Institute was financing exploration of the Canyon during the cave discovery: "Discoveries which almost conclusively prove that the race which inhabited this mysterious cavern, hewn in solid rock by human hands, was of oriental origin, possibly from Egypt, tracing back to Rameses. If their theories are born out by the translation of the tablets engraved with hieroglyphics, the mystery of the prehistoric peoples of North America, their ancient arts, who they were and whence they came, will be solved. Egypt and the Nile, and Arizona and the Colorado will be linked by a historical chain running back to ages which stagger the wildest fancy of the fictionist."[31]

The Master Teachers further claim that during this phase of Akhenaten's spiritual development, he studied with the Lord of the Christ Consciousness, Quetzalcoatl. This may explain Akhenaten's spiritual presence among indigenous peoples of the ancient American Southwest.

Akhenaten wrote the celebrated poem, "Great Hymn to Aten," synthesizing many of the religious and spiritual teachings of Atenism:

How manifold it is, what thou hast made!
They are hidden from the face (of man).
O sole god, like whom there is no other!
Thou didst create the world according to thy desire,
Whilst thou wert alone: All men, cattle, and wild beasts,
Whatever is on earth, going upon (its) feet,
And what is on high, flying with its wings.
The countries of Syria and Nubia, the land of Egypt,
Thou settest every man in his place,
Thou suppliest their necessities:
Everyone has his food, and his time of life is reckoned.
Their tongues are separate in speech,
And their natures as well;

APPENDIX G

FIGURE 7-G
Akhenaten and Family
This relief depicts the ancient Egyptian royal family: Akhenaten, Nefertiti, with three of their children. Note the sun, extending its Rays of light, a religous symbol of Aten.

[Gerbil, The royal family: Akhenaten, Nefertiti and their children, Wikimedia Commons (2008).]

FIGURE 8-G
Akhenaten and the Blue Crown
The Blue Crown evolved from the Crown of War and was worn by Egyptian Kings. It is associated with royal ceremonies. Cairo Museum.

[Jon Bosworth, Akhenaten with Blue Crown, Wikimedia Commons (2007).]

APPENDIX G

The Golden City of Gobean Lineage of Gurus:

QUETZALCOATL
Lord of the Christ Consciousness

Guru to:

AKHENATEN
ONE God

Reincarnation of:

SERAPIS BEY
Ascension

Guru to:

EL MORYA
*Transformation
Harmony
Peace*

FIGURE 9-G
The Golden City of Gobean Lineage of Gurus (Master Teachers)

Quetzalcoatl, known by many esoteric historians as a form of the Egyptian deity Thoth—an archetypal deity that dates as early as Atlantean times (52,000 BC) to ancient Egypt (1292 BC)—is known in Master Teachings as the Lord of the Christ Consciousness. The Master Teachers claim Akhenaten traveled in the ethereal planes to receive training from Quetzalcoatl Akhenaten was the reincarnation of the incarnated angel and architect of Shamballa, Serapis Bey. Serapis Bey, the Master of the White Ray of Purity and the Ascension Process, is guru to the Ascended Master El Morya, steward of the Golden City of Gobean. El Morya steps-down the ancient energies of Quetzalcoatl into Gobean through the spiritual energies of Transformation, Harmony, and Peace.

APPENDIX G

Their skins are distinguished,
As thou distinguishest the foreign peoples.
Thou makest a Nile in the underworld,
Thou bringest forth as thou desirest
To maintain the people (of Egypt)
According as thou madest them for thyself,
The lord of all of them, wearying (himself) with them,
The lord of every land, rising for them,
The Aten of the day, great of majesty.[32]

[Editor's Note: For more information regarding Serapis Bey, see *Points of Perception, Appendix H, Serapis Bey.*]

Projection of Consciousness

This ability acquired through a Mastery of meditation enables individuals to split their consciousness (existence, sensations, and cognitions) to another physical location or plane, while retaining the physical body in the physical dimension. Masters of this technique project their consciousness both to teach and to learn. As this technique is perfected, an ethereal body is often used for projection. This body is similar in appearance to the physical body. *Projection of Consciousness* is a pre-requisite skill for bi-location—the ability to physically exist in more than one location or spiritual plane—a talent often employed by an Ascended Master.

Star of Knowledge

The *Star of Knowledge* is yet another term for the Star of a Golden City Vortex, the center of the Vortex, or the apex. [Editor's Note: For more information, see *Points of Perception, Appendix G, Golden City Star.*]

---

[1] *Encyclopedic Theosophical Glossary*, http://www.theosociety.org/pasadena/etglos/etg-hp.htm, (2011).

[2] *Top 10 Civilizations with Advanced Technology*, http://ufo.whipnet.org/creation/ancient.advanced.civilizations/index.html, (2011).

[3] *Gobi Desert Mysteries, China Pyramids and Mounds*, http://www.edgarcayce.org/AncientMysteriesTemp/gobidesert.html, (2011).

[4] *Modern Genetic Research Confirming Cayce's Story*, http://www.edgarcayce.org/AncientMysteriesTemp/geneticevidence.html, (2011).

[5] *Wikipedia, Sanat Kumara*, http://en.wikipedia.org/wiki/Sanat_Kumara, (2011).

[6] Ibid.

[7] Joshua Stone, *The Complete Ascension Manual: How to Achieve Ascension in This Lifetime*, (Light Technology Publishing, 1994, Sedona, AZ), pages 178–9.

[8] *Wikipedia, Sanat Kumara*, http://en.wikipedia.org/wiki/Sanat_Kumara, (2011).

APPENDIX G

[9] Joshua Stone, *The Complete Ascension Manual: How to Achieve Ascension in This Lifetime,* (Light Technology Publishing, 1994, Sedona, AZ), page 179.

[10] Lori Toye, *Points of Perception: Prophecies and Teachings of Saint Germain,* (I AM America Seventh Ray Publishing, 2008, Payson, AZ), page 248.

[11] Joshua Stone, *The Complete Ascension Manual: How to Achieve Ascension in This Lifetime,* (Light Technology Publishing, 1994, Sedona, AZ), page 181.

[12] Lori Toye, *Points of Perception: Prophecies and Teachings of Saint Germain,* (I AM America Seventh Ray Publishing, 2008, Payson, AZ), pages 248–9.

[13] Joshua Stone, *The Complete Ascension Manual, How to Achieve Ascension in This Lifetime,* (Light Technology Publishing, 1994, Sedona, AZ), page 182.

[14] Lori Toye, *Points of Perception: Prophecies and Teachings of Saint Germain,* (I AM America Seventh Ray Publishing, 2008, Payson, AZ), pages 248–9.

[15] Ibid.

[16] Joshua Stone, *The Complete Ascension Manual: How to Achieve Ascension in This Lifetime,* (Light Technology Publishing, 1994, Sedona, AZ), page 138.

[17] Ibid.

[18] A. D .K. Luk, *Law of Life,* (A. D. K. Luk Publications, 1989, Pueblo, CO), Book II, page 310.

[19] Lori Toye, *New World Atlas, Volume One: Prophecies and Teachings for the New Times,* (I AM America Seventh Ray Publishing, Revised Edition 2010, Payson, AZ), pages 187–9.

[20] Ibid., pages 191–3.

[21] Ibid., pages 195–201.

[22] Ibid., pages 207–209.

[23] Lori Toye, *Points of Perception: Prophecies and Teachings of Saint Germain,* (I AM America Seventh Ray Publishing, 2008, Payson, AZ), page 172.

[24] A. D. K. Luk, *Law of Life,* (A. D. K. Luk Publications, 1989, Pueblo, CO), Book II, page 306.

[25] Joshua Stone, *The Complete Ascension Manual: How to Achieve Ascension in This Lifetime,* (Light Technology Publishing, 1994, Sedona, AZ), page 185.

[26] *Encyclopedic Theosophical Glossary,* http://www.theosociety.org/pasadena/etglos/etg-hp.htm, (2011).

[27] Ibid.

[28] Manly P. Hall, *Twelve World Teachers: A Summary of Their Lives and Teachings,* (Philosophical Research Society, Inc., 1965, Los Angeles, CA), page 21.

[29] *Wikipedia,* Akhenaten, http://en.wikipedia.org/wiki/Akhenaten, (2011).

[30] Manly P. Hall, *Twelve World Teachers: A Summary of Their Lives and Teachings,* (Philosophical Research Society, Inc., 1965, Los Angeles, CA), page 16.

[31] David Hatcher Childress, *Lost Cities of North and Central America,* (Adventures Unlimited Press, 1992, Stelle, IL), page 317.

[32] *Wikipedia,* Great Hymn to the Aten, http://en.wikipedia.org/wiki//Great_Hymn_to_the_Aten, (2011).

APPENDIX H

Topics and Terms for The Light of a Thousand Suns

Possible Earthquakes and Volcanic Eruptions
Saint Germain's Teachings on Relationships and Working with Others
Teachings on the Will and Choice
Kuthumi Prophesies Changes in the Elemental and Nature Kingdoms
Telepathy and the Bridge of Awakening
The Ruby Ray —a Catalyst
Path of Desire
The Golden City of Malton
The Gold Ray of the Lords of Venus
Prayer of a Thousand Suns
Telepathy and Vibration

On Predicted Events

Master Teachers will often predict events. However, accompanied with their projections are their calculations of probability and whether or not forecasted circumstances might have a negative effect. Therefore, along with predictions, Masters will often share the appropriate remedies to lessen or avert catastrophe. This type of prediction is known as a *prophecy*. In the teaching *The Light of a Thousand Suns,* Saint Germain informs listeners of a possible coastal earthquake in California, and says that prayer and consciousness will play an invaluable role in its outcome. A large quake has never occurred in this area, yet interestingly, the same year the quake was predicted, an earthquake swarm—the Long Valley Caldera (1998) occurred.

According to the Ascended Masters' teachings on prediction and prophecy, once events are prophesied, recognition by those who hear the prophecy has an effect upon individual and collective consciousness. Students, chelas, initiates, and their Master Teachers work appropriately to alter possible tragedy through adjusting collective energy and light fields. [Editor's Note: References to the Ring of Fire in this lesson refer to the 1998 eruptions of Mount Merapi (Java, Indonesia) and the Popocatepetl Volcano (Mexico).]

Out-picturing

This is a Co-creative process taught by the Master Teachers that includes meditation, focused attention, and visualization. Students and chelas are encouraged to use the *Out-picturing Process* especially in the realization of objectives and goals. The process may also include the use of specific breathing and energy techniques together with holding precise mental pictures.

APPENDIX H

Saint Germain on Relationships with Others
1. Encountering those on a spiritual path that is a bit different than yours does not mean that your path is superior or more evolved. Remember to understand and respect the concept, "Equal to."
2. Working toward Unity with others is imperative. One way to achieve this is joint ventures in consciousness efforts through prayer and conscious attunement toward worldwide events.
3. When you feel stress and turmoil in relationships, Saint Germain suggests that the use of the Violet Flame can shift negative energies and wipe away conflicting Karmas. Once the muddy waters of others' agendas are cleared from your thoughts, you can see your *own* path.
4. Saint Germain states: "Know thyself; and know thyself, first." Self-knowledge assists you in finding your purpose in a relationship and provides a bridge into Unity—*two as* One. From this point, the relationship can evolve and grow.
5. This evolutionary process with others can be difficult, and filled with judgments and doubts. Saint Germain, however, gives this guidance: "When there is natural harmony, the consequence of that harmony is always a good action."
6. Even in relationships, as we strive to unite as One, we are still individuals, and our challenge is to remain focused and to not be diverted from our own choices and spiritual path. Saint Germain reminds us that as we develop and grow through relationships, we are tuning and practicing our instruments of will and choice. This invaluable experience ultimately grooms our consciousness for entrance into a *larger symphony* with others.
7. Our knowledge and understanding of the individual roles we play in relationships and partnerships ready our consciousness to unite into the One. *Know thyself first, and harmony is assured.*

Saint Germain's Teachings on the Will
1. Raising human consciousness completely out of animal states requires the development of the will. Tempering this spirit strengthens the will.
2. Saint Germain assures that we are not victims of predestination. "You are the purveyor of your own will," he says. This means that through our conscious perceptions and choices, each of our thoughts is carefully cultivated and inevitably creates our world of experiences. [Editor's Note: For additional insight, see definition of *purveyor* below.]

Purveyor

Purveyor, or *purvey*, is derived from an old French word: *porveeir*, which in turn comes from the Latin word *providere*. Providere means to *foresee; provide for;* or *make provision. Videre* is a later Latin word which means *see; look at;* or *consider*. When considering the development of the will and Saint Germain's statement that we play a role as its purveyor, we understand that the derivation of the word suggests that indeed, an honest assessment of self is absolutely necessary to understand personal strengths, weaknesses, and past

APPENDIX H

choices—in order to navigate the spiritual path ahead. Purveyor is also synonymous with the word *promulgate*, which means to *make known; decree;* or *declare.*[1]

Prophecies of Change by Master Kuthumi

1. The earth is beginning its process of purification. This is also foretold in earth's astrology.
2. Prayer can change many things, including humanity. Master Kuthumi suggests we pray to change from the *inside* first.
3. There is great deceit and manipulation in world politics which places the United States economy in grave danger.
4. The Elemental Animal, Plant, and Mineral Kingdoms are all evolving, and their consciousness affects humanity's evolution. These Kingdoms serve us in various ways:
    a. Pets offer the consciousness of friendship and companionship.
    b. The Mineral Kingdom emits various qualities of Ray Forces.
    c. The Plant Kingdom offers its life force so we can live in and experience the physical plane.
    d. As each Kingdom experiences great change, so will humanity.
5. As we all spiritually awaken telepathically, connections form between humans, animals, plants, and minerals. This helps to create awareness and knowledge of the power of consciousness. Master Kuthumi calls this the *Bridge of Awakening*.

Harmonization with the Great Central Sun

Vedic and Western astrologers alike agree regarding the earth's winter solstice position's current conjunction with the Galactic Center, or in Ascended Master terminology: Great Central Sun. This position is calculated within one degree, and while there is some speculation as to the exact conjunction point, it is placed at 6° 40′ sidereally or approximately 29° tropically. The sidereal zodiac is used primarily by Eastern, or Vedic, astrologers; the tropical zodiac is a calculation commonly used in Western astrology. The difference between the two zodiacs, in a nutshell, is precession, or the slight wobble of the earth as it rotates on its axis.

Precession of the equinoxes is the slow backward shifting of the earth as it rotates. This slight tilting of the pole is calculated at approximately 23.5°; this is the source of the Vedic Ayanamsha, which differentiates planetary movements against the movement of stars—sidereal astrology. In contrast, tropical, or Western astrology tracks planets in reference to seasonal points according to a point of view from earth. Vedic astrology adjusts for precession; the Western system does not.[2]

The precise conjunction point of the Galactic Center with the earth will not be exact for about fifty to one hundred years; however this influence is currently producing many changes on earth and among humanity. Prominent Vedic astrologers, such as Dr. David Frawley, contend that the current conjunction is responsible for new collective spiritual beliefs, akin to the Spiritual and Cellular Awakening in Ascended Master teachings. Contrasting this profound opportunity for spiritual growth is the potential for worldwide catastrophes and possible Earth Changes. Frawley writes, "Much of the new spiritual think-

APPENDIX H

ing and the potential cataclysmic changes on the planet may be from this attunement process that insists we enter into a new ascending age of light and cast off the shadows of the dark ages of strife and dissension."[3] Our ability to enter the New Times and receive the benefits of the Golden Age, albeit in its infant stages, is subject to our capacity to integrate and apply the energies from the Galactic Center. This harmonization process demands our attunement with the great cosmic laws and forces of the universe, and initiates either humanity's spiritual enlightenment or retributive destruction.

Kuthumi's Teachings on the Ruby Ray

1. The Ruby Ray acts as a catalyst for the fulfillment of desires. Desires are not perceived as trappings of materiality or sinful craving, but as another aspect of God's promise of fulfillment. Hindu philosophies similarly teach that until man fulfills his desires, it is difficult to achieve liberation. Ultimately, Master Kuthumi views the human core of desires as, "an urge to know God."
2. Once all desires are obtained, often all that is left is the desire to know God. Master Kuthumi observes the quest to fulfill long-held desires as the greatest of all initiations, as it comes directly from the heart. Students and chelas who work intentionally to achieve desires through the Ruby Ray follow the *Path of Desires* as a liberation process.
3. As one becomes a practiced Master in the achievement of desires, the transparent cause of Unity and the ONE is realized. However, humanity is still in its infant stages of understanding this spiritual truth. In fact, Master Kuthumi claims that the simple desires of Peace and Happiness, which are constantly within the grasp of any individual, become almost impossible to obtain.
4. Since human nature craves demonstration of all things physical and is obsessed with materiality, one of the Golden City of Malton's purposes is to satiate desires.
5. Malton's higher purpose brings completion to the long-held desires of the human experience. Kuthumi asks students and chelas to assemble a list of the many unfulfilled desires held lifetime after lifetime. This step is critical before entering the upcoming initiatory steps of liberation—the Ascension process.
6. The Elemental and Nature Kingdoms assist the preparatory *Path of Desire* in the Golden City of Malton.
7. During the New Times, conscious phases of instant-thought-manifestation demonstrate to humanity the supreme truth that this unseen world of heaven—the spiritual planes—exist.

Kuthumi's Teachings and Prophecies on the Gold Ray

1. The Gold Ray will initiate human consciousness into a new vibration.
2. The New Energies through air, water, earth, and fire are currently utilized by the Nature Kingdoms: Elementals, Plants, Animals, and Minerals. This is heightening of the overall vibration of the earth.
3. As humanity rises in consciousness and understands the new vibration, the consequent energy gives further assistance to these various Kingdoms creating a type of evolutionary spiritual eco-system (the *Spirito-System*).

APPENDIX H

4. Around the year 2000 AD, the earth was flooded with the Gold Ray. While the first infusions of this higher energy cause discomfort and disharmony, the overall outcome for the New Times will be determined by the qualification and utilization of this Ray Force for higher consciousness.
5. Master Kuthumi suggests a simple prayer for harmony and to adjust humanity's vibratory rate and frequencies to the Gold Ray:

The Prayer of a Thousand Suns
"(Golden Ray) Bring Harmony forth to my Brothers and Sisters,
Let us be united as ONE, for we truly are."

The Master claims that as the Gold Ray grows in strength and radiance on earth, it will create the *Light of a Thousand Suns* to illumine minds with understanding; open hearts that are willing.

6. The Gold Ray is a collective outpouring of illumined wisdom and love from the Lords of Venus.
7. According to Kuthumi, vibration is keenly increased in Golden City Vortices, and this increase in vibration is a key to telepathy with Nature Kingdoms, Master Teachers, and Spirit Guides.
8. In the New Times, personal suffering and worldwide misery will be lessened. This is due to shifts in energy and the rise in vibration of the earth. This changes many of the perceptions individuals and humanity currently hold. Master Kuthumi prophesies that our perceptions of misery and suffering can be shifted into new realities.
9. Two critical tools: Worldwide Peace and Unity are taught by Master Kuthumi to obtain this Co-creative Consciousness. However, consciousness must be honed without denying or judging desires in order to obtain peace. And desires need to be fueled by the *Fire of Co-creation* in order to obtain worldwide Unity.

The Gold Ray

The Gold Ray in classic astrology and teachings on the Rays is often identified with our Solar Sun, an archetype of the Divine Father, and associated with leadership, courage, independence, authority, and justice. In fundamental Ascended Master teachings, the Gold Ray is often paired with the Ruby Ray, and this celestial partnership refines the energies of Mars (the Ruby Ray) from its base energies of war and aggression into passion, skill, determination, and duty. In later teachings on the Rays, the Gold Ray is also coupled with the Aquamarine Ray (Neptune), as a moderator of this Ray's association with illusion and fantasy, evolving the blue-green Ray's mysticism into perception, self-realization, transparency, and spiritual Unity. The Gold Ray is also associated with the Great Central Sun, the Solar Logos; our Solar Sun is a step-down transformer of its energies. According to the Master Teachers, the Gold Ray is the epitome of change for the New Times. The Gold Ray is the ultimate authority of Cosmic Law and carries both our personal and worldwide Karma and Dharma (purpose). Its presence is designed to instigate responsible spiritual

APPENDIX H

growth and planetary evolution for humanity's aspirations and the development of the HU-man. The Gold Ray, however, is also associated with Karmic justice and will instigate change: constructive and destructive. The extent of catastrophe or transformation is contingent on humanity's personal and collective spiritual growth and evolutionary process as we progress into the New Times.

Vibration

In common English, *vibration* comes from the word vibrate, which means to move, swing, or oscillate. In Ascended Master teachings, *vibration* is associated with light's movement in both physical and spiritual presence. In this context, light is affiliated with Wisdom, Love, and Power—attributes of the Unfed Flame and the expansion of the heart-flame through spiritual enlightenment. According to Master Kuthumi, increased light results in spiritual evolution, and this produces greater intuitive and psychic abilities; harmony with others, including the Animal and Fourth Dimensional Nature Kingdoms. Our vibration is calibrated by our thought processes—which consciousness grows out of—and these processes are fed by personal perceptions and choices. Kuthumi calls this the *Eye of Consciousness*, which is crucial to our personal level of vibration. States and levels of consciousness are perhaps the most powerful tools of vibration, and they create through the *Out-picturing Process* our recognition of human or HU-man experience.

---

[1] http://www.thefreedictionary.com, (2009).
[2] Lori Toye, *Points of Perception: Prophecies and Teachings of Saint Germain*, (I AM America Seventh Ray Publishing, 2008, Payson, AZ), page 259.
[3] David Frawley, *The Astrology of the Seers: A Guide to Vedic (Hindu) Astrology*, (Passage Press, 1990, Salt Lake City, Utah), page 63.

APPENDIX H

The Golden City of Denasha

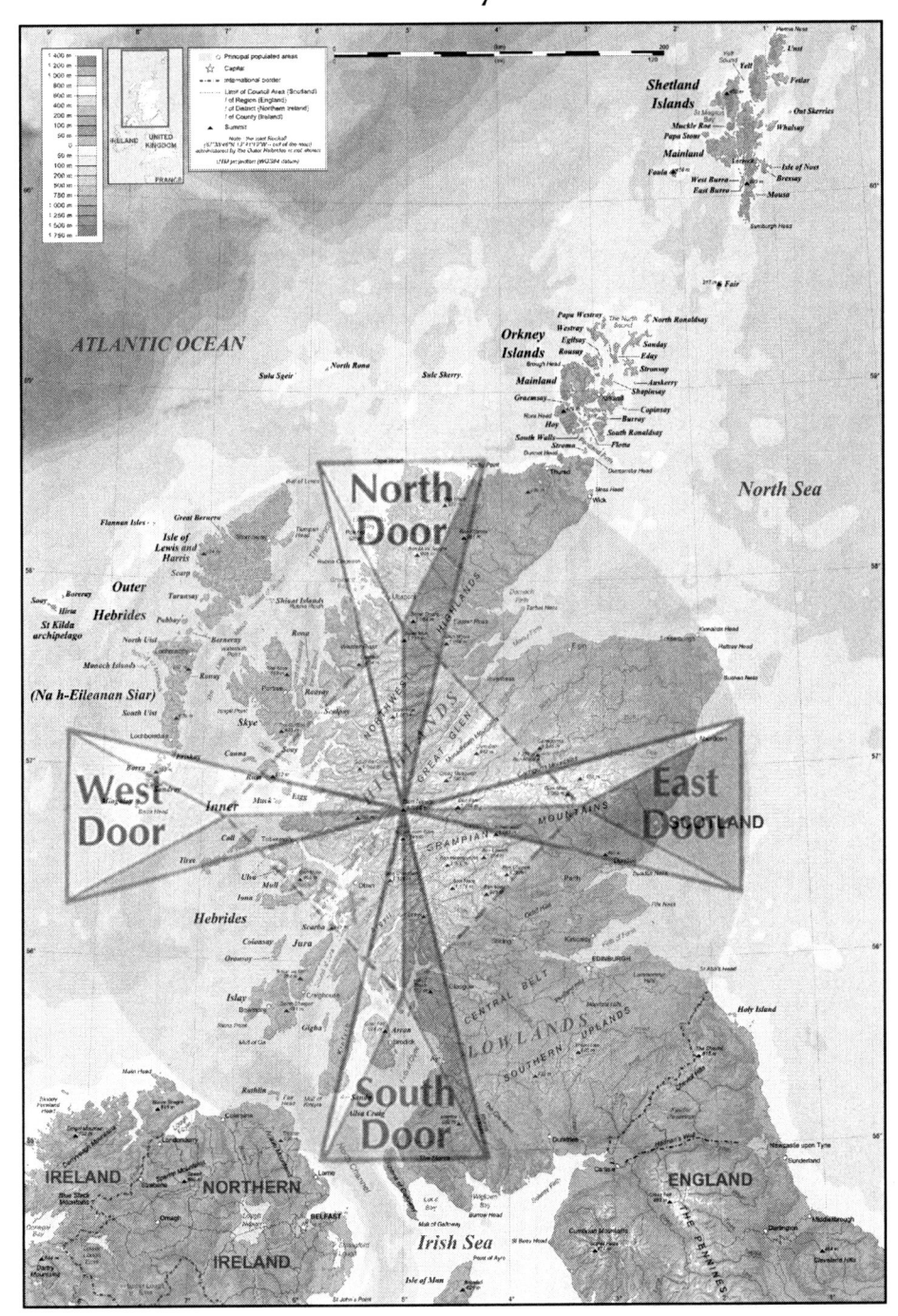

FIGURE 1-H
Golden City of Denasha

The *Golden City of Denasha* is primarily located in Scotland. The apex or center of this spiritual haven is Ben Nevis, the highest mountain in the British Isles (4,409 ft.) The Community of Findhorn is located in the Northeastern sector on the Moray Firth coast. Denasha is the Sister Golden City to Malton (Illinois and Indiana, USA) and both Vortices mutually distribute energies to the Nature and Elemental Kingdoms during the New Times. The Master Teacher of Denasha is Nada; the Ray Force is Yellow; and Denasha's meaning translates to the "Mountain of Zeus." (Golden City Figure not to scale.)

[Map Base Art: Sting. File:Scotland Topographic Map-en.jpg. Wikimedia Commons. 12 Dec. 2007. Web. 14 Jan. 2011. <http://commons.wikimedia.org/wiki/File:Scotland_topographic_map-en.jpg>.]

Bibliography

Bailey, Alice. *Esoteric Psychology*, New York, N.Y: Lucis Publishing Co., 1962.

Cayce, Edgar.
Gobi Desert Mysteries, China Pyramids and Mounds, http://www.edgar-cayce.org/AncientMysteriesTemp/gobidesert.html, 2011.
Modern Genetic Research Confirming Cayce's Story, http://www.edgarcayce.org/AncientMysteriesTemp/geneticevidence.html, 2011.

Childress, David Hatcher. *Lost Cities of North and Central America*, Stelle, IL: Adventures Unlimited Press, 1992.

Cumot, Franz. *The Mysteries of Mithra*, http://www.sacred-texts.com, 2010.

Dale, Cyndi. *The Subtle Body, An Encyclopedia of Your Energetic Anatomy*, Boulder, CO: Sounds True e-book, 2009.

de Fouw, Hart. *Light on Life, an Introduction to the Astrology of India*, New York, NY: Penguin Books, 1996.

Donaldson, Craig. How to Get Great Results When You Pray, http://www.ascension-research.org, 2010.

Every Culture. *Countries and Their Cultures: Gonds*, http://www.everyculture.com/wc/Germany-to-Jamaica/Gonds.html, 2010.

Free Dictionary. http://www.thefreedictionary.com, 2009.

Frawley, David. *The Astrology of the Seers: A Guide to Vedic (Hindu) Astrology*, Salt Lake City, Utah: Passage Press, 1990.

Funderstanding. Right Brain vs. Left Brain, http//www.funderstanding.com, 2010.

Hall, Manly.
The Secret Teachings of All Ages: An Encyclopedic Outline of Masonic, Hermetic, Qabbalistic and Rosicrucian Symbolical Philosophy, Los Angeles, CA: The Philosophical Research Society, Inc., 1988.
Twelve World Teachers: A Summary of Their Lives and Teachings, Los Angeles, CA: Philosophical Research Society, Inc., 1965.

BIBLIOGRAPHY

Kazlev, M. Alan. *The Higher Mind and Transformation,* http://www.kheper.net/Aurobindo/Higher_Mind.html, 2010.

Klemp, Harold. *HU: A Love Song to God,* http://www.eckandar.org/hu.html, 2010.

Kybalion, The. http://www.kybalion.org, 2010.

Levacy, William. *Beneath a Vedic Sky,* Carlsbad, CA: Hay House, Inc., 1999.

Luk, A. D .K. *Law of Life, Book I and II,* Pueblo, CO: A. D. K. Luk Publications, 1989.

McIntosh, Christopher. *A Short History of Astrology,* United Kingdom: Barnes and Noble Books by arrangement with Random House, UK, Ltd., 1994.

Murphy, Barbara. *The Clairs,* http://www.quantumpossibilities.biz/clairs.htm, 2010.

Saint Germain Foundation, *I AM Angel Decrees Part Two,* Chicago, IL: Saint Germain Press, Inc., 1974.

Stone, Joshua. *The Complete Ascension Manual: How to Achieve Ascension in This Lifetime,* Sedona, AZ: Light Technology Publishing, 1994.

Svoboda, Robert. *Light on Life, an Introduction to the Astrology of India,* New York, NY: Penguin Books, 1996.

Theosophical Society. *Encyclopedic Theosophical Glossary,* http://www.theosociety.org/pasadena/etglos/etg-hp.htm, 2011.

Toye, Lenard and Lori. *School of the Four Pillars: Illustrations and Notes:* Payson, AZ: 1992-1997.

Toye, Lori.
Blue Flame of Gobean Transcript, Payson AZ: Seventh Ray Publishing, 1998.
Points of Perception: Prophecies and Teachings of Saint Germain, Payson, AZ: I AM America Seventh Ray Publishing, 2008.

Twain, Mark. *The War Prayer,* http://www.ntua.gr/lurk/making/warprayer.html, 2010.

UFO Whipnet. *Top 10 Civilizations with Advanced Technology,* http://ufo.whipnet.org/creation/ancient.advanced.civilizations/index.html, 2011.

BIBLIOGRAPHY

Venefia, Avia. http://www.whats-your-sign.com/diamond-symbol-meaning.html, 2009.

Webster's Online Dictionary. *Multilingual Thesaurus Translation*, http://www.websters-online-dictionary.org, 2011.

Wikimedia Commons. http://commons.wikimedia.org, 2010-2011.

Wikipedia. http://www.wikipedia.org, 2009-2011.

Yogananda, Paramahansa. *Autobiography of a Yogi,* Los Angeles, CA: Self-Realization Fellowship, 1946.

Discography

This list provides the recording session date and name of the original selected recordings cited in this work that provide the basis for its original transcriptions.

Toye, Lori

Light a Candle, I AM America Seventh Ray Publishing International Audiocassette. © February 19, 1998.

Emanation, Instruction on the Rays, I AM America Seventh Ray Publishing International, Audiocassette. © April 10, 1998.

Behind the Interplay, The Service of the Rays, I AM America Seventh Ray Publishing International, Audiocassette. © April 14, 1998.

A New Day, I AM America Seventh Ray Publishing International, Audiocassette. © June 26, 1998.

A Quickening, Gobean Ready, I AM America Seventh Ray Publishing International, Audiocassette. © June 3, 1998. ℗ No. 070398, 1998.

Golden City Rays, Rays of the Golden Cities, I AM America Seventh Ray Publishing International, Audiocassette. © July 23, 1998. ℗ No. 072398, 1998.

Blue Illumination, Gobean and El Morya, I AM America Seventh Ray Publishing International, Audiocassette. © July 31, 1998.

The Light of a Thousand Suns, Golden Harmony, I AM America Seventh Ray Publishing International, Audiocassette. © September, 9, 1998.

Index

A

Absolute Harmony, 65
abundance, 201
 definition, 89
Adamic language, 204
Adept, 128, 222
Adjatal
 Golden City of
  meaning, 205
Adjutant Points, 58, 192
 Gobean, 186
Afrom
 Golden City of
  meaning, 205
Ahura Mazda, 216
Ahura Mazda Investiture, 224
Ajna Chakra, 154
Akasa
 and the HU-man energy system, 226
Akashic Records, 55, 212, 225
 and the Flower of Life, 137
 and the Golden City of Gobean, 76
 definition, 89
Akhenaten, 77, 89
 and Gobean, 213
 biography, 226
Akhenaten and Family, 228
Akhenaten and the Blue Crown, 228
Amerigo
 Golden City of
  meaning, 205
Anahata Chakra, 152
Anandamay Sheath, 156
Anasazi
 ancient influences, 77
Ancient Golden Cities
 alignment to Golden City of Klehma, 69

Ancient of Days, 216
 by William Blake, 223
Andeo
 Golden City of
  meaning, 205
Angelica
 Golden City of
  meaning, 205
apex
 and mantras, 70
 of Shalahah, 67
Apollo, 220
Aquamarine Ray, 161
 and the Gold Ray, 237
Aquarius, 149
Archangel Crystiel
 and the Seventeen Initiations of the Map of Exchanges, 199
Archangel Michael
 and the Seventeen Initiations of the Map of Exchanges, 199
Archangels
 and Ray Forces, 114
Arhat, 221
Aries, 151
Arkana
 Golden City of
  meaning, 205
Aryan, 131
 definition, 89
"As above, so below.", 74
Ascended Master, 171
 and specific Golden Cities, 175
 and their sound, 168
 consciousness
  definition, 89
 individualization upon a Ray Force, 114
 role in assisting humanity and the Earth, 45
 "...we take form at will.", 45

Ascension, 42, 76, 171, 174, 176
 and Babajeran, 173
 and Spiritual Migration, 197
 and the Golden City of Klehma, 69
 "...a new wine skin.", 42
 beyond the HU-man, 44
 body, 173
 definition, 89
 "...discard old beliefs, illusions.", 44
 El Morya's teachings, 177
Ascension Process, 141, 155, 172, 199
 and the Violet Flame Angels, 203
Ascension Valley, 67, 128, 200
 definition, 90
ashram
 definition, 90
Asonea
 Golden City of
  meaning, 205
Aspirant, 221
 definition, 90
Astral
 body, 23, 26, 31, 36, 128
 and Ray Forces, 63
 and the rebuilding of Shamballa, 74
 definition, 90
Astral Light, 226
Astrological Body, 29
Astrology, 23
Aten, 226, 228
 Great Hymn to Aten, 227
Atlantean Genetic Type, 214
Atlantis, 131, 213
 definition, 90
Atma, 167
Atmakaraka
 soul indicator through Ray Forces, 201
Aura, 25, 140, 173
 and Ray Forces, 63
 Auric Blueprint, 147
 Layers of the Human Aura, 146

The Golden City Series: Book Two

Auric Blueprint, 140
auric vision, 37
Aurobindo, Sri, 116
avatar
    definition, 91
Awaken
    definition, 91

B

Babajeran, 21, 36
Bailey, Alice, 216
    definition of a Ray, 106
Ballard, Edna, 203
beauty, 85
beliefs, 36, 42, 172
    inhibition, 173
    structuring new beliefs, 173
        El Morya's teachings, 175
belief versus experience, 77
Besant, Annie, 218
Bija-seed mantra, 111, 165
    definition, 91
    HU, 185
    Sanskrit mantras for the seven planets, 111
bi-locate
    definition, 91
bilocation, 68, 76, 200, 230
    Projection of Consciousness, 230
Binary Intellect, 134
    definition, 91
birth
    moment of, 63
Blake, William, 223
Blavatsky, H. P., 114, 218
Blue Flame, 37
    decree for, 177
    definition, 91
Blue Race, 74, 211
Blue Ray, 45, 58, 64, 67, 107, 186, 193
    and the manifestation of Shamballa, 74, 211
    definition, 92
    qualification, 27

Braham
    Golden City of meaning, 205
brain
    left and right brain experiences, 134
Braun
    Golden City of meaning, 205
breathwork, 65
    definition, 92
Brennan, Barbara, 193
Bridge of Awakening
    prophecy by Master Kuthumi, 235
Bronze Age, 143
Brotherhood, 67
Buddha, 154, 219—See also Lord Gautama
Bull of Truth
    Cycle of the Yugas, 143
butterfly symbology, 183

C

Caduceus, 142
    ancient symbol of Hermes, 140
    Crown Chakra, 141
Cancer, 155
Candle Meditation from El Morya, 75, 225
Capricorn, 149
causal body
    definition, 90
cause and effect, 42, 172
Cayce, Edgar, 214
Cellular
    Awakening, 76, 132
        definition, 92
    Fear, 21, 67, 172, 174
        definition, 92
Cellular Acceleration, 133
ceremony, 58, 62
Ceres, 166

Chakra, 159
    Base (root), 140, 149
    breathing, 191, 193
    Crown, 67, 155
    definition, 92
    Fifth, 153
    First, 149
    Fourth, 152
    Heart, 68, 152
    intersection, 141
    movement, 25, 159
    seal, 37
    Second, 150
    Seventh, 155
    Sexual, 150
    Sixth, 154
    Solar Plexus, 151
    sub-vortices, 159
    Third, 151
    Third Eye, 141, 154
    Throat, 64, 153
Chakra of One-Thousand Petals, 155
Chakras—See also Chakras: Ray Forces
    and disease, 144
    and sound vibration, 29, 63, 168
    and the endocrine system, 144
    electromagnetic output, 145
    Ray Forces, 22, 63, 65
character, 54
Chela, 212, 221—See also Quilian
    and preparation, 38
    definition, 92
    "...each chela is individualized.", 38
Chiron, 166
Chohan, 24
    Green Ray, 24
Choice, 25, 53, 79
    and the New Times, 57
    "...sparked within.", 43
    "...you begin anew.", 43

Light of Awakening

Christ
    consciousness, 197, 219
        and the Golden City of Gobean, 78
        definition, 92
        Quetzalcoatl, 227
    Cosmic, 219
Ciampi, Carolo Azeglio, 136
City of the Kumaras, 218
Clair Senses, 171
clairvoyance, 171
Clayje
    Golden City of
        meaning, 205
Closure of Understanding, 28, 138
Co-creation, 133
    and Ray Forces, 26
    definition, 18, 19, 35, 54, 55, 56, 57, 58, 59, 60, 61, 62, 64, 65, 66, 67, 68, 69, 70, 71, 165, 166, 167, 168, 169
    mudra, 161
Co-creative Thought Process, 181
Co-creator, 37, 42, 53, 80—See also HU-man
Co-creatorship, 30, 59
color, 38
    and frequency-wave patterns, 145
compassion, 32, 37
    definition, 92
conductivity, 74, 134
conscience, 42, 173
conscience and consciousness, 42
conscious human, 221
Conscious Immortality, 172
Consciousness, 22, 32, 83
    and Ascension, 44
    and immortality, 173
    and the Animal State, 234—See also will: Saint Germain's Teachings
    and the Golden Cities, 58
    and the Violet Flame, 29
    averting Earth Changes, 79
    ethereal, 76
    from animal to human, 79
    projecting, 77, 230
Continuity of Consciousness, 77
Coomaraswamy, Ananda, 115
cooperation, 69
Cosmic Law
    and the Gold Ray, 237
Cosmic Man
    and the planets, 166
courage, 46
Creative Chakra, 150
Cresta
    Golden City of
        meaning, 205
Crotese
    Golden City of
        meaning, 206
Crown Chakra, 155, 173
    and the Violet Ray, 67
Cumot, Franz, 119, 142

D

Dagaz, 183
    symbol, 183
Daityas, 213
Dale, Cyndi, 145, 156
Dark Side
    definition, 93
da Vinci, Leonardo, 136
death
    and consciousness, 42
    "...down with death.", 42, 66
    urge released through the White Fire of Klehma, 69
Death
    and fear, 43
    consciousness, 211
    decree, 110
    and chakras, 111
Denasha
    Golden City of, 85
        definition, 93
        Map, 239
        meaning, 206
desire, 45, 53
    and Golden Cities, 65
    body, 129
    into fruition, 83
    to know God, 82, 236
Devas, 65
Dharma, 22, 127
    definition, 93
Dharmic Bull of Truth, 143
diamond
    symbology, 183
Dimensional leaping
    and the Mayan culture, 69
discernment
    "By their fruits, you shall know them.", 80
discouragement, 46
dis-ease, 61
Divine
    Father, 152
    Feminine, 150, 152
    Guru, 155
    Language, 204
    Melodies, 167
    Messenger, 154
    Mother, 153
    Rain, 155
    Warrior, 149
Divine Destiny, 171
    and human evolution, 41
    and immortality, 42
Divine Grace, 18
Divine Intervention, 47, 67
    and the Golden Cities, 76
Divine Plan
    and forgiveness, 49
Divineship
    definition, 93
Divine Will, 152, 172
    alignment, 176
    and harmony, 186
    birth of, 44
    definition, 93
    releasing to, 46

249

The Golden City Series: Book Two

divinity
  within, 60, 82
DNA
  and identifying Ray Forces, 193
  and X Haplotype, 214—*See also Atlantis*
Donjakey
  Golden City of
    meaning, 206
doubt
  overpowering, 44
dreaming, 144
Dunlap, S. F., 114
Dvapara-Yuga, 143
dysfunctional patterns, 175

E

Eabra
  Golden City of
    meaning, 206
earth, 166
  purification, 81
Earth Changes, 235—*See also Galactic: Center: earth's conjuction with*
  and balance, 65
  and inner change, 49
  and the Ruby and Gold Ray, 65
  and Unana, 65
  "...birth a New Time.", 80
  California
    earthquake, 79
  cataclysmic changes obstructed by Galactic Light, 132
  earthquake swarm: Long Valley Caldera, 233
  increased light, 21
  Ring of Fire, 79, 233
Earth Changes Prophecies
  embrace constructive change, 174
  Master Teachers adjust collective energy, 233
Earth Plane
  definition, 93

Earth Plane and Planet
  definition, 127
Eastern Door, 61
  definition, 93
Ecological Alchemy
  and the Seventeen Initiations of the Greening Map, 198
economy
  deceit and manipulation, 235
Egyptians, Ancient
  presence in the Grand Canyon, 227
Eighth Ray, 132
Eight-Sided Cell of Perfection, 59
  activation, 25
  and the Violet Flame, 56
  and the Will Chakras, 158
  definition, 93
  Directional Movement of Energy, 130
  eight sectors, 130
  Location and Movement of the Rays through the Eight-Sided Cell of Perfection, 129
  microcosm and macrocosm, 131
  movement of the Rays, 129
  Overlaid the Human Body, 131
Elemental Force, 65
Elemental Kingdom
  and the Ruby and Gold Ray, 65
  mantra for, 69
Elementals
  definition, 93
El Morya, 82, 175
  definition, 93
  "...have to courage to feel it, live it, and act it out.", 176
  "...seek your own perfection.", 211
  "...seize life for life!", 177
Elohim, 174
  definition, 93

emanation, 23, 24, 26, 73, 127
  definition, 93
emotion
  development, 131
E-Motion, 54, 184
  definition, 94
Endocrine System
  chakras, 144
Energy Balancing
  for integrating Ray Forces, 66, 193
Energy Merdians, 140
equality
  and divinity, 176
  "Equal to", 44
  and relationships, 234
Ever-present now, 23, 50, 172, 175
evolution
  through the Rays, 63
experience, 36
  "...the difference is experience.", 36
Eye of Consciousness, 85, 238—*See also Vibration*
"Eyes to see; ears to hear", 41

F

fear, 21
  cellular
    removal of, 43
  genetic, 21, 132
  releasing, 44
feeling
  "...binds or lifts thought into harmony.", 54
feet
  chakras, 144
feminine, 132, 184
feminine energy
  astrological signs, 141
Fifth Dimension
  Akashic Records, 226
  and Golden City Names, 204
  and Ray Forces, 106
  and Star Seed evolution, 199

Light of Awakening

Fire of Co-creation, 237
Fires of Purification, 179
Fire Triplicity, 113
    definition, 94
    transmits the energies of the Galactic Center—*See also Fire Triplicity*
Flower of Life, 137
focus, 77, 179
    definition, 94
    "focus aligns", 59
forgetfulness, 56
Forgiveness, 48, 174
form languages, 204
Four Kumaras, 222
Fourth Dimension, 171, 226—*See also Ascension;See also Golden City Vortices*
    and Ray Forces, 106
    Klehma—*See Ascension*
Frawley, Dr. David, 113, 156, 165, 235
Freedom
    "...one is allowed to expand.", 29
Fron
    Golden City of
        meaning, 206

G

Galactic
    Center, 113, 127, 199
        earth's conjuction with, 235
        earth's position, 165
    Light, 128, 132
        definition, 94
        percentages through the Yugas—*See also Yuga(s)*
        Yuga percentages, 143
Ganakra
    Golden City of
        meaning, 206
Gandawan
    Golden City of
        meaning, 206
Gemini, 153

gemstones, 138
    and Ray Forces, 112
geometrical shape
    and conductivity, 134
Giza
    and the Golden City of Gobean, 77
Gobean, 50, 58, 64
    Golden City of, 73, 175
        Adjutant Points, 186
        affiliation with the Golden City of Gobi, 211
        align to the Golden City of Gobi, 75
        ancient location, 77
        and the Blue Ray, 186
        and the Giza Plateau, 213
        conncection to Shamballa, 76
        definition, 94
        doorways, 189
        meaning, 206
        to cultivate inner peace, 49
    integrating Ray Forces, 66
    Star, 19, 57
Gobi
    Desert, 213
        ancient civilizations, 74
    Golden City of, 73, 212
        definition, 94
        Map, 214
        meaning, 207
God, 82
    within, 38
God force, 44
Godhead
    definition, 94
God-state
    definition, 94
Golden Age, 41, 80, 143, 167
    of Kali-Yuga, 144
Golden City Doorways—*See also Spiritual: Migration*
Golden City Mantras, 202
    and centrifugal force of the Ray, 70

Golden City Names
    and myths, 204
    meanings, 205
Golden City Network
    Template of Consciousness, 186
Golden City of Gobean Lineage of Gurus, 229
Golden City Vortex, 57
    and a new consciousness, 42
    and the human energy system, 27
    and vibrational acceleration, 50
    apex, 64
    assimilating energies, 50
        during Spiritual Migration, 192
    astral body, 133
    development of, 27
    energies, 76
    Fifth Dimension, 135, 137
    Fourth Dimension, 135
    network, 58, 73
    of Gobean, 49
    of Malton, 65
    of Shalahah, 67
    of Wahanee, 49
    Star, 185
    Third Dimension, 135
    vibration of water, vegetables, 49
Golden City Vortices, 27, 42, 49, 174—*See also Ascension*
    activation, 185
        date, 187
    and mineral energies, 189
    and Ray Forces, 132, 192
    and the Eight-Sided Cell of Perfection, 131
    and the New Times, 62
    dominant Ray and attraction, 66
    dominant sound, 64

doorways
   Eastern Door, 61
   North Door, 61
   Southern Door, 61
   Western Door, 61
   energies, 61
   evolutionary process, 133
   higher energies, 21
   initiation, 195
   living in, 58
   moving to, 70
   the Star, 57, 62
   travel to, 58, 175
   water, air, and plant life, 174
Golden Perfections, 76, 224
   definition, 94
Golden Thread Axis, 25, 140
   and the Major Chakra System, 148
   definition, 94
Gold Ray, 65, 67, 160
   and the Elemental Kingdoms, 83
   definition, 95, 237
   Master Kuthumi's Teachings, 236
grace, 62
Grand Teacher, 173
Great Central Sun, 64, 113, 127, 155
   and the flow of light, 36
   and the Gold Ray, 237
   definition, 95
   harmonization with, 235
   "...is the light that shall free you all.", 21
   Ray Forces, 22
Greater Mind, 116
   definition, 95
Great Law
   definition, 95
Great Mystery
   definition, 95
Great Silence, 17, 105

Great White Brotherhood, 175, 219
   mudra, 161
Greek language, 204
Greening Map
   Seventeen Initiations, 196, 198
   Archangels Chamuel, Jophiel, Raphael, Gabriel and Uriel, 198
Green Ray, 23, 67, 107, 152, 194, 201—*See also Ray Forces: color*
   definition, 95
Grein
   Golden City of
   meaning, 207
Group Mind, 54, 110
   definition, 96
Gruecha
   Golden City of
   meaning, 207
guilt, 48

H

Hall, Manly, 167
Hall of Wisdom, 78
hands
   chakras, 144
   flow of the Rays, 160
   index finger, 160
   middle finger, 161
   ring finger, 160
   thumb, 161
Harmony, 23, 81, 179
   and relationships, 234
   definition, 96
   of the spheres, 166
   definition, 96
healing, 132—*See also Eight-Sided Cell of Perfection*
   and the Green Ray, 67
Heart, 152
   frequency range, 145
   of the Dove, 19, 116

Heart Chakra, 152
   affected by Green Ray in Golden City of Shalahah, 68
   and the Violet Ray, 194
Heart's Desire, 44
   definition, 96
   "...is the source of creation.", 220
Heaven and Earth, 76
   and the Seventeen Initations of the Map of Exchanges, 198
Hebrew language, 204
hertz frequency, 145
higher energies, 132
Higher Self, 37, 167
history
   as direct perception, 77
Holy Trinity, 137
Hopi culture
   influenced by the teachings of Akhenaton, 77
Hue
   Golden City of
   meaning, 207
HU-man, 24, 28, 36, 132, 155
   and Ray Forces, 22
human body
   symmetry and sacred geometry, 136
Human Energy System, 140
human evolution
   affected by the evolving Elemental, Animal, Plant, and Mineral Kingdoms, 235
   seven levels, 221
Humanity's Heart Opening
   Saint Germain's emblem, 184
Hunt, Dr. Valerie, 145
HU, the, 37, 56, 167
   and Violet Flame decrees, 37
   definition, 97
hypnotism
   "...through collective illusion.", 46

Light of Awakening

I

I AM
 Presence, 140, 173, 175
 revealed to all, 22
I AM America
 Seventeen Initiations, 195, 198
I AM America Map, 41, 171
I AM Presence
 engendered by Sanat Kumara, 221
I AM Race, 198
Ida Energy Current
 lunar current, 140
illusion, 45
immortal consciousness, 42
immortality, 183
 conscious, 172
 physical, 76
immortals
 of Shamballa, 74
Initiate, 221
innocence, 83
Instant-Thought-Manifestation, 53, 133, 179, 225
 and the Golden City of Malton, 65
 definition, 97
integration, 45, 191
 of Ray Forces, 64
intelligence
 development, 131
intention, 31, 35, 43, 47, 69, 167, 175
interplay, 168
 of the Rays, 36, 114

J

Jeafray
 Golden City of
  meaning, 207
Jehoa
 Golden City of
  meaning, 207
Jesus the Christ
 Akhenaten, spiritual forerunner, 227
judgment, 60, 80
"...exists within yourself.", 36
Juno, 166
Jupiter, 150, 151, 161, 166
Jyotish, 107, 143

K

Kali-Yuga, 75, 105, 143, 198, 212
 and the Violet Plume, 185
 definition, 97
 Iron Age, 143
Kalki Kings
 of Shamballa, 217
Kantan
 Golden City of
  meaning, 207
Karagulla, Dr. Shafica, 144
Karma, 36
 and cause and effect, 64
 and the Violet Flame, 80
 release of, 29
karmic debt, 35
Karmic Justice
 and the Gold Ray, 238
Kartikkeya, 216, 224
Kepler, Johannes, 166
Ketu, 166
Kirlian photography, 111
Klehma
 Golden City of, 68, 194, 200
  definition, 97
  meaning, 207
  Star, 19
Klemp, Harold, 167
"Know Thyself", 81, 178, 234
 "...and the truth shall set you free.", 55
 through meditation, 38
Kreshe
 Golden City of
  meaning, 208
Krita-Yuga, 143
Kuan Yin, 87
 scent, 112
Kumaras, the, 216

Kundalini, 22, 25, 134, 140, 168, 173, 226—See also Akasa
 and Crown Chakra, 67
 and OM, 28
 and sound vibration, 38
 definition, 97
 Kundalini System and the Golden Thread Axis, 142
 Kundalini System and the Seven Major Chakras, 157
 rising of, 144
Kuthumi, 81

L

Larito
 Golden City of
  meaning, 208
Law(s) of
 Cause and Effect, 172
 Love
  definition, 97
 Mercy and Compassion, 56
 Trinity, 37
Leadbeater, C. W., 216
leadership, 68
lei-lines, 192
Lemuria, 131
 definition, 98
Levacy, William R., 156
liberation, 31
 through the Path of Desires, 236—See also Ruby Ray: Master Kuthumi's Teachings
Libra, 152
Light
 acceleration, 22
 increase, 21
 internal, 41
 of a Thousand Suns, 84
 of Awakening, 128
  definition, 98
 "...seeds the vehicle of consciousness.", 85
 "...within is without judgment or shame.", 60

Light and Sound, 106, 168
lightning
  as Babajeran's will, 43
Light Side
  definition, 98
Lineage of Gurus
  definition, 98
Lineage of Shamballa to the
    Golden Cities, 215
"little steps", 47
Lord Gautama, 218
  earth's first Buddha, 219
Lord Maitreya, 218
  leader of the Great White
    Brotherhood, 219
Lords of the Flame, 218
Lords of Venus, 84
  and the Gold Ray, 237
Love one another, 60
Luk, A. D. K., 219

M

magnetic fields
  human sensitivity, 144
magnetite, 144
Mahabharata
  and Sanat Kumara, 216
Mahatma
  definition, 222
Mala, 111
male tyranny, 132
Malton, 65
  Golden City of, 79, 82, 199, 236
    and Kundalini energies, 65
    definition, 99
    meaning, 208
    purpose, 83
  Star, 19
manifest destiny—See also Instant-Thought-Manifestation
Manipura Chakra, 151

mantra, 110, 138
  anatomy, 202
  bija-seed, 91
  definition, 99
  Golden Cities, 69
    centrifugal force, 70
Map of Exchanges
  Seventeen Initiations, 197, 198
Marnero
  Golden City of
    meaning, 208
Marriage
  Inner—See Thought, Feeling, and Action
Mars, 110, 149, 151, 160, 166
  and the Ruby Ray, 237
masculine energy
  astrological signs, 141
Massey, Gerald, 115
Master, 222
Master Builder, 192
mastermind, 222
Mastery, 63
  of perfection and bilocation, 212
  of Ray Forces, 37
Mayan culture
  and ancient influences, 77
  dimensional leap, 69
meditation—See also Seven Rays of Light and Sound: Saint Germain's teachings
  and silence, 184
  and sound vibration, 168
  on the ONE, 45
  preparation through mantra or decree, 111
  Ray Forces, 28, 38, 138—See also Seven Rays of Light and Sound: Saint Germain's teachings
  to access Akashic Records, 226—See also Akashic Records
  to quell emotions, 55

mediums
  frequency range, 145
Medullar Shushumna
  Golden Thread Axis, 140
Mentgen, Janet
  Healing Touch, 193
Mercury, 107, 166
  and the history of Shamballa, 74
Merkabah, 134
Meru
  Lord
    definition, 98
Mesotamp
  Golden City of
    meaning, 208
Mexico
  Ancient Golden Cities, 69
mind
  "...as builder; body will follow.", 68
Mineral Kingdom
  and Golden City Vortices, 189
  and Ray Forces, 81
Miraculous Draught of Fish, 137
mistakes, 49
Mithra
  Ancient Chaldeans, 114
  and King Antiochus, 119
  as Boundless Time, 142
  Investiture of Sassanid Emperor Shapur II, 119
  Roman Mithraeum of Ostia, 141
  The Sun God, 119
moon, 160, 166
Mother Earth
  and the Golden Cities, 50
  the Grand Teacher, 173
  "...the witness.", 42
Mother Mary
  scent, 112
Mousse
  Golden City of
    meaning, 208
mudra, 161

Muladhara
  Base Chakra, 149
music, 166
mystics
  frequency range, 145

N

Nadis, 140, 173
Native American Butterfly Symbol, 183
Native American Leaders
  and the Golden City of Klehma, 200
Nature
  Kingdoms, 85, 236
Neal, Viola Petitt, 144
Nefertiti, Queen, 226
negativity
  discharging, 184
Neptune, 166
New Age
  definition, 99
New Atlantis, 199
New Day
  definition, 99
  release old patterns, 46
New Dimensions, 41, 54, 194, 200
  and the White Ray, 68
  definition, 99
New Lemuria, 199
new mind
  and beginning anew, 43
Nomaking
  Golden City of
    meaning, 208
Northern Door, 61, 76, 225
  definition, 99
Number: 17
  symbology, 197
Number:21
  symbology, 192
Number: 22
  symbology, 192

O

octahedron
  rotating, 137
OM—See also Bija-seed mantra
Om Eandra
  Golden City of Klehma, 69
  Golden City of Malton, 69
Om Hue
  Golden City of Wahanee, 69
Om Shanti
  Golden City of Gobean, 69
Om Sheahah
  Golden City of Shalahah, 69
ONE, 80—See also Light: of Awakening
  and Akhenaten, 226
  and El Morya's Candle Meditation, 225
  and relationships, 234
  and the Ever-present Now, 172
  and the Golden Cities, 174
  and the principle of conductivity, 75
  "...choose, choose, choose for the ONE.", 60
  "...two shall become as ONE.", 54
  uniting polarities, 60
Oneness
  of Kuthumi, El Morya, and Saint Germain, 81
  through telepathy, 41
Oneship, 64
  and Ascension Valley, 67
Oral Tradition, 153
  definition, 99
out-picturing, 233, 238
overshadowing, 219
Owaspee, 204

P

Pashacino
  Golden City of
    meaning, 208
Peace, 55, 82—See also White Candle Meditation

Pearlanu
  Golden City of
    meaning, 208
Perception, 22
  and Ray Forces, 133
  tool of consciousness, 85
Perfection—See Violet Flame
  "...is an emanation.", 74
perseverance, 48
pets, 81
Pierrakos, John, 193
pineal gland, 144
Pingala Energy Current
  solar energy current, 140
Pink Flame, 37
Pink Ray, 45, 107, 160, 201
  definition, 99
pinoline, 144
Pisces, 150
pituitary gland, 144
Planetary Logos, 216
planetary systems
  and Ray Forces, 36
planets
  are life forces, 36
Pluto, 166
Point of Perception, 18, 53, 80, 115
  definition, 99
polarity, 60
political leaders, 17
Political tipping point, 105
pollution
  and the Elemental Kingdom, 65
portal
  interdimensional, 67
Portals of Entry, 21, 128
  definition, 99
prana, 141, 173
  condensed in Golden City Stars, 66
  definition, 100
Prana
  Golden City of
    meaning, 208

Pranayama, 191
prayer, 18, 84, 167
   can change prophecies, 235
   for humanity, 81
   for our world leaders, 105
   Prayer of a Thousand Suns, 237
precession, 235
predicted events, 233
prediction and prophecy, 233
Presching
   Golden City of
      meaning, 208
Priesthood of Amen, 226
Prophecies of Change
   Elemental, Vegetable, and Mineral Kingdom, 81
Prophecy
   "...a gentle birth.", 82
   and the Gold Ray, 83
   and the Oneship in the Nature Kingdoms, 199
   a quickening, 61
   Bridge of Awakening, 82, 235
   Cellular Awakening, 224
   changes in Human Aura, 41
   changes in the Elemental, Animal, Plant, and Mineral Kingdoms, 235
   changes within, 58
   definition, 100, 233
   divine intervention of Golden Cities, 225
   earth cleansing, 199
   Elemental Kingdoms, 199
   end of Kali-Yuga, 224
   for a New Day, 49
   Golden City strategic points, 185
   humanity's acceleration into Light, 49
   increased Galactic Light, 132
   Klehma is one of the first Crystal Cities, 68
   misery and suffering can be shifted into new realities, 237
   national economy in grave danger, 81
   of Unana, 53
   purpose of, 50
   "...suffering and misery will be lessened.", 85
   the Golden Perfections, 224
   the HU-man, 133
   Time Compaction, 42, 179
   unconscious fear, 22
   water and vibration, 83
Prophet, Mark, 111
prosperity
   and the Golden City of Shalahah, 68
   definition, 100
psychic experience
   and the dream state, 144
psychics
   frequency range, 145
Puranas, 144
Puresk
   Golden City of
      meaning, 209
purification
   definition, 100
   fire of, 53
   in Golden Cities, 64
purveyor, 234
   "...you are a purveyor of your own Will.", 80
Pythagoras, 134, 166

Q

Quetzalcoatl
   definition, 100
   the Christ energies of Cooperation, 68
   the first Christ, 78
Quickening, 61
   spiritual teachings, 185
Quilian
   pronounced Chee-layn: chela, 212

R

radiation, 57
Rahu, 150, 166
Rama, 213
Ray Chart
   Deities: Rays Five through Eight, 123
   Rays Five through Eight, 109
   Rays One through Four, 108
Ray Forces
   absorbing new energies, 193
   and gemstones, 112
   and human endeavor, 106
   and scents, 112
   color, 23
   movement of, 113
   qualification, 24
   recognition, 138
Ray(s)
   Flow of the Rays through the Human Hands, 160
   Gold, 65
   Green, 23, 68
   history, 114
   interplay, 30
   lower qualities, 24
   Movement of the Rays through the Human Feet, 162
   of human evolution, 131
   qualification, 133
   Ruby and Gold, 65
Ray Systems, 106
re-embodiment
   of historical World Leaders in Golden City of Klehma, 68
regeneration
   and the Violet Ray, 66
reincarnation, 26
relationships
   Saint Germain's teachings, 234
releasing the past, 50
Rod of Asclepius, 141
Rod of Power, 140, 141
Root Chakra, 149, 173

Ruby and Gold Ray, 65, 66, 81, 82, 110, 201
   and natural disasters, 199
Ruby Ray, 160
   definition, 100
   Master Kuthumi's Teachings, 236
Russell, George William, 204

S

Sacred Fire
   definition, 100
Sacred Geometry, 27, 134
   definition, 100
   diamond, 183
safety, 194
   "...is a matter of the Heart.", 68
Sagittarius, 150
Sahasrara Chakra, 155
Saint Germain, 177
   "life is for life.", 174
   scent, 113
   "...the hands of God are your hands.", 174
   "...through your own practice", 169
Samadhi, 156
Sananda
   mudra, 161
Sanat Kumara, 74, 212
   biography, 216
   definition, 100
   return to Venus, 219
   "...your enlightenment has always been.", 220
Sanskrit, 204
Saturn, 110, 149, 153, 161, 166
Satyaloka, 155
scents
   and Ray Forces, 112
School of the Four Pillars, 156, 193
schoolroom earth, 55
Scorpio, 151
Seraphic Host, 218
Serapis Bey, 77, 218, 227
   definition, 101

service, 35, 44, 81, 167
   and detachment, 35
Seven Rays of Light and Sound, 30, 37, 105, 222
   and ancient astrology, 143
   and the Christian dove, 115
   and the Secret Doctrine, 114
   and the Seventh Chakra, 155
   base of Ancient Religions, 114
   cosmic bondage, 128
   definition, 101
   harmonize, 138
   mantras, 139
   Saint Germain's teachings, 138
Seventh Ray
   and immortality, 115
sexual energy, 161
Shadbala
   for Ray Forces, 201
Shalahah
   definition, 101
   Golden City of, 67, 69, 194, 200
   and health retreats, 68
   meaning, 209
   Star, 19
Shamballa, 73, 211
   and the Gobi Desert, 212
   annual opening and celebration, 220
   a state of consciousness, 221
   definition, 101
   earth's Crown Chakra, 216
   in Buddhism, 217
   influence on Ancient America, 77
   the Hall of Wisdom, 213
   timeline, 217
shatki, 134
Sheahah
   Golden City of
      meaning, 209
Shehez
   Golden City of
      meaning, 209

Shroud of Darkness, 42, 172, 173
Silver Age, 143
simplicity, 45, 82
sin
   against self, 48, 178
Sircalwe
   Golden City of
      meaning, 209
sleep, 26, 50, 128
   during Ray Force integration, 193
Solar Plexus, 151, 194
   affected by energies of Shalahah, 68
   and transmutation of death consciousness, 67
solar system, 165
   and Time Compaction, 55
Sons of Will and Yoga, 213
Soul
   completing lessons, 138
   growth, 226
Soul Family, 199
Sound, 28, 110, 168
   and harmony, 38
   and Ray Forces, 37, 168
   and the E-motion, 54
   consonants and vowels, 38
   vibration, 38
   and the Violet Flame, 38
South America, 69
Southern Door, 61, 76, 224
   definition, 101
Spirito-System, 236
Spiritual
   Development
      and Astral Light—See also Astral: body
   maturity, 192
   Migration, 191, 197
      definition—See Golden City Vortices
   World, 83
Spiritual Prophecies
   I AM revealed to many, 133

Spleen Chakra, 144
Star, 62
   definition, 101
   Golden City, 64, 66, 70, 185
      moving to, 185
      template of perfect thought, 58
   meditation technqiue, 199
   tetrahedron, 134
Star of Freedom, 56
Star of Gobean, 60
   activated, 57
Star of Klehma, 69
Star of Knowledge, 77, 230
Star Seed, 66, 74, 199, 213
Star Seed consciousness—
     See Golden City Vortices
   definition, 101
Step-down Transformer
   our Solar Sun, 237
Stienta
   Golden City of
      meaning, 209
Stone, Dr. Joshua, 216
Strategic Points
   definition, 101
strife among families, 41
suffering
   "...when suffering is lessened.", 32
sun, 110, 151, 160, 166
   companion dwarf star theory, 143
Super Senses
   and Ray Forces, 106
Svadhisthana Chakra, 150

T

Taurus, 153
Tehekoa
   Golden City of
      meaning, 209

telepathy
   between the Plant, Animal, and Mineral Kingdom, 82
   definition, 101
   prophecy, 41
   with teachers and spirit guides, 84
Temple of Mercy, 87
Temple to the Formless One, 227
Third Eye, 64, 141, 154
Thirteenth School, 213
Thought—See also Thought: cultivation of
   and action create, 54
   and a New Day, 46
   and collective reality, 55
   and reincarnation, 42
   compaction, 54
   cultivation of, 234
   Projection, 77
   under Time Compaction, 184
Thought and Time Compaction, 182
Throat Chakra, 153
Time, 23
   "...must be cast aside.", 45
   of Acceleration, 22
   of Peace, 17
   of Tribulation, 57
Time Compaction, 42, 53, 174, 224
   and Babajeran, 54
   definition, 102
Time of Change, 58
   definition, 102
   earth's rising vibration, 83
Time of Opportunity, 53
Time of Tribulation, 184
   definition, 102
Transformation, 61
transgression, 56
Transmutation, 45
   definition, 102
Transportation Vortex, 67, 128, 200

Treta Yuga, 143
truth, 55
tsunami, 65
Twain, Mark
   The War Prayer, 115
Twelve Jurisdictions
   Abundance, 201
   Abundance in Shalahah, 68
   and Sanat Kumara, 220
   Charity, 220
   Cooperation: Masculine Principle, 220
   Desire, 220
   Harmony, 58, 179
   Service, 167
   Stillness, 220
Twleve Jurisdictions, 28
Tzu, Lao, 214

U

Unana, 31, 41, 59, 174
   and Gobean, 49
   and interconnectedness, 44
   definition, 102
Unfed Flame, 238
   and Sanat Kumara, 221
   history of, 74
unification of self, 42, 59
United States
   new capitol, 68
Unity, 85
   and relationships, 234
   Consciousness, 41, 54, 132, 180
Universal Seed of Life, 137
Unte
   Golden City of
      meaning, 209
Uranus, 110, 166
Usui, Mikao
   Reiki, 193
Uverno
   Golden City of
      meaning, 209

V

Vedic
  astrology, 107
  Rishis, 110, 143, 165
Vegetable Kingdom
  and Golden City Vortices, 189
  and human evolution, 81
Venefia, Avia, 183
Venus, 107, 150, 166
  lunar half, 153
  Shamballa's founders, 74
  temples of, 217
Vertical Power Current, 43, 64, 173, 175
  definition, 102
Vesica Piscis, 137
Vesta, 166
Vibration, 83
  definition, 102, 238
  movement of light, 85
Violet Flame, 29, 178
  and difficult relationships, 234
  and Divine Intervention, 56
  and fulfillment of intention, 48
  and gaining momentum, 31
  and growth of peace, 55
  and the Divine Law, 57
  and the HU, 37
  application for a specific focus, 47
  birthed from the Blue Flame, 37
  conductor of Ray Forces, 139
  Decree
    for assistance, 56
    for higher emanation of a Ray, 138
    for overcoming difficult karma, 29
    for overcoming discouragement, 47
    to diminish fears, 177
    to discharge negativity, 184
    to harmonize the Rays, 30, 138
  Decrees, 111
    and Karma, 37
    definition, 103
    for disharmony, 55
    Forgiveness, Compassion, Mercy, 139
    for identifying personal Ray Tones, 169
    invocation at sunrise, sunset, 87
    Spiritual Lineage, 87
    use for stress, 80
Violet Flame Angels, 69, 203
  definition, 103
Violet Plume, 56, 185
Violet Ray, 45, 66, 110, 161
  and immortality, 66
  and transmutation, 67
  definition, 103
  physical symptoms, 67
Virgo, 154
Vishuddha Chakra, 153
Vishvakarma
  the world architect, 219
visualization
  technique for Gobean, 51
Vitruvian Man, 134
  by Leonardo da Vinci, 136
Vortex
  creation of, 75
  Tube Torus, 137

W

Wahanee
  Golden City of, 66, 69, 194
    and healing clinics, 67
    and the Violet Flame, 174
    definition, 103
    meaning, 209
    release injustice, 49
  Star, 19, 200
war
  effect on human consciousness, 115
  prophecy, 17
wars, 105
water, 83
Western Door, 61
  definition, 103
Wheel of Karma, 155
White Candle Meditation, 116
white candles
  burning of, 18
White Fire, 69
White Ray, 68, 107, 150
  and release of the death urge, 194
  and Venusian energies, 68
  definition, 103
will, 43, 79, 161
  alignment, 45
  and the collective, 43
  development, 131
  Saint Germain's Teachings, 234
Will Chakras, 140, 159
  and the Golden Thread Axis, 158
  Concentrative-Receptive, 159
  Creative Will, 159
  Expressive, 159
  Solar Will, 159
  Will to Live, 159
  Will to Love, 159
Write and Burn Technique, 176
  definition, 103

Y

Y2K
  Flood of Light, 84
Yellow Ray, 107, 198, 201
  definition, 103
Yogananda, Paramahansa, 128, 144
Yuga(s)
  Cycle of, 143
  definition, 103
  four, 143
Yuteswar, Sri, 144
Yuthor
  Golden City of
    meaning, 210

Z

Zadkiel
  and the Seventeen Initiations of
    I AM America, 198
Zaskar
  Golden City of
    meaning, 210
Zodiac
  Sidereal and Western, 235
  Vedic Ayanamsha, 235

About Lori Toye

Lori Toye is not a Prophet of doom and gloom. The fact that she became a Prophet at all is highly unlikely. Reared in a small Idaho farming community as a member of the conservative Missouri Synod Lutheran church, Lori had never heard of meditation, spiritual development, reincarnation, channeling or clairvoyant sight.

Her unusual spiritual journey began in Washington State, when, as advertising manager of a weekly newspaper, she answered a request to pick up an ad for a local health food store. Upon entering, a woman at the counter pointed a finger at her and said, "You have work to do for Master Saint Germain!"

The next several years were filled with spiritual enlightenment that introduced Lori, then only twenty-two years old, to the most exceptional and inspirational information she had ever encountered. Lori became a student of Ascended Master teachings.

Awakened one night by the luminous figure of Saint Germain at the foot of her bed, her work had begun. Later in the same year, an image of a map appeared in her dream. Four teachers clad in white robes were present, pointing out Earth Changes that would shape the future United States.

Five years later, faced with the stress of a painful divorce and rebuilding her life as a single mother, Lori attended spiritual meditation classes. While there she shared her experience, and encouraged by friends she began to explore the dream through daily meditation. The four Beings appeared again, and expressed a willingness to share the information. Over a six-month period, they gave over 80 sessions of material, including detailed information that would later become the I AM America Map.

Clearly she had to produce the map. The only means to finance it was to sell her house. She put her home up for sale, and in a depressed market, it sold the first day at full asking price.

She produced the map in 1989, rolled them on her kitchen table, and sold them through word-of-mouth. She then launched a lecture tour of the Northwest and California. Hers was the first Earth Changes Map published, and many others have followed, but the rest is history.

From the tabloids to the New York Times, The Washington Post, television interviews in the U.S., London, and Europe, Lori's Mission was to honor the material she had received. The material is not hers, she stresses. It belongs to the Masters, and their loving, healing approach is disseminated through the I AM America Publishing Company operated by her husband and spiritual partner, Lenard Toye. Working together they organized free classes of the teachings and their instructional pursuits led them to form the School of the Four Pillars which included holistic and energy healing techniques. In 1995 and 1996 they sponsored the first Prophecy Conferences in Philadelphia and Phoenix, Arizona.

Other publications include three additional Prophecy maps, four books, a video, and more than 60 audio tapes based on sessions with Master Teacher Saint Germain and other Ascended Masters.

Spiritual in nature, I AM America is not a church, religion, sect, or cult. There is no interest or intent in amassing followers or engaging in any activity other than what Lori and Lenard can do on their own to publicize the materials they have been entrusted with.

They have also been directed to build the first Golden City community. A very positive aspect of the vision is that all the maps include areas called, "Golden Cities." These places hold a high spiritual energy, and are where sustainable communities are to be built using solar energy alongside Classical Feng Shui engineering and infrastructure. The first community, Wenima Village, is currently being planned for development.

Concerned that some might misinterpret the Maps' messages as doom and gloom and miss the metaphor for personal change, or not consider the spiritual teachings attached to the maps, Lori emphasizes the Masters stressed that this was a Prophecy of choice. Prophecy allows for choice in making informed decisions and promotes the opportunity for cooperation and harmony. Lenard and Lori's vision for I AM America is to share the Ascended Masters' prophecies as spiritual warnings to heal and renew our lives.

About I AM America

I AM America is an educational and publishing foundation dedicated to disseminating the Ascended Masters' message of Earth Changes Prophecy and Spiritual Teachings for self-development. Our office is run by the husband and wife team of Lenard and Lori Toye who hand-roll maps, package and mail information and products with a small staff. Our first publication was the I AM America Map, which was published in September, 1989. Since then we have published three more Prophecy maps, five books, and numerous audios/CDs based on the channeled sessions with the Spiritual Teachers.

We are not a church, a religion, a sect or cult, and are not interested in amassing followers or members. Nor do we have any affiliation with a church, religion, political group, or government of any kind. We are not a college or university, research facility, or a mystery school. El Morya told us that the best way to see ourselves is as, "Cosmic Beings, having a human experience."

In 1994, we asked Saint Germain, "How do you see our work at I AM America?" and he answered, "I AM America is to be a clearinghouse for the new humanity." Grabbing a dictionary, we quickly learned that the term "clearinghouse" refers to "an organization or unit within an organization that functions as a central agency for collecting, organizing, storing and disseminating documents, usually within a specific academic discipline or field." So inarguably, we are this too. But in uncomplicated terms, we publish and share spiritually transformational information because at I AM America there is no doubt that, "A Change of Heart can Change the World."

With Violet Flame Blessings,
Lori & Lenard Toye

For more information or visit our online bookstore, go to:
www.iamamerica.com

To receive a catalog by mail, please write to:
I AM America
P.O. Box 2511
Payson, AZ 85547

CPSIA information can be obtained at www.ICGtesting.com
Printed in the USA
BVOW050525220413

318753BV00002B/12/P